GW01607168

SNOWDONIA
AND
NORTHERN WALES

To my son Gareth

SNOWDONIA AND NORTHERN WALES

John B. Hilling

B. T. BATSFORD LTD
LONDON

First published 1980

ISBN 0 7134 3793 6

Printed in Great Britain
for the publishers, B. T. Batsford Ltd
4 Fitzhardinge Street, London W1H 0AH
by Redwood Burn Ltd
Trowbridge and Esher

CONTENTS

List of illustrations vi
List of maps vii

Preface

PART ONE: POWYS

1 Powys 3

2 The Brecon Beacons and the Usk Valley 11

3 The Wye Valley 24

4 Montgomery and the Severn Valley 37

PART TWO: CLWYD

5 Clwyd 51

6 Dyffryn Ceiriog and the Vale of Llangollen 60

7 Maelor and the Dee Estuary 72

8 Dyffryn Clwyd 87

PART THREE: GWYNEDD

9 Gwynedd 99

10 Vale of Conwy and Nant Ffrancon 111

11 Anglesey 128

12 Caernarfon, Snowdon and Llŷn 145

13 Meirionnydd 160

Index 175

LIST OF ILLUSTRATIONS

Black and white photographs, between pages 104 and 105

Powys

1 The Wye Valley above Hay
2 The bridge over the River Usk at Crickhowell
3 Powis Castle, Welshpool
4 The Market Hall, Llanidloes
5 Elan Valley reservoirs, near Rhayader
6 Looking across Llan-gors lake towards the Brecon Beacons

Clwyd

7 The Vale of Clwyd near Denbigh
8 The River Dee near Llangollen
9 Flint Castle, on the estuary of the River Dee
10 The church at Bodelwyddan, known as the Marble Church
11 St Asaph Cathedral
12 Part of the ruins of the Abbey of Valle Crucis

Gwynedd

13 Afon (River) Conwy at Llanwrst
14 The Swallow Falls at Betws-y-coed
15 Llyn Ogwen, looking towards Nant Ffrancon
16 Llyn Gwynant and Yr Aran
17 Harlech Castle
18 Caernarfon Castle
19 The cliffs of Cadair Idris, and Llyn Cau
20 Looking from the top of Snowdon towards Lliwedd
21 Telford's suspension bridge across the Menai Straits
22 Amlwch Harbour, Isle of Anglesey

LIST OF MAPS

1 Powys: South 4
2 Powys: North 5
3 Clwyd 52
4 Gwynedd: West 100
5 Gwynedd: East 101

ACKNOWLEDGEMENTS

The Publishers would like to thank the following for permission to reproduce their photographs in the book: Barnaby's Picture Library, Nos 7, 9, 10, 11, 13, 14, 20, 21, 22; J. Allan Cash Ltd, Nos 1, 2, 4, 5, 8, 15, 16, 18; A. F. Kersting, Nos 3, 6, 12, 17, 19.

Preface

It is difficult to divide Wales equally into a northern and a southern half. There are, of course, differences in the accent and spoken Welsh of people living in the north and south just as there are differences in the topography and density of population. But these are mainly differences of emphasis. There is, however, no hard and fast line where the south ends or the north begins. In earlier times it was possible to divide Wales arbitarily into six northern counties and seven southern counties. With the new arrangement of fewer and larger counties any division into north and south is impossible.

This book covers the area of three of the new counties – Clwyd, Gwynedd and Powys – and therefore includes not only northern Wales but a large part of mid-Wales as well. The Usk Valley and the Brecon Beacons of Powys are, perhaps, more closely related to southern Wales than with the rest of mid-Wales; they have, however, been included in this book in order to make the coverage of Powys complete.

The new counties came into being in 1974 and as a result the old county boundaries, which had been established by Edward I in 1284 and Henry VIII in 1536, became redundant. The new county and district names have been used in this book. Most of the new names have, in fact, been derived from ancient Welsh kingdoms and administrative units and are therefore not as inappropriate as they might at first appear. Gwynedd and Powys, for instance, are the names of two of the old Welsh kingdoms. The name Clwyd, however, is taken from the name of a river and range of hills in that same county. The composition of the new counties is as follows: Powys includes most of Breconshire, Montgomeryshire and Radnorshire; Gwynedd includes the island of Anglesey, Caernarfonshire, most of Merionethshire and a small part of Denbighshire east of the Afon Conwy; Clwyd includes Flintshire, most of Denbighshire and a small part of Merionethshire.

The book has been arranged in three parts. Each part deals with one of the new counties and begins with an introductory chapter outlining the topographical features and historic events of the area.

This is followed by three or four tours describing places of interest and the people connected with those places.

PART ONE

Powys

Map 1 Powys: South

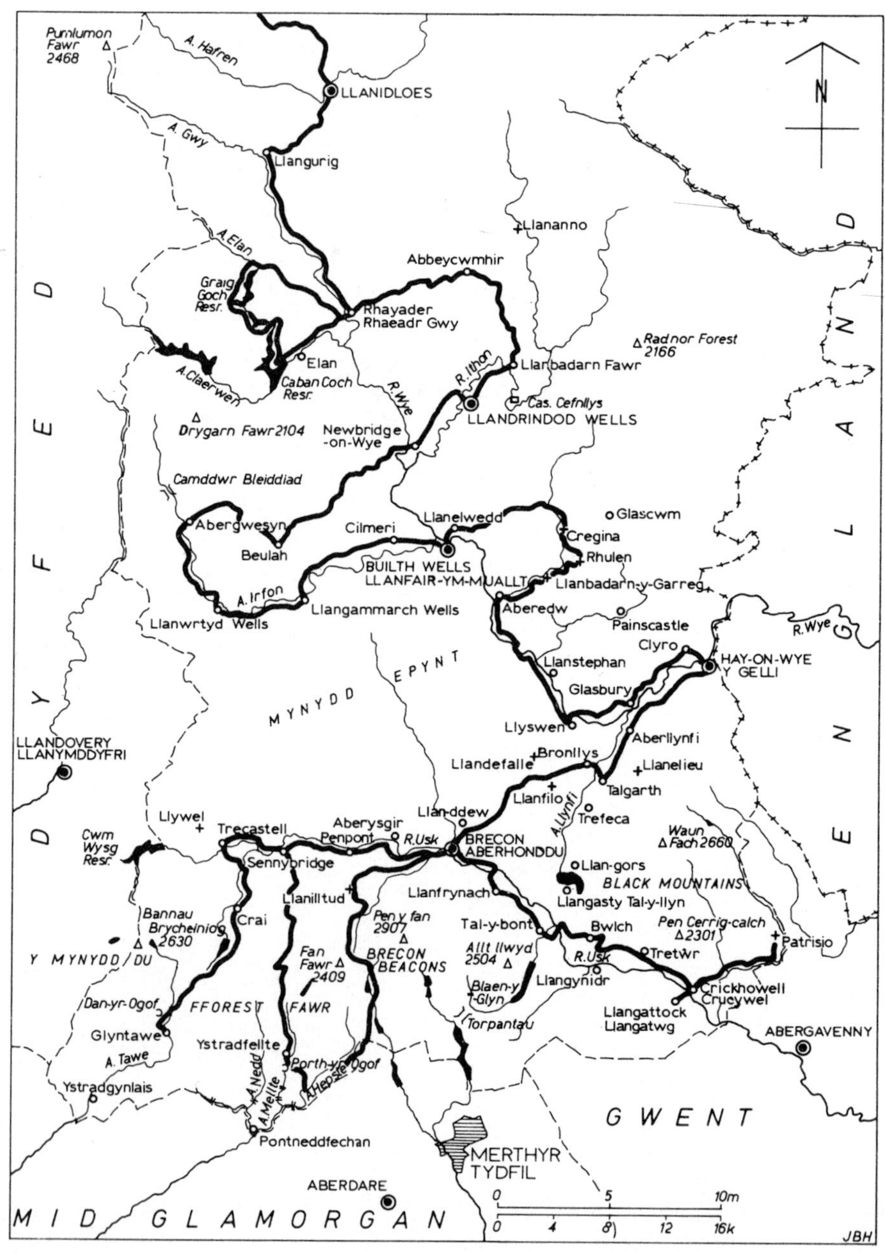

Map 2 Powys: North

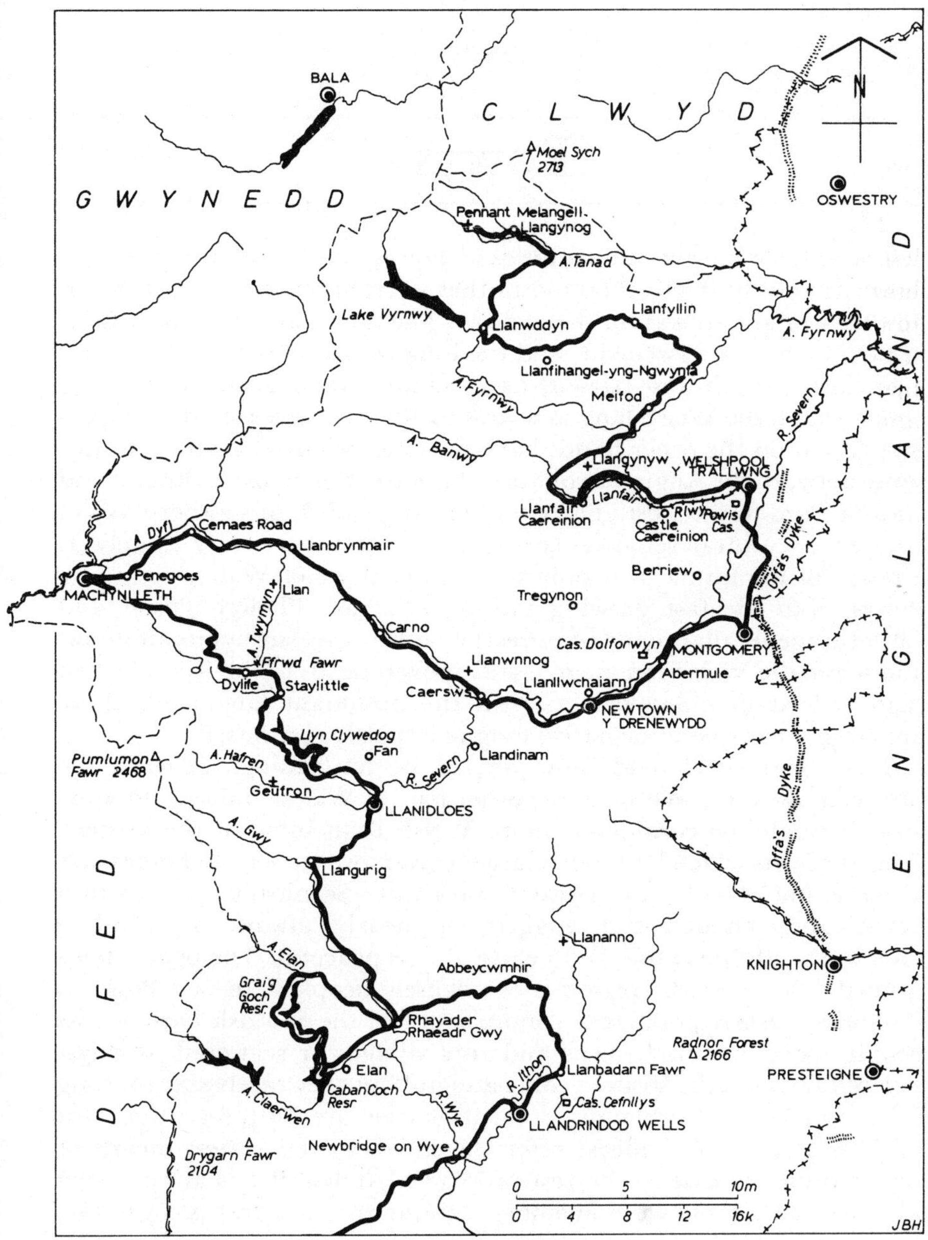

ONE

Powys

The eastern borderland counties of Powys and Clwyd are, perhaps, less distinctively Welsh than most other parts of Wales; at least that is how they might appear on the surface. The mountain fastness of Eryri in the north-west (Gwynedd) and the long curving valleys of Teifi and Tywi in the south-west (Dyfed) have retained their distinctive Welshness through the Welsh language and by their relative isolation. Powys and Clwyd on the other hand, have for long centuries acted as buffer zones between the Anglo-Saxons (and later the Normans) to the east and *Gwalia Pura* to the west. The deep, mining valleys of southern Wales enjoyed a cultural renaissance in the nineteenth century largely as a result of the influx of people from other parts of Wales, including Powys, into the fast growing industrial areas. Though Powys and Clwyd are generally upland counties they are not excessively mountainous and while the Welsh language is still spoken north of the River Severn (and indeed in many parts is still the dominant language), there are large areas where the native tongue is hardly ever heard.

Superficial views tend, however, to be misleading. Beneath the surface Powys is as Welsh as any other part of Wales – indeed, in some ways it might be considered more Welsh than some of the western coastal resorts which have been largely given over to second homes and become inundated with visitors' caravans. Scenically, the eastern borderland, though not rugged, is nearly always beautiful – sometimes sublimely so – and nearly always peaceful. The peace stems from the fact that the region is not densely peopled. In fact Powys is the most sparsely populated county south of the Scottish border – its people living in small towns and tiny villages or scattered amongst isolated farmsteads. Visitors come and go, but they rarely stay for long for the eastern borderlands, divided as they are by three important and beautiful river valleys, offer the quickest and easiest means of access from the east to the rest of Wales. And so it has always been whether the visitors were invaders, conquerors, mineral prospectors, railway navvies or simply tourists.

For the most part, Powys presents a relatively consistent scene of rich vales divided by gently sweeping hills and mountains interspersed with delectable little valleys dotted with cottages, farms and villages. Here and there, where tributaries join their mother rivers, a few small market towns still serve their modest hinterlands, as they have done for centuries. The main valleys formed by the Usk (Afon Wysg), Wye (Afon Gwy) and Severn (Afon Hafren) rivers divide Powys into three districts each corresponding roughly with the old counties of Breconshire, Radnorshire and Montgomeryshire.

The beautiful Usk rises in the mountainous crags of the Brecon Beacons National Park and traverses the southern part of Powys from west to east. The richly verdant upper Usk valley stands out in splendid contrast to the wilder uplands on either side. To the east the bare Black Mountains rear up in a solid phalanx of parallel ridges which end in a cluster of isolated hills around Abergavenny. West of the Usk the Brecon Beacons themselves fan out from a central trio of shapely peaks almost 3,000 feet high. Beyond are the now empty expanses of the ancient Fforest Fawr (Great Forest) and Y Mynydd Du and its mysterious lakes. Immediately south of the Brecon Beacons and Fforest Fawr a narrow band of limestone, grey white in colour in contrast to the rich red-browns of the rocks and soils elsewhere, forms the limit of the National Park. The action of water on the limestone has resulted in a strip of landscape which is totally different and includes spectacular waterfalls, swallow-holes and caves. North of the Usk there are quiet valleys descending from the moorland plateau of Mynydd Epynt which is now partly used as an artillery range.

The Wye valley is the most dramatically picturesque of the three main valleys. It can be followed on a twisting course from the English border at Hay through the heart of mid-Wales to its source on Pumlumon a few miles east of Aberystwyth. The triangular area north east of the Wye is mainly a region of upland farms and moorlands. Before local government reorganisation reshaped the Welsh counties in 1974 it was known as Radnorshire and before that it was known to the Welsh princes simply as Rhwng Gwy a Hafren (literally 'Between Wye and Severn'). Radnor Forest at the centre of the old county is the highest point at 2,166 feet above sea level; it is almost 400 feet higher than any other hill in the area and although it possesses no jagged peaks it somehow manages to look as wild, particularly in winter, as many a higher mountain.

The River Severn starts from almost the same point on Pumlumon as the Wye, but flows north-eastwards through broad vales to Welshpool, the ancient capital of the kings of Powys. The northern side of the Severn is fed by a number of tributary rivers – Banwy,

Fyrnwy and Tanat – which come down from the Berwyn Mountains. This region is the old county of Montgomeryshire and comprises a landscape of wooded hills, endearing valleys, stone farms and a peppering of black and white half-timbered houses.

The northern rim of Powys is formed by an almost continuous chain of mountains extending from Cardigan Bay in the West to the English border on the east. This ridge, including Cadair Idris (in Gwynedd) and the Berwyn range is really the edge of an immense geological fault which, slicing across Wales from south-west to north-east, separates the subdued uplands of central Wales from the severely glaciated mountains of the north.

The rocks underlying the landscape fall into three groups. In the south the peaks of the Brecon Beacons and the ridges of the Black Mountains are composed of colourful Old Red Sandstone rocks. The rest of Powys, north of the Wye, is made up of the harder and greyer Ordivician and Silurian rocks gradually worn down and eroded by weathering over millions of years to their present gentle outlines. The rocks were named after the Iron Age tribes of Ordivices and Silures living in Powys at the time of the Roman advance into Wales.

In Roman times, Powys, like the rest of Wales, formed part of the military zone of Roman Britain. Roman forts were mostly in the main river valleys at Brecon, Clyro, Caersws and Forden with an additional fort at Castell Collen centrally placed near Llandrindod Wells. None of these, however, were on the scale of the great legionary fortresses controlling northern and southern Wales at Chester and Caerleon. Mid-Wales was not particularly important to the Romans except in offering routes for the connecting links of their road network between north and south.

After the Roman departure mid-Wales developed politically into a series of princedoms and small kingdoms. Brycheiniog in the south was a compact little state whose princes traced their descent to Brychan the son of an Irish king. Many of Brychan's numerous children became saints of the Celtic Church and founded new churches throughout mid-Wales. The most important kingdom was Powys itself which in its heyday included all the land between the River Wye and the River Dee and probably also extended for a time eastwards to include large parts of Shropshire and Cheshire. Later the eastern border of Powys was moved westwards to the line of Offa's Dyke, and the northern and southern parts of the kingdom, known as Powys Fadog and Rhwng Gwy a Hafren, passed to secondary branches of the dynasty.

Powys was one of the first parts of Wales to be threatened by the advancing Normans after the Battle of Hastings. Well before the end of the eleventh century Roger, Earl of Shrewsbury, had built Montgomery Castle (named after his home in Normandy) and from there he attacked and laid waste much of the Severn valley. Further south Norman lords from Herefordshire set off to conquer lands in the Wye and Usk valleys. Philip de Braose seized Radnor about 1090 and then moved on to Builth, and three years later Brycheiniog fell to Bernard de Newmarche.

In the twelfth century the Normans managed to strengthen their hold over the southern half of modern Powys. In the northern part, however, the Normans were ousted from the Severn valley and the ancient kingdom of Powys, though much reduced in size, remained independent. From time to time Powys was aligned, either forcibly or voluntarily, with Gwynedd which at this period was the leading Welsh state. The union was a precarious one and for a few years in the middle of the thirteenth century the rulers of Powys transferred their allegiance to the king of England. By 1263 the whole of Powys, including Radnor, Builth and Brecon, was once again reunited with Gwynedd and an independent Wales. It was to be a short-lived reunion, however, for in 1282 Llywelyn ap Gruffydd, the last Prince of Wales, was ambushed and killed near Builth during the Second War of Independence and not only Powys but all Wales fell into English hands.

During the early years of the fifteenth century the eastern borderland had become, once again, part of a united and independent Wales under Owain Glyndŵr. Two of Glyndŵr's victories, at Hyddgen on the northern slopes of Pumlumon and at Bryn Glas in Radnorshire, were fought in Powys. He also set up a parliament at Machynlleth at the western extremity of the county. Three quarters of a century later Powys witnessed another Welsh army marching through the land. This was the army of Henry Tudor which after traversing Dyfed from Pembroke to Aberystwyth wheeled right at Machynlleth and followed the Severn valley down to Welshpool. On 13 August 1485, Henry and his supporters gathered together for the last time in Wales, on the Long Mountain just outside Welshpool, before going on to Bosworth Field and victory. Half a century later the Act of Union of 1536 formally united Wales with England. At the same time the Act deprived the Marcher lords of their political powers and created instead the counties of Montgomeryshire, Radnorshire and Breconshire.

When the Civil War started a century later the whole of Powys, in common with the most of Wales, was strongly in support of the Royalists. In 1644, however, Parliamentary forces turned their attack to the Severn valley area and captured Welshpool, Newtown and Montgomery. The Royalists counter-attacked at Montgomery but were heavily defeated, leaving the way open for the Parliamentary forces to advance on Shrewsbury and north-eastern Wales.

Thereafter Powys was uninvolved in politics and wars and life settled down to a slow rural pace that hardly changed in the succeeding centuries. Conditions gradually improved and the population slowly increased in numbers—helped by lead mining and the flannel industry in the Severn Valley—to a peak in the mid-nineteenth century. Non-conformism also began to flourish under the leadership of Howell Harris of Trefeca in the Black Mountains. Fortunately, none of these intrusions have had much affect on the landscape for each, whether leadmines, the flannel industry or chapels, was on a comparatively small scale. Railways too have come and gone and the scars of cuttings and embankments have healed with time.

The greatest change in the Powys landscape has been the construction of reservoirs. There are more reservoirs in Powys than in any other Welsh county and few, if any, are for the local inhabitants; they are there to quench the thirsts of the industrial areas of southern Wales, the English Midlands and Merseyside. Most of the reservoirs were built in the nineteenth century although some of the larger ones were constructed quite recently. They fall into three groups: a scatter of smaller reservoirs in the Brecon Beacons, a mini-lake district in the Elan Valley and some larger reservoirs along the tributaries of the River Severn. It is possible to argue the politics of siting so many reservoirs in mid-Wales and about the loss of agricultural land or even about the design of their dams. Undeniably, however, they add interest to the scene and have become popular tourist areas, providing new roads across hills and mountains where before there was nothing but moorland and sheep tracks. Ironically, it is the farmers and their families – who might have benefited most from the new roads – which have been ousted from the flooded valleys.

TWO

The Brecon Beacons and the Usk Valley

Although on the edge of a densely populated area and nearer to London than any other national park in Britain, the Brecon Beacons National Park is undeservedly the least well-known of the three national parks in Wales. The Brecon Beacons cannot compare in grandeur with the rocky and historically symbolic vastness of Snowdonia in the north or in dramatic qualities with the sea-cliffs of the Pembrokeshire Coast in the west, but for sheer pastoral beauty they are unsurpassable. The mountains of the Brecon Beacons National Park do, indeed, have precipices and cliffs but unlike the Alpine crags of the north, they do not dominate the scene; rather, they are highlights in a splendid panoramic landscape of luxuriant valleys and softly rounded peaks and ridges. Added to the apparent gentleness of the mountains (at least when viewed from below) is the genial loveliness of the valleys themselves with their lush tree planting, warm stone buildings and rich red-brown ploughed fields. Together the gentle shapes and warm colouring have created a unique landscape that is richly attractive and human.

And yet for all their apparent mildness the uplands never look like mere hills – they are mountains good and proper, rising to almost 3,000 feet above sea level with large expanses of bare wilderness, long lines of escarpments and remote corrie lakes all of which can be dangerous to the unwary. Like every real mountain they should always be treated with respect and caution.

From Abergavenny in the east to Llandeilo in the west there are four main mountain ranges. They are the Black Mountains, the Brecon Beacons, Fforest Fawr and Y Mynydd Du. From their northern summits long ridges sweep grandly away to the southern boundary of the Park where a narrow rim of limestone gives rise to some of the most fascinating scenery in the Park. Here, on the very borders of the coalfield are picturesque waterfalls, towering gorges, craggy out-crops and vast cave systems.

The river valleys vary considerably from the geologically young

V-shaped valleys to the distinctive U-shaped glaciated valleys. Each is delightful but surpassing all is the Usk valley crossing the Park from west to east. Starting on the northern slopes of Y Mynydd Du the Usk river turns west along a beautiful valley to Brecon and then veers south-eastwards, paralleled by a canal, in a trench-like vale between the Brecon Beacons and the Black Mountains down to Crickhowell.

Crickhowell (Crucywel) is delightfully situated on the east side of the Usk, cradled between the Old Red Sandstone slopes of the Black Mountains and the limestone cliffs of Mynydd Llangatwg. Its most prominent feature is the pretty broach spire of the fourteenth-century church (St Edmunds) on the western edge of the town. Just beyond the church and on a corner where the two main roads meet is Porth Mawr, a medieval castellated gateway which once formed the entrance to a Tudor mansion long since demolished. In a small park on the other side of the town the fragmentary remains of a motte-castle with a shell keep bear witness to Owain Glyndŵr's war of independence at the beginning of the fifteenth century. In the more peaceful centuries that followed Crickhowell became an important centre of the flannel industry and later still it acquired a good collection of Georgian houses.

In the early years of the nineteenth century, Crickhowell was the home for nearly 30 years of Thomas Price. One of the foremost Celtic scholars of the day, Price was noted as a historian and antiquary and did much to make the Welsh and the Bretons in France aware of their kinship and was largely instrumental in getting the Bible translated into Breton. As an ardent advocate of the language and culture of Wales, he successfully established as far back as 1820 a Welsh school in the district and also set up a school for blind harpists in Brecon.

Crickhowell was also the home of Sir George Everest (1790–1866), the Surveyor General of India after whom Mount Everest was named. Gwern-vale, the late eighteenth-century mansion where Everest lived, still stands (though much altered) on the hillside above the Brecon road. It is now a hotel. At the entrance to Gwern-vale there is Stone Age burial chamber, recently exposed as a result of road improvements.

A lovely thirteen-arch, seventeenth-century bridge spans the Usk and connects Crickhowell to Llangattock (Llangatwg) on the west side of the river. Nearly half of the bridge is built over dry land. Llangattock crawls up the hill towards a delightful stretch of the Brecon Canal which here winds lazily around the base of the mountains. At the lower end of the village there is a massively towered church inside a circular churchyard. The old village stocks and whipping post can still be seen in the north aisle.

In the little valley beyond Llangattock the great limestone cliffs of

Craig y Cilau rise up like a miniature Grand Canyon. Here amongst the rocky clefts, is one of the habitats of the lesser Whitebeam, an indigenous plant related to the mountain ash and not known anywhere outside the Brecon Beacons National Park. Craig y Cilau is also caving country. The mountain behind the cliffs is honeycombed with a network of caverns, passages and underground water courses that include some of the longest cave systems in the British Isles. Ogof Agen Allwedd ('Keyhole Cave'), for instance, was first discovered in 1948 and has now been explored for a length of 13 miles underneath Mynydd Llangatwg. Most of the caves are difficult to locate and are accessible only to experienced cavers but Ogof Eglwys Faen ('Stone Church'), half-way along the base of the cliffs, is fairly easy to find and has free access.

Many of the ridges and valleys of the Black Mountains can be reached most easily from Crickhowell. The nearest peak is Pen Cerrig-calch (2,302 feet), two and a half miles away. Its summit is an isolated limestone cap which represents the last remnant of the vast limestone sheet which in prehistoric times must have lain right across the Usk valleys and the Black Mountains. On the shoulder of the mountain are the oval ramparts of Crug Hywel hill-fort (after which Crickhowell gets its name). Beyond Pen Cerrig-calch there is a marvellous ridge walk where one can walk northwards for nine miles without going below the 2,000 foot contour.

Patrisio church, buried deep in the hills above the Grwyne Fawr valley to the east of Crickhowell, is one of the rare monuments that have survived, almost by accident, virtually intact. Progress has by-passed it and its very isolation has been the means of preserving its treasures. Without the aid of a good map it is difficult to find, so snugly and delightfully is it hidden away in the folds of the valley, but it is well worth the effort to discover. Inside there is an eleventh-century font, a large number of wall murals, including one with a skeletal figure of Death, and an oak cradle-roof. But the finest prize of this simple but enchanting church is the exquisitely carved screen to the medieval rood-loft (*c.* 1500). Based on a restrained repetitive pattern the screen has the diffident charm and slender grace of delicate lace-work and one wonders how it could possibly have been fashioned by hand out of wood.

To the north of Crickhowell lies Tretŵr at the junction of two important routes, one to Brecon and the west via the pass of Bwlch and the other to Talgarth and the north via the pass of Pengenffordd. To control this strategic point between the Usk and Wye the Normans built themselves a castle at the first opportunity. Originally a typical motte-and-bailey castle, it was later rebuilt with a polygonal shell keep, but this was not sufficient to deter the Welsh and sometime about the end of the twelfth century it was overwhelmed and gutted. On regaining control the Anglo-Norman lord decided to rebuild again, but this time with a single round tower of massive proportions and it is this great tower, rising up out of the earlier ruins, that can still be seen standing alone amongst the flat meadows. By the fourteenth century the conditions of life were somewhat quieter and the castle, which had now outlived its usefulness, was abandoned in favour of Tretower Court nearby. It was still necessary, however, to take some protective measures and thus a large fortified gateway was built in the late fifteenth century at the entrance to the courtyard of the mansion and linked to the stone and timber dwelling by a high level wall-walk.

The little village of Bwlch (meaning 'a pass'), is appropriately named for it is situated high up in a narrow col between Buckland Hill and Mynydd Llan-gors and away from the Usk Valley which here would have been too narrow and difficult to accommodate an invading army on the march. The main road climbs up from Tretŵr following the route taken by the Romans and Normans. Just north of Bwlch and hidden amongst trees at Blaenllyfni are the meagre remains of a Norman castle. Below Bwlch the River Usk is crossed by a fine six-arch bridge at Llangynidr. Though not as long as Crickhowell bridge it is narrower and higher and has a splendid setting.

On Buckland Hill Colonel Gwynne Holford, a veteran of Waterloo, undertook a novel form of memorial by planting a forest in which the lines of trees represented the ranks of infantry at the great battle. Holford's own memorialial is at Llansanffraed, a mile further along the main road, in the church that he had rebuilt in red sandstone in 1884. The religious poet Henry Vaughan (1621–95), often known as the Silurist (after the Silures who occupied this part of Wales during the Roman period) and also as The Swan of Usk, was buried in the churchyard. After studying law at London and working for a time in Brecon, Vaughan turned his attention to medicine and returned to live at Newton farm near Llansanffraed. Here, beside the peaceful Usk which he dearly loved, he wrote his poetry including the collection known as *Silex Scintillus.* After his wife's death Vaughan returned to a cottage at Scethrog a mile further upstream.

A secondary road north of Bwlch leads, in a couple of miles to Llangors Lake (Llyn Syfaddan), a shallow stretch of water lying at the headwaters of the Afon Llynfi. Five miles in circumference, it is the second largest natural lake in Wales. An excellent view of the lake and its surroundings can be had from the top of Mynydd Troed, a bare outlier of the Black Mountains just under 2000 feet high. In the middle ages the lake was a sufficiently rich fishing ground to give rise to a Parliamentary survey in 1650 and was particularly renowned for the immense size of its fish which inspired the saying *cyhyd a llyswen*

Syfaddan ('as long as a Syfaddan eel'). It is also rich in legends. It is reputed to be bottomless and the water of the Llynfi which flows through it on its way to join the Wye is said not to mix with that of the lake. Another legend (according to Giraldus Cambrensis) was that the birds sung of Gruffydd ap Rhys as being the rightful owner of the surrounding land and not the Norman invaders. Better known is the story of a submerged city, the walls and roofs of which it is said can be seen below the water in certain lighting conditions. This is probably a genuine relic of folk memory for the small island at the northern end and was in fact inhabited in the distant past. In 1925 a *cafn unpren* (a dug-out canoe now in Brecon Museum) was found there, along with the remains of a prehistoric lake-dwelling which had been supported on wooden piles. In summertime the lake is busy with yachts and boats, but in winter it is deserted by man and becomes an important gathering ground for the handsome great crested grebes and for little grebes, goosanders, herons and other wildfowl. It is also the most westerly limit of the pretty little reed warbler and the home of the now rare medicinal leech. The last golden eagle is said to have been seen near Cathedin at the southern corner of the lake in the 1930s.

Cathedin was also the home for a time of the playwright Christopher Fry, who once lived at the Regency-fronted house known as Trebinshwm. Nearby, at Llangasty Tal-y-llyn there is a delightful group of buildings comprising an austerely designed church, school and master's house at the side of the lake. They were built for Robert Raikes of Treberfedd, the founder of Sunday Schools, between 1848 and 1850 to the designs of J. L. Pearson. Treberfedd, higher up the hill to the south, was originally a simple eighteenth-century house and was enlarged and rebuilt in Tudor style by Pearson at the same time.

Tal-y-bont, opposite Llansanffraed on the other side of the Usk, is a good centre to explore the wild and beautiful country behind the Brecon Beacons. The hamlet stands at the side of the Monmouthshire and Brecon Canal (opened in 1801, and now one of the few Welsh canals still in use) and was in the nineteenth century the terminus of the old Bryn-oer tramroad that led across the mountains to the coal-mining valleys further south. The site of the tramroad now makes a delightful footpath for walkers. For the Brecon Beacons themselves take the road westwards alongside Tal-y-bont reservoir and through lovely Glyn Collwn between the arête-like ridge of Allt-lwyd (2,100 feet) and the shapely dome of Tor-y-foel. At the head of the valley there is a splendid waterfall (Blaen-y-Glyn) half-hidden in the woods and beyond that the road climbs steeply up to the pass at Torpantau (1,446 feet high). From there the peaks of the Brecon Beacons can be approached by a fairly easy four-mile walk along the track of an old Roman road. Alternatively one can continue on down hill to the Taf

Fechan Forest and sample its delightful picnic places amongst the woodland glades or explore its interesting nature trails.

The road from Tal-y-bont to Brecon follows the canal past Pencelli and Llanfrynach. At Pencelli there are slight earthworks and masonry remains of a medieval castle, but the unexpectedly large church of St Meugan with its fifteenth-century tower and cradle-roofed nave is half a mile away on the slopes of the mountains. In the churchyard there are the graves of a bride and groom and their friends all of whom were drowned while crossing the Usk in 1753 on their way to the marriage service.

Llanfrynach is a quiet village, closely-knit around a church (rebuilt in the nineteenth century except for the tower) and a large churchyard, a mile further on. The un-Welsh layout of the village is compensated by a monumental slab (1616) in the church listing in typically Welsh fashion the pedigree of Thomas ap John ap Thomas ap John ap Rosser ap John ap Ieuan ap Philip ap Howell Gam. Behind the village is the site of a Roman bathhouse discovered in the late eighteenth century. Part of its mosaic floor is now in the National Museum at Cardiff.

Just before joining the main road the way goes near an aqueduct at Brynich and passes near to Abercynrig, a small two-storeyed sixteenth-century mansion with steep hipped roofs. Most of the building was refurbished at the end of the seventeenth century in an attempt to give it an (almost) symmetrical and formal appearance. The house is unusual in that it has retained intact a pair of seventeenth-century paintings (with scenes from the legend of Diana and Actaeon) above the two fireplaces in the hall. John Lloyd, who inherited Abercynrig in 1818, was a poet of some standing in his day but is now chiefly remembered for his long and not very profound narrative poem entitled 'The English Country Gentlemen' written in 1849.

Few towns anywhere in Britain are so beautifully situated as Brecon (Aberhonddu), standing as it does on the gently rising north bank of the graceful Usk, where the fast-running Afon Honddu (after which the town gets its Welsh name) has its confluence. Across the Usk are the Brecon Beacons, not so near as to be overwhelming but not too far away to appreciate the magnificent outline of their peaks. As with many old towns Brecon itself, however, is inward looking and for views of the mountains one must go beyond the medieval core down to the riverside or up to the modern outskirts on the hills behind the town.

Much of Brecon's distinctive charm is due to its irregular layout of narrow medieval streets developing from a triangular market place in the centre of the town. One side of this open space is dominated by St Mary's parish church with its 100-foot-high tower built by the Duke of Buckingham at the beginning of the sixteenth century for the sum of

£2,000. Though few medieval buildings now remain, the street layout belongs to the walled borough established first by the Normans in 1093. Fragments of the old town walls and a tower still survive alongside the Captain's Walk, a promenade built during the Napoleonic wars by French prisoners. Rather more of the castle sited on the west bank of the Honddu has managed to withstand the ravages of time and weather. Originally built by Bernard de Newmarche, the half-brother of William the Conqueror, the castle now consists of the twelfth- or thirteenth-century Ely Tower (named after the Bishop of Ely who was imprisoned here by Richard III) in the grounds of the Bishop of Swansea and Brecon's private gardens and, on the opposite side of the road (in the grounds of the Castle of Brecon Hotel), the ruins of a thirteenth-century great hall.

Before the Industrial Revolution Brecon was one of the principal towns of Wales and a fashionable centre of social life. The numerous Jacobean and Georgian town-houses of the local gentry are still a notable feature of the older part of the town. There was also a theatre and it was in Brecon that the great tragic actress Sarah Siddons was born in 1755 at the Shoulder of Mutton Inn (47 High Street). Contemporary with Mrs Siddons were Theophilus Jones and Thomas Coke. The former, born in 1759 at 12 Lion street, was the author of *A History of the County of Brecknock* while the latter, born in 1747, became a missionary of the Wesleyan Foreign church and was responsible for the establishment of the Wesleyan Foreign Mission Committee. The Wesleyan Chapel in Lion Street was built in 1835 to commemorate Dr Coke. Another native of the town was Sir John Price, a barrister, Secretary of the Council in Wales and the Marches and principal ecclesiastical registrar to Henry VIII. He was one of the earliest collectors of Welsh manuscripts and also published the first printed book *Yn y Lhyvr hwnn*, in 1546.

Of Brecon's nineteenth-century buildings, the most outstanding is the Brecknock Museum designed in 1842 by T. H. Wyatt as the Shirehall with its stately Neo-Greek portico. Inside, the Court Room has been refurnished with its original fittings. There are good examples of Celtic inscribed stones, a dug-out canoe of the Dark Ages and Roman finds as well as natural history and folk-life exhibits. For military history there is the Regimental Museum of the South Wales Borderers at the Watton Barracks nearby, where there are fine collections of uniforms, weapons and medals. The South Wales Borderers are remembered for their heroic defence at Rorke's Drift in the Zulu War of 1879, for which nine Victoria Crosses were awarded to its members.

The important religious buildings stand outside the medieval town. On the hill overlooking the Honddu is the Cathedral. It was once the

Benedictine priory of St John. Its tithe barn, Deanery and four-storeyed Canonry still stand within a fifteenth-century precinct wall adjacent to the church and together form the most complete group of medieval ecclesiastical buildings in the Principality. The cruciform church has a massive central tower giving it a fortress-like appearance belying the elegance of the interior, particularly the beautiful thirteenth-century choir with its walls filled with deeply recessed lancet windows. St Keynes Chapel, on the north side of the nave, was originally the guild chapel for corvizors (or shoe-makers) and tailors. It still retains its ancient screen with a fine ogee arch and has a recessed tomb of a layman (Bloxham) who is thought to have been the builder of the nave. On the bank between the Cathedral and the Honddu is the start of the delightful Priory Groves, a walk laid out some 150 years ago, and now a nature trail.

Rather less of the Dominican friary at Llanfaes (beyond the sixteenth-century arched bridge across the Usk) has survived. It is now incorporated in the nineteenth-century buildings of Christ College, one of Wales' pair of Public Schools. The thirteenth-century choir of the friary church remains and now functions as the college chapel, whilst the nave stands as a roofless shell. There is also a fourteenth-century refectory. Most of the remaining buildings were built between 1861 and 1864 by John Prichard, the restorer of Llandaf Cathedral.

There are further religious connections at Llan-ddew, a mile north-east of Brecon. St David's was once one of the mother (or *clas*) churches of Wales and is one of the oldest still standing in Powys. It is massively built, with tiny windows and a tower that has its piers inside the transept crossing. On the opposite side of the road an arched doorway stands as almost the only reminder of a bishop's palace which once stood here. For a few years, at the end of the twelfth century, it was the home of Gerald de Barri (Giraldus Cambrensis) when he occupied the position of Archdeacon of Brecon which was then an outpost of the far-flung diocese of Tyddewi (St David's) in Dyfed.

A short walk to the north-west of Brecon brings one to Pen-y-Crug, an Iron Age hill-fort. The triple line of ramparts and ditches which once defended it are still well preserved and the summit of this bracken-covered hill commands a superb panoramic view southwards over the town and across the vale of Usk towards the Brecon Beacons, the Black Mountains, Fforest Fawr and Y Mynydd Du. Northwards, there are views across Mynydd Epynt. A mile and a half further west at Aberysgir is Y Gaer, the largest Roman auxiliary fort in Wales. Originally built of timber in the first century to house the Spanish Vettonian Cavalry, it was partly rebuilt in stone about the middle of the second century. It was reoccupied in the third century and finally abandoned in the latter part of the fourth century. Sir Mortimer Wheeler excavated the fort in 1924 and parts of it, including the foundations of three gateways, a portion of the wall and the corner towers, have been left exposed.

The easiest way to the Brecon Beacons from Brecon is by road to the Storey Arms (originally a hostelry but now an outdoor activities school) situated at the top of the pass at 1,440 feet above sea level. From Storey Arms there is an easy two mile walk to Pen-y-fan which at 2,906 feet above sea level is the highest peak south of Cadair Idris in Gwynedd. A far more interesting circular route is from Cantref (three miles south of Brecon) and then up the Bryn-teg ridge to Cribyn (2,608 feet) and Pen-y-fan; the way back is over the shoulder of Carn Du (2,863 feet) and down to lonely Llyn Cwmllwch (a small tarn with a legendary island), past some waterfalls and into the pretty Ffrwdgrech valley. In fine weather, the Beacons make superb hill-walking country with glorious views all around (south across the Severn Sea to Exmoor and north to Pumlumon and even, on occasions, as far as Cadair Idris, 60 miles away), but in misty weather the northern escarpments, etched by glaciers of the Ice Age into almost precipitous cliffs, can be as dangerous for the unwary as the cliffs of Snowdonia. To emphasize the point there is a stone monument near Carn Du commemorating the death of little five-year-old Tommy Jones who got lost when out walking on his own.

To the west of the Beacons is Fforest Fawr (Great Forest), a barren, undulating moorland area dissected by parallel rivers flowing south towards Swansea Bay. Originally a royal hunting forest, it was farmed out after the Middle Ages but remained Crown land until the early nineteenth century. North of Fan Fawr (2,409 feet), the highest peak of the Fforest, is Craig Cerig-gleisiad, an armchair shaped cwm formed by glacial erosion. It is now a National Nature Reserve and here an arctic tundra type of vegetation (a relic of the last Great Ice Age), which includes Cowberry, Green Spleenwart and Purple Saxifrage, has survived on the craggy cliffs as well as the more temperate Welsh Poppy. Here also is the home of the Buzzard.

The more friendly common of Mynydd Illtud lies further north. Amongst its heathland and marshy pools is the Mountain Centre, a purpose-built building opened in 1966, providing a lounge, viewing terraces, picnic area and car park, as well as information on all aspects of the Brecon Beacons National Park. Llanilltud church nearby is nineteenth-century and of no particular interest, but the circular *llan* (churchyard) surrounding the church dates from the Dark Ages and in May and June is a colourful carpet of bluebells. Sarn Helen, one of the Roman roads that crosses mid-Wales from north to south and a Bronze Age cromlech (Bedd Illtud) add an air of mystery to the place while not far away are the ruins of Castell Cwmcamlais (or Maescar Castle as it is otherwise known), a reminder of one of the Welsh Wars of Independence. The castle, probably built by Llywelyn ap Gruffydd and destroyed by Edward I, now comprises the stump of a large mid thirteenth-century circular tower surrounded by a deep dry moat.

South of Fforest Fawr the scenery changes dramatically from open moorland to deep, narrow and densely wooded valleys. As the rivers that water these valleys come down from Fforest Fawr, on their way to the sea, they cross from the Old Red Sandstone rocks to Carboniferous Limestone rocks giving rise in the process to numerous waterfalls, underground rivers and caves. The area is of exceptional scenic and geological interest, but requires time to explore and can only really be seen on foot. The little village of Ystradfellte is a good centre to start from.

The first place of interest is Porth-yr-Ogof ('Gateway of the Cave') where the Mellte, after running underground for some distance, reappears briefly only to disappear again into a vast cavern. The cave with its mass of side passages can be entered in dry weather for some distance without equipment except a light, but in flood conditions it is impossible. The river reappears from the cave about a quarter of a mile further on. There are many other caves near Ystradfellte and at Pwll-y-rhyd on the Afon Nedd, including one with five miles of underground passages, but these are all potentially dangerous and are for experts only.

Below Porth-y-Ogof, a footpath leads in about a mile to the first of the three Clun-gwyn waterfalls. Of the three falls, the most beautiful is the middle Clun-gwyn with its single leap followed immediately by a tumbling cascade. The footpath continues through the woods well above the Mellte river to a tributary, the Afon Hepste. Here there are two splendid falls. The lower one is a rapid and like most of the other falls in the district is best seen after wet weather. A short way further up the Hepste is Scwd-yr-Eira a well-named fall meaning the 'spout of snow'. This is perhaps the best of all the falls and is unusual in that one can walk (with care) behind the 50-foot curtain of water as it drops in a graceful curve over the ledge above. Below the confluence of the Mellte and Hepste the way, though exquisitely beautiful, is extremely difficult because of the steepness of the ravine's sides, which here is a 200- to 300-foot deep gorge.

To explore the valleys west of Ystradfellte take the road along the ridge southwards to Pontneddfechan (Pontneath Vaughan) and join the footpath alongside the Afon Nedd. About a mile upstream the Nedd is joined by the Afon Pyrddin with its two beautiful waterfalls.

Scwd Gwladys, the nearer of the two falls, is graceful and easily accessible while Scwd Einon-gam is perhaps more spectacular but difficult to approach except along the bed of the river when it is dry. After crossing over the Pyrddin by a footbridge continue a mile up the west bank of the Nedd to Pont Melin-fach, passing on the way two cataracts and two fine falls known as Scwd Ddwli Isaf and Scwd Ddwli Uchaf. At Pont Melin-fach one can continue upstream for a further two and a half miles to Pwll-y-Rhyd, where the river disappears underground for a short distance or, alternatively, take the road again and continue to Ystradfellte.

From Ystradfellte, a mountain road follows the line of the Roman road Sarn Helen northwards again to the Usk valley. Near the highest point it passes Maen Llia, an isolated Early Christian memorial stone, and then zig-zags down a steep escarpment into the Senni valley leading eventually to the upper part of the Usk valley at Sennybridge.

Sennybridge was largely developed in the early nineteenth-century when, after the opening of the turnpike road, it took over the sheep and cattle market which had originally been held in nearby Defynnog. The Sennybridge sheep sales were started by Scottish farmers who bought large areas of sheep-walks after the enclosure of Fforest Fawr in 1815–19. On the opposite side of the river there is an army camp serving the Mynydd Epynt artillery range.

Betws Pen-pont lies a short way east of Sennybridge in a delightful situation along a fine stretch of the Usk. There is an unusual church and two large mansions but no village. Between them they form a fascinating group of buildings. The earliest of the two mansions is Pen-pont, which was built in the late seventeenth century by Daniel Williams with money acquired by successive marriages to two rich heiresses. The classical colonnade in front of the house was added about 1810. Nearby is a small dower house, with a richly carved pediment, built for Daniel Williams's son in 1686. The unusual church at Betws Pen-pont has a circular tower and steeple and a semicircular east end. It is the result of rebuilding in 1865 by Sir George Gilbert Scott. Abercamlais, the other mansion in this group, was built about 1710 by another branch of the Williams family. It is also three storeys high and has a grand staircase. Both houses still retain their dovecotes. Pen-pont's is plain and square but the two-storey octagonal dovecot at Abercamlais is more ornamental and also has a multipurpose use; the upper part is for the doves while the lower part serves as a privy and also forms a bridge across the stream.

A couple of miles west of Sennybridge is Trecastell. The large motte-and-bailey castle which towers above the road was built by the Lord of Brecknock in the twelfth-century to guard the valley from the west. A mile further on is Llywel church with its tall fifteenth-century tower, churchyard stocks and inside a colony of Natterer's bats and two early Christian stones with Ogham (Irish) inscriptions.

The last major mountain in the chain of mountains that stretch from east to west across the Brecon Beacons National Park is Y Mynydd Du (otherwise known as the Black Mountain—a needless Anglicization that only results in confusion with the Black Mountains at the eastern end of the Park). It forms the boundary between two counties (Powys and Dyfed) and has two peaks (Bannau Brycheiniog, 2,632 feet, and Bannau Sir Gaer, 2,460 feet) which look down precipitously onto two lakes (Llyn y Fan Fawr and Llyn y Fan Fach) 700 feet below.

Emerging from the northern slopes of Y Mynydd Du are the sources of two important rivers, the Usk (or as it is known here, Afon Wysg) and the Tawe. For the first few miles the Usk stream goes steadily north passing a number of small Bronze Age stone circles, each accompanied by an avenue of small stones and all largely hidden now by undergrowth, and then after passing through the very attractive Cwmwysg reservoir turns suddenly eastwards on its journey, now as a fully-fledged river, towards Sennybridge and Brecon.

The Tawe, on the other hand, starts by going east and then makes a sharp turn south following a course below the long, dark escarpment of Fan Hir. At Glyntawe the river crosses a narrow band of limestone and the scenery changes once again from open moorland to a deep, winding and well wooded valley with rocky outcrops. Here within the short space of half-a-mile are two places of unusual interest, one natural and the other man made.

The natural feature is Dan-yr-Ogof, a marvellous cave system which is illuminated and open to the public. The caves were first discovered and explored in 1912 by two local brothers, Ashwell and Jeff Morgan, who found a chain of underground lakes, natural bridges and an underground waterfall as well as some fine stalactites and stalagmites. For 25 years no more was heard of the caves and then in 1938 they were re-explored by properly trained cavers and a year later opened to the public. The guided tour of just over a mile lasts about 45 minutes. In 1971 an adjoining cave known as the Cathedral cave, because of its vast 80-foot high cavern, was also opened to the public. Ogof Ffynnon Ddu, the largest cave in Wales with 16 miles of caverns and passages, is situated on the opposite side of the Tawe valley amongst the Carreg-lwyd quarries.

The man-made curiosity of this romantic valley is Craig-y-Nos ('Rock of the Night'), a Gothic castle first built in 1842 (to designs by T. H. Wyatt) for Rhys Davies Powell and later extended with Italianate additions. For 40 years it was the home and refuge of Adelina Patti, the Victorian *prima donna*, who returned here by special train after each triumphant tour of the world's opera houses; at the station she had her own private waiting room. Born in Madrid of Italian parents and brought up in New York, Madam Patti was 36 when she came to Wales and bought Craig-y-Nos, but by then she was well on the way to amassing one of the largest fortunes ever made by an opera singer. In 1886 Madam Patti married the French tenor Ernesto Nicolini and together they set about transforming Craig-y-Nos. Wings were added on, a clock-tower was built, a winter garden with tropical plants was constructed, a private theatre opened and, in addition to all this, a suite of rooms was prepared and set apart for the use of the Prince of Wales—later King Edward VII. In 1898 Nicolini died and Patti married again, this time to Baron Cederstrom, who was then 26 years her junior. Adelina Patti died in 1919 and left Craig-y-Nos for the last time to be taken to Paris and buried in the Père Lachaise Cemetery there. Craig-y-Nos later became a tuberculosis sanatorium and the Winter Garden was re-erected at Swansea. The beautiful grounds around the Castle, with lakes stocked with fish and wildfowl, have now become a country park and the delightful little theatre is still occasionally used by local opera groups.

A couple of miles downstream the Tawe turns southwest and, as industry takes over from the rural landscape at Aber-craf and Ystradgynlais, the valley becomes known as the Swansea Valley and Powys and the National Park are left behind.

THREE

The Wye Valley

The middle reaches of the Wye Valley can be easily reached from Brecon a few miles to the south-west. The neck of land between the Usk at Brecon and the Wye at Llyswen was always of strategic importance for this was the route that invaders used to penetrate into mid-Wales and for centuries strife must have been part of the normal pattern of life in these parts. At Talgarth, just below the bend of the Wye and sheltering amongst the northern foothills of the Black Mountains, there is a medieval tower-house (called simply Tower) four storeys high and similar in construction to the peel-towers of the Scottish border. Another tower-house still survives a few miles south of Talgarth at Scethrog in the Usk Valley. Not far away, the medieval mansion of Porth-aml Fawr has a detached and fortified gatehouse. On the far side of the river and standing on a mound surrounded by trees is the thirteenth-century Bronllys Castle, which like Tretŵr, now has a single round tower. Detached towers seem to have been the rage in this area for even the church at Bronllys has a free-standing tower, possible intended as a place of refuge.

Yet in spite of all this concern for defence Talgarth itself appears to have had a quiet existence undisturbed by military events. Of its two most eminent residents one of these, Jane Williams, is now almost forgotten. She lived at Neuadd Felin in Church Street in the nineteenth century and during her lifetime was well known as the author of historical and biographical works; *The history of Wales, Literary Women of the Seventeenth Century*, and a book about the Rev Thomas Price (Carnhuanawc).

The other celebrity was Howell Harris, one of the chief leaders of the Methodist Revival in Wales. He was born in 1714 at Trefeca Uchaf, a mile south-west of Talgarth. Harris was destined for the established church but his methods of preaching brought him into conflict with the local vicar and he soon became a Methodist. In 1752, after a quarrel with Daniel Rowland—another Methodist leader, the autocratic Harris founded a religious community at Trefeca based on the experiments of the Moravians in England and Germany. Harris added to and altered the original house so that it became a 'castellated monastery' in Strawberry Hill Gothic style. The semi-monastic community aimed at a self-sufficient economy in which all members lived as a family, practising a large variety of crafts, woollen-making, and planned agriculture. The community was supported by the Countess of Huntingdon and with her help a college for training young preachers was set up at College Farm nearby. This rich and pious lady became a widow after 18 years of marriage and then devoted her remaining 45 years of widowhood to founding a religious sect and building 64 chapels in addition to supporting Harris in his work. After the death of Harris the community languished and Trefeca was eventually taken over in 1842 by the Welsh Calvinistic Methodist Church as a theological college. Part of Harris' additions were demolished to make way for a new chapel (1872) which has become a museum with an excellent exhibition dealing with Harris' life and work. The house is now part of a residential missionary centre.

A feature of some of the small churches embedded in the hills around Talgarth is their delicate rood-screens. Excellent examples can be seen at Llandefalle and Llanfilo on either side of the Brecon road and at Llanelieu tucked away at the edge of the Black Mountains. The very remoteness of these country churches probably explains the preservation of these miracles of the carpenter's art. The church at Llanfilo is particularly attractive. Long and low-slung on the outside with gravestones on the walls, the white-washed interior is unexpectedly fresh and bright. In addition to the graceful rood-loft and screen the church still retains its seventeenth-century pulpit and pews and plaster ceiling.

Half way between Talgarth and Hay on the southern side of the Wye is the hamlet of Aberllynfi, or Three Cocks as it is otherwise known from the name of the railway station (now gone) and the old coaching inn. There are a number of Stone Age burial tombs in the vicinity as well as a castle motte and remains of two ancient camps. The most interesting building, however, is Old Gwernyfed, a fascinating mansion, built about 1600, with a symmetrical front. One wing of the house has been a shell since a fire in 1780. Two circular dovecotes with conical roofs stand at the forecourt entrance. Gwernyfed Park, near the main road, is a late nineteenth-century house (now a school) designed by W. E. Nesfield in Jacobean style.

Hay stands just within the Welsh side of the boundary with England, on the south bank of the River Wye. The border itself is marked by the tiny Dulas brook as it tumbles down from the Black Mountains to meet the mother river. The name Hay (officially

Hay-on-Wye), or 'The Hay' as it is sometimes referred to locally, is derived from the Norman-French *La Haie* meaning hedge or enclosure. The Welsh name, Y Gelli, similarly means 'The Grove'. Hay itself is a delightful little town and, though mostly built up during the nineteenth century, has a quaint kind of medieval air about it. This is due to its numerous narrow little streets which wind up and down in an apparently aimless pattern, but in fact still follow the constrictions of centuries' old lanes and thoroughfares, jig-sawed into the confines of the walled borough. The town walls have gone completely – the last remnants unceremoniously demolished when the railway was built in 1864 – and there is nothing to show that the walls ever existed except for the shape of the town on the ground. The railway has now gone too, its place being taken by an attractive riverside walk stretching from the bridge back to the Warren, a 'natural' recreation area formed by a double bend in the river. Surprisingly, the most flourishing industry in the town now is the second-hand book trade which is carried on in the old cinema and nearly a dozen other small shops.

In the centre of the town the diminutive Market House and the Butter Market, both with Classical colonnaded fronts and both dating from the early nineteenth century, are the chief buildings of architectural interest. The shell of Hay Castle frowns over the town just outside the line of the old walls. This, however, was not Hay's first castle, but replaced an earlier Norman fortification the earthen *motte* of which can be seen at the side of St Mary's Church, near the river. Little remains of the medieval fortress erected by the ruthless and malicious Marcher Lord William de Braose at the beginning of the thirteenth century apart from a single tower and gateway. In the seventeenth century a large Jacobean gentry house was built on the site of de Braose's fortress and this, with its nineteenth-century remodelling is the gaunt 'castle' which now overlooks the town. In the nineteenth century Hay Castle was leased out as a vicarage and here in the 1870s the Rev Francis Kilvert, the diarist, was a frequent visitor. In one of his entries Kilvert described Hay as 'the picturesque little border town with its slate-roofed houses climbing and shining up the hill crested by the dark long mass of the old ivy-grown castle with its huge war-broken tower.'

Clyro, on the opposite side of the Wye, has a fine setting with views across the valley to the Black Mountains. Apart from a tree-covered mound denoting the site of a medieval castle the only place of interest is Ashbrook House where a plaque informs the visitor that the Rev Francis Kilvert lived here as a curate of Clyro from 1865 to 1872. Kilvert's fame rests entirely on his fascinating diary in which he recorded, with a keenly observant eye, the daily life of his parish and its surroundings. He was a great walker and covered a considerable area during his time at Clyro. Mostly his walks were with the purpose of visiting his far-flung flock and friends, but often it was just for the sheer joy of exploring the countryside, a countryside made even more mellow by his writings.

The road, now much improved as far as Glasbury, keeps to the side of the flat alluvial plain through which the Wye meanders. From this side of the valley the Black Mountains look at their best, especially in early spring when the fields are green and the mountains still have a coating of snow.

Llowes is little more than a hamlet in size. The Early Christian wheel-cross, carved after the Irish fashion, which used to stand in Llowes churchyard is now inside the church. A mile beyond Llowes and in a field near a by-road stands Maes-yr-onen Chapel, the oldest nonconformist chapel still in use in Wales. Attached to the end of the chapel is the caretaker's cottage where the key is kept. Utterly simple in appearance outside and inside, the chapel has survived remarkably intact and still contains its original furniture. Nearby Maesllwch Castle stands just above Glasbury enjoying fine views across the valley to the Black Mountains. Originally built in 1830 in a castellated Norman and Gothic style, to designs by Robert Lugar, the house was extended eastwards about 40 years later in a more austere manner. The main block was demolished in 1951 to make way for a garden and now only the later building remains.

At Glasbury, a compact and comparatively large village for this part of the world, the main road crosses to the south side of the Wye. Near this point once stood Glasbury's medieval church, but a tremendous flood in 1660 swept it away and changed the course of the river leaving the remains of the church on the opposite bank of the river. When the church was rebuilt in 1837 it was sited still further away from the village, south of the river, which at that time formed the old county boundary. Thus Glasbury stood on one side of the Wye in Radnorshire and its church stood on the other side in Breconshire.

Northwards from Llyswen the valley becomes narrower towards Builth and its character changes to that of an upland valley. This part of the Wye valley is almost continuously attractive. The western bank is well wooded, while the eastern bank is generally bleaker and more mountainous with, here and there, rocky cliffs breaking through the thin cover of earth. Between the banks the river swirls and rushes along at a madding pace over the rocks and boulders. The main road on the west bank follows close to the river; a quieter, but equally attractive secondary road follows, on the east bank, the line of an old railway through cuttings alongside the river from Boughrood to Llanelwedd.

Between Llyswen and the suspension bridge at Llanstephan the main road passes close to the eye-catching mansion of Llangoed Castle which was largely rebuilt as recently as 1919 to designs by the late Sir Clough Williams-Ellis in a grand Tudor manner. The centre porch, with its stone doorway dated 1632, still stands as a survivor of the original. Just beyond Llanstephan on the east side of the Wye there is a delightful little wooded valley, known as Craig Pwll-du, with a miniature gorge and waterfall. At the highest end of the valley, accessible by a zig-zag road from Llandeilo Graban, there is a perfect specimen of a castle motte encircled by a ditch and bank. A mile to the north lies Llan Bwch-llyn, a pleasant lake (now uncomfortably fenced in by the Water Board) nestling below rugged hills.

Further east is Painscastle, a straggling village lying beneath the massive ramparts of a large motte-and-bailey castle built by Payn fitzJohn in the early twelfth-century. It was of critical importance in the affairs of Powys and for a century and a half continually changed hands between the princes of Wales, the Marcher lords and the English king. For a while it was the chief centre of the hated baron William de Breos who reconstructed it and renamed it Castrum Matildis after his wife Matilda (Maude de St Valerie). William was the favourite of King John and quickly became lord of vast areas in mid-Wales much to the annoyance of the Prince Gwenwynwyn of Powys. When de Breos had Gwenwynwyn's cousin Trahaiarn brutally murdered the Prince of Powys laid siege to Painscastle. At first the siege seemed set for success, but was later turned to disaster in a decisive battle. Following this even the all-powerful de Breos fell into disgrace with the king (for failure to pay his debts) and was forced to flee with his family to Ireland. His wife Matilda was caught and sent to Windsor where she was starved to death, but William de Breos managed to escape again to France. In the thirteenth century Painscastle was once again a trouble spot and when Prince Llywelyn marched against Brecon and Radnor in 1231, King Henry III retaliated by rebuilding the castle in stone on a monumental scale. A generation later Painscastle was attacked and destroyed and eventually ceded back to the Welsh prince.

The road on the east bank of the Wye skirts a rocky landscape which eventually culminates in the great pile known as Aberedw Rocks. Towering 500 feet above the road the striated rocks, weathered and dissected into giant rectangular blocks, look like the walls of some long-forgotten Inca fortress. The church at Aberedw stands high above the Afon Edw which is here a rushing torrent cleaving a narrow passage through the rocky gorge on its way to meet the Wye. The church is solidly built and disarmingly simple outside with a large stone porch (with arched timber roof) and a massive tower. The stately interior has a high timber roof and a fine open rood-screen.

Just behind the church are the earthwork remains of the outer bailey of a superbly sited stone castle. The steep castle motte is at the highest point and is protected on the landward side by a sunken dry ditch and bank. The motte, only large enough for a small circular keep tower, stands right on the edge of a dangerously sheer rock face a hundred feet or more above the Edw. This must have been the castle to which Llywelyn ap Gruffydd came in 1282 on his last fateful journey southwards, before being traitorously betrayed and then assassinated at the Irfon Bridge near Builth. This castle, in an area which was mostly under the control of the Marcher lords, was a Welsh outpost and according to some writers was used by Llywelyn as a hunting lodge when he was able to get away from the affairs of state at his headquarters in Gwynedd. High up amongst the rocks on the opposite side of the gorge, but difficult to find, is the cave where local tradition claims that Llywelyn hid just before his untimely death in December. It is an unlikely story which has only been corroborated by another unlikely tradition telling that when the snow lay on the ground the Prince came to the local blacksmith to ask him to reverse the shoes of his horse in order to mislead the English; unfortunately for Llywelyn the blacksmith, so it is said, betrayed the prince to the English and they were able, as a result of this double deception, to follow his tracks.

The castle at Aberedw, which is most often referred to as Llywelyn's castle, is a quarter of a mile away towards the Wye and was not, in fact, built until 1284, two years after the Prince's death. Very little remains of this small castle as it was largely destroyed to make way for the mid-Wales railway in 1864.

There is an interesting detour along the Edw valley to Rhulen. The valley is steep sided and the flanking hills look like mountains despite their low height, but the chief interest is a group of tiny, utterly simple churches. At Llanbadarn-y-Garreg the church is merely a stone box, without even a porch, standing alone in a field beside the stream. The stonework details are so sparse that it is impossible to date the church accurately. White-washed inside and out, it has a large faded painting of the Royal Arms on the rood beam. St David's Church at Rhulen, high up in the hills, has both porch and wooden belfry, but these only make the rest of the building look even smaller. The walls lean out and the interior is lit by two small windows in the chancel which, until recently, were only supplemented by gas lights. St David's at Cregina is to the same minute scale set in a circular churchyard and has an open timber roof inside and a primitive rood-screen.

A minor road follows a tributary stream to Glascwm where, at the end of a narrow valley, the thirteenth-century church is a giant in comparison with the previous ones. Glascwm is the mother church of the surrounding parishes and is said to have been founded by St David in the sixth century. The chancel was added in the fifteenth century as was the massive braced roof over the nave. There is a large timber belfry rising through the roof. At Hundred House, with its old corn-mill, the roads from Glascwm and Rhulen join the main road back to Builth. There are no other buildings of any interest, but one can see from a glance at the Ordnance Survey map that the surrounding hills abound with remains of ancient camps and burial tombs.

Llanelwedd, at the side of the Wye again, shelters below a large igneous rock outcrop which is slowly being quarried away for road-stone. The neat church dates from 1877 and has good stained glass in the east window.

Pencerrig, the home of Thomas Jones (1742–1803) the landscape painter, lies a mile north of the village. Jones was the son of a Radnorshire country squire and, after spending several years painting in Italy, retired to Pencerrig in 1787. Prior to that he had been a pupil of Richard Wilson and though his work reflects the master's teaching he never achieved Wilson's fame. Jones had an individual touch, however, and his paintings vary from a vividly portrayed *Bard* (now in the National Museum at Cardiff), to a highly realistic series of *Radnorshire Landscapes* completed in the 1790s.

Just before crossing the six-arched bridge into Builth Wells (Llanfair-ym-Muallt) the road passes the permanent site of the Royal Welsh Show. In July when the show opens the field is busy and full of life, but, save for some pre-fabricated sheds, for most of the year it is empty and devoid of interest. Builth Wells is now a quiet market town, but was once well known as a health spa. The mineral waters at Builth were known as far back as 1740 but the little town achieved its greatest popularity during the last decades of the nineteenth century and the period up to the First World War. The two wells (Glannau and Park), both about a mile to the west of the town, are now closed.

Builth Castle (south-east of the Wye Bridge) had a stormy history but little remains now apart from some impressive earthworks on the edge of the town. For centuries it was an English thorn in the midst of Welsh-held territory and remained isolated from the rest of the Norman Marchlands. It was captured in 1168 and 1215, rebuilt in 1219 and attacked by Llywelyn Fawr in 1223. By 1231 it had fallen into Llywelyn's hands, but on his death it was retrieved by the English King and rebuilt, this time probably in stone. The castle was captured once again in 1260 by Llywelyn's son Llywelyn ap Gruffydd and razed to the ground. In the war of 1276 the lordship was regained by Edward I who immediately set about rebuilding the castle on a magnificent scale. Although at one time it had a great keep tower, a twin-towered gateway and six lesser towers along the curtain wall, not a stone now remains above ground; most of the masonry having been taken away, according to Theophilus Jones (the eighteenth-century historian of Brecknock), to build new mansions in the neighbourhood.

The irony of Builth, however, is not that it was the very first of the great Edwardian castles to be built in Wales, but that it was the scene of the last act of Llywelyn ap Gruffydd, the last independant prince of Wales. The second war of independance was started on Palm Sunday by the Prince of Wales' brother David after many months of fighting during which both sides had scored victories and the outcome of the struggle still hung in the balance. Llywelyn had already succeeded in reversing the English army's advance up the Tywi valley in the south and had seriously damaged the king's fleet in the Menai Strait in the north; then the prince made his way south again to Aberedw, ostensibly to rouse the people of the south, but possibly to meet Edward de Mortimer who is said to have pretended to have turned traitor on the king in order to lure the prince into a trap. Llywelyn captured the lordship of Builth, but failed to take the strongly-held and newly-built castle itself. In the ensuing battle, fought two miles to the west of Builth at Irfon Bridge, the Prince of Wales became separated from his small expeditionary force who were attacked from the rear by a much larger English army. The prince, without his armour (for according to tradition he had been coerced away to confer with de Mortimer) and hearing the noise of battle, hurried back to his men but was mortally struck down by a certain Stephen de Frankton. After the prince's body had been identified, the head was cut off and sent to London for exhibition. The prince's brother David continued to battle with the English until the following June (when he too was captured and executed), but the death of Llywelyn had decisively tipped the scales of war in the king's favour. A monument to Llywelyn the Last, in the form of a simple stone slab, stands near the side of the main road at Cilmeri, not far from the site of Irfon Bridge.

The Irfon valley is spa country for in addition to Builth Wells there are also medicinal wells at Llangammarch and Llanwrtyd, all lying within ten miles of each other. Llangammarch Wells is a tiny village, on a by-road between Builth and Llanwrtyd, and its wells – like those at the other two towns – have known better days. The barium chloride waters were said to be the best in Britain and comparable to the more famous Kreuznach waters in Germany. The Pump Room still stands in the grounds of the Lake Hotel just east of the village. Two miles beyond Llangammarch is Cefn-brith, the farmhouse birthplace of the religious reformer John Penry (1563–93). Penry's books and his reforming zeal brought him into trouble with both the government and the church. He was arrested and fled to Scotland, but was eventually caught, tried and executed at the early age of 30.

Llanwrtyd Wells, on the road to Llandovery, is a minute town, profusely endowed with mineral water springs. The earliest public knowledge of these wells dates from 1732 when the Vicar of Llangammarch, Theophilus Evans, was induced to try the sulphurous waters to cure his scurvy. Somewhat dubious at first, the reverend gentleman saw a frog hop out of the water and, noticing that the frog seemed none the worse from the experience, tried the water himself, and after two months of this treatment the disease disappeared. Later, other wells were opened, notably the Victoria Wells (sulphur discovered in 1897 and lithia saline in 1908) and Henfron Wells (saline sulphur and chalybeate discovered in 1922). For a century and a half the main source of employment for the local people was the local woollen mills. The Cambrian Factory, which is still worked as a woollen mill, was originally a corn mill. It turned to the production of flannel in the 1820s and has, since 1926, been run by the British Legion to provide employment for disabled people. It is now open to the public and visitors can see tweeds and garments being made from Welsh wools. The Esgair Moel Woollen Factory was closed soon after the Second World War and was then removed to the Welsh Folk Museum near Cardiff where it was rebuilt and still produces woollen blankets and other textiles.

North of Llanwrtyd the countryside becomes more rugged and wilder. Just beyond the town the river has carved a narrow valley through a hard belt of igneous rock. This is part of a band of volcanic magma which oozed through the Silurian shales and flagstones to become the source of mineral waters with which the Irfon valley is blessed. At the tiny hamlet of Abergwesyn the road continues northwards alongside the Irfon through the beautiful pass of Camddwr Bleiddiad to the uninhabited moorlands of Elenydd. In the nineteenth century the district was reasonably well populated, but now the village's inn has closed and of its two churches (one on each side of the river) only the graveyards remain. Camddwr Bleiddiad ('Wolf's Leap') is a romantic gorge and though it hardly seems possible that any animal could actually leap across the valley its name is a reminder that this was once wolf country. Beyond is the open moorland and 150 square miles of fell walking uninterrupted by any through-roads. Apart from an occasional farm the nearest villages to Abergwesyn are Tregaron (12 miles west), Cwmystwyth (14 miles north-west), Llangurig (18 miles north) and Elan Village (9 miles north-east).

From Abergwesyn the road follows the Cnyffiad stream back through a beautiful winding, forest-clad valley to Beulah. From there the secondary road runs through open and unspoilt countryside to Newbridge-on-Wye. On the high points between the numerous little valleys along the way there are a number of good views southwards to the hills of Mynydd Epynt and the Wye Valley. Newbridge is delightfully situated on the east bank of the Wye, but its red-brick buildings seem out of place here as also does its large multicoloured nineteenth-century church.

Even more out of place is Llandrindod Wells, the largest and most famous of the mid-Wales spa towns. After all the cosy stone and half-timbered buildings of the surrounding countryside, the harsh red and yellow brick and purple-blue slate of Llandrindod's terraces comes as something of a shock. It is as if a nineteenth-century town from the English seaside had been bodily up-rooted and set down in the heart of rural Wales. The town should not be missed, however, for despite its non-conforming architecture it has a pleasant and cheerful atmosphere and is uncommonly well blessed with parks and open spaces. Indeed, there seem to be gardens, parks and recreation grounds everywhere, most of which are linked to a dingle running through the town. The Temple Gardens at the town centre are named after a Stone Age circle that once stood on the site, the stones of which have now found their way into the garden walls of nearby houses. Almost next door to this is the Recreation Ground, its Grand Pavilion now converted into a cinema and conference hall. From here a path alongside the Dingle leads under the railway into the Rock Park where an attractive wooded valley follows the stream down to a bend of the River Ithon and Lover's Leap. The Pump Room and Spa Treatment Centre stands in the middle of the Rock Park. The Pump House Hotel is now the County Council Offices.

Although Llandrindod did not really become popular as a spa until after the opening of the railway in 1865, the efficacy of its mineral waters had been known two centuries earlier. Thirty springs supply the town with the saline, sulphurous, magnesian and chalybeate waters used both for drinking and bathing. The first two springs were re-discovered by a Mrs Jenkins in 1736 and were used with some success in curing the sick, but the first real effort to advertise the town's waters came a few years later in 1749 when a Mr Grosvenor of Shrewsbury converted a local farm into a hotel. On the eastern side of the town is The Common, a fine wooded stretch of countryside with a large boating lake (complete with an island) in the centre. On the hill beyond is Llandrindod's old church, a small thirteenth-century building which was, until recently, the venue for election of the archbishops of the Church in Wales. The elaborate Holy Trinity church in the town was built in 1871. In order to persuade people to go to the new church the old church was deliberately un-roofed until 1894 when it was restored.

The Ithon River twists and turns along a series of tight bends and loops in a great semi-circle around Llandrindod. The ramparts of

Castell Collen, a Roman fort from the first century A.D., stands on the west bank of the Ithon a mile north of the town centre. A Roman Centurial Stone from the fort is preserved in the west wall of the church at Llanbadarn Fawr two miles away. In Roman times the fort must have been of considerable importance, for just south of Llandrindod there are the scanty remains (barely visible to the eye) of 18 practice camps, the largest known group of practice camps in the Roman Empire. One and a half miles east of Llandrindod (but almost nine miles if one follows the river) the Ithon loops back around the base of a steep peninsula-like hill on which Castell Cefnllys was built. The siting of the castle, 300 feet above the river, was magnificent and although little now survives apart from earthworks the hill is well worth climbing for the superb views. The castle had two keeps and there was a medieval borough with a charter dating back to 1297.

The quickest way from Llandrindod to Rhayader is to go back to the Wye Valley and then along the A470 road. It is, however, worthwhile taking a longer and more circuitous detour alongside the Clywedog Brook to Abbeycwmhir. The most obvious things in this tiny village are The Hall, with its many high gables ornamented with decorative bargeboards, and the church with its peculiar square tower and stumpy spire over the porch. Both date from 1867. Far older are the ruins (which are minimal) of the once famous abbey lying in the meadow between the road and the stream. The low walls and bases of columns that remain give only a very inadequate idea of the scale on which this church was built, making it by far the largest church in Wales and one of the largest in Britain. The 14-bay nave, measuring 242 feet by 70 feet, was longer than the naves of Canterbury or Salisbury cathedrals and twice as long as the nave of St David's Cathedral in Dyfed. The abbey's great size was probably due to Llywelyn Fawr's patronage and it was here that the body of Llywelyn the Last is said to have been buried. After the Dissolution of the Monasteries in the sixteenth century part of the nave arcades were removed to Llanidloes in the Severn Valley to be re-built into the church there. The marvellously intricate rood-screen from Abbeycwmhir was reputedly transferred to the little church of Llananno across the hill in the next valley. Just below the abbey is the monk's fishing pool.

Rhayader (Rhaeadr Gwy), a grey and compact little town, is centred on a cross-roads and each street (almost the only streets in the town) is named after the four points of the compass. 'The Waterfall on the Wye' from which Rhayader derives its name has virtually disappeared, the unfortunate consequences of building a new bridge across the river at the end of the eighteenth century.

The bridge leads westwards through Llansanffraed Cwmteuddwr to the Elan Valley, the so-called 'Welsh Lake District'. The 'lakes', five in number varying from one-and-a-half-miles to four miles in length, are in fact reservoirs. They were constructed (1892 to 1904 and 1946–52) in the narrow Elan and Claerwen valleys to supply water to Birmingham 75 miles away. Although man-made, the reservoirs, particularly the earlier ones, are extremely attractive, twisting and turning along the valley floor between tree-clad hills on one side and rocky crags on the other side. Just below the lowest dam stands Elan Village, an early example of a model village, prettily sited by the side of the river and constructed in 1906–9 to house maintenance staff. Caban Coch, the lowest of the chain of reservoirs in the Elan Valley, also includes a long inlet in the Claerwen valley. Submerged under the waters of this reservoir are Cwm Elan and Nantgwyllt, two houses where the poet Shelley lived for a short period between 1811 and 1812 with his young wife Harriet. Also under the water is a chapel and a church. Near the junction of the Elan and Claerwen valleys a branch road crosses Caban Coch Reservoir on a viaduct built over the submerged Garreg Ddu dam; it is at this point that the water is drawn off to be taken by aqueduct to the English Midlands. A small chapel stands at the far end of the viaduct and then the branch road continues alongside the Afon Claerwen for a further four miles to the Claerwen Reservoir. This, the largest and most recent of the reservoirs, has a mass concrete dam 184 feet high. The main road continues along the Elan Valley at the side of Garreg Ddu, perhaps the most attractive of all the reservoirs, and at its northernmost end, where the hillside is hung with cliffs, the road crosses over the opposite bank just below Pen-y-garreg. The Pen-y-garreg Dam is best seen in flood conditions when the water sweeps over the lip of the dam in one tremendous waterfall. Craig Goch Dam is another fine piece of nineteenth-century engineering crossed by a curving road viaduct. Craig Goch, like the Claerwen Reservoir, is sited amongst the bare, open moorlands and is therefore perhaps less attractive than the three lower reservoirs. Nevertheless, it is worthwhile continuing along the road to the head of the reservoir at Pont ar Elan and then turning right to follow the winding road back to Rhayader via the delightfully secluded Esglog valley with its own natural lake.

North of Rhayader the road closely follows the Wye between bulging headlands as mountains close in on the young river. Bwlchgwyn ('White Pass') must have once been the upper limit of the Wye as the contorted shapes of four converging valleys here testify, but millions of years ago a tributary of the River Severn, diverted by glaciers at Llangurig (six miles north), forced its way through the mountain pass to join the Wye and became henceforth its main stream.

Llangurig stands isolated, almost like an oasis amongst bare hills, at the junction of three important routes; one westwards, one north-eastwards and the other from Rhayader and the south. It is, to all intent, the centre of Wales, being eight miles from the sources of the two longest rivers, the Wye and the Severn. In the nineteenth century Llangurig was an important lead-mining centre and the Welsh Potosi Company prospected here hopefully for silver; now all has gone apart from some of the tips and earthworks. So too has the unfortunate Manchester and Milford Railway. Part of the railway line, which would have given mid-Wales a new outlet for the flannel trade, was actually built between Llanidloes and Llangurig about 1860, but the ambitious venture failed to get enough financial support and the railway was never completed. One can still trace the track of the ill-fated scheme along a footpath east of the village.

Railways and silver-mining might have turned Llangurig into an industrial town, but, fortunately, it was not to be and today it is still the ancient church which unquestionably dominates the village. The church tower is medieval (mid-fourteenth century) but much of the rest of the building is a nineteenth-century reconstruction carried out in 1877–8 at the then high cost of £11,000. Included in the re-building was a very fine set of stained-glass windows depicting scenes from the life of St Curig (the founder of the church in the sixth century), the royal families of Wales and heraldry of the local benefactor, J. Y. W. Lloyd of Clochfaen. The screen, which was made in 1878, is a re-creation of the beautiful fifteenth-century screen taken down and broken up in 1834.

FOUR

Montgomery and the Severn Valley

Though small in size Llanidloes manages, with only 500 or so houses, to convey an urban appearance, yet its street layout today is very much the same as it was in the thirteenth century. An ancient half-timbered Market Hall stands in the middle of the crossroads at the centre of the town. It dates from 1609 and has survived intact despite the hazards of traffic while others in less fortunate market towns have long since disappeared or been rebuilt. The cobbled ground floor is open and arcaded with heavy oak pillars and arches. The upper floor, which was originally used as a courtroom, now contains a small museum of local history and industry and has relics of the Chartist uprising of 1839.

The buildings of Llanidloes are an interesting mixture of old and not so old, some constructed in stone, some of brick or half-timbering and others clad with slate-hanging. The tree-lined streets and a few of the shop fronts still have a pre-First World War look about them, yet for a small town the Town Hall in Great Oak Street has an unusually imposing appearance. It was built in 1908 in Neo-Jacobean style as a gift to the town from the Davies family of Llandinam. Opposite is the Trewythen Arms, the scene of a mini-siege when in 1839 three London policemen (sent to quell industrial unrest in the neighbourhood) were imprisoned by the Chartists. It is difficult now to believe that in the early nineteenth-century Llanidloes was both an industrial and a market town. At that time trade was booming. The town had its own flannel factory and the population was twice as high as today. The boom, however, was short-lived and unrest soon developed as a result of low wages and unemployment. In an acrid atmosphere Chartism grew strong and at the time of the siege the Chartists were able, for five days, to rule the town; then the Yeomanry arrived and the Chartists fled, only to be caught and later sentenced to transportation to the colonies and hard labour. A flannel mill and two early nineteenth-century rows of three-storey weaver's houses can still be seen alongside the river near the Short Bridge.

Llanidloes has some good chapels; the best, Sion (1878) in Short Bridge Street, is distinguished by columns on the main façade linked by round-headed arches – a favourite device of its architect John Humphreys. The large parish church is hidden away in a corner of the town near the river. Its square, stubby tower at the west end is topped by a timber belfry. Inside the church there is a splendid early thirteenth-century arcade of clustered columns on the north side of the nave and a glorious oak hammer-beam roof carved with angels. The arcade was brought here from Abbeycwmhir in 1542 after the dissolution of that monastery; the roof is also reputed to have come from Abbeycwmhir although it was constructed at least two centuries after the arcade.

From the Long Bridge a secondary road can be followed to the Clywedog Valley and Llyn Clywedog, about four miles away. This very long serpentine lake is really a man-made reservoir and is set against a mountainous background softened by odd patches of trees. The lake twists back and forth between the folds of the high intervening ridge-like peninsulars which prevent a complete view of the water. The main concrete dam – less obtrusive than most as it is largely hidden away in the valley below the road – is, at 237 feet, the highest dam in Wales. It was built between 1964 and 1968 mainly to regulate the Severn and avoid the flooding that periodically threatened the valley. A second and smaller dam was constructed a mile upstream to prevent water spilling over from the east side of the reservoir into the adjoining valley below Fan Hill. At the foot of the main dam a track leads across a long, narrow wooden footbridge to Bryn-tail Lead Mine, an industrial monument now partly restored and open to visitors. The remains comprise some of the nineteenth-century industrial buildings and stone settling tanks associated with processing the ore from the mine. Beyond the main dam, where there is a carefully designed viewing platform and snack bar, a narrow road can be followed up into the hills above one side of the reservoir and then down through Coed Hafren – one of the more picturesque forestry estates (with some delightful picnic spots) – past slate-covered Geufron Chapel in its conifer setting and alongside the infant Severn. The source of the Severn (or Hafren in Welsh) is at the edge of Coed Hafren on the slopes of Pumlumon, about five miles back from Geufron.

From Staylittle at the head of Llyn Clywedog a detour can be made to the most westerly part of Powys at Machynlleth which lies almost within sight of Cardigan Bay. The road continues up and down over the hills for a few miles before crossing the end of the deep Twymyn valley. The western side of the valley is edged with craggy escarpments and at the upper end there is a spectacular waterfall, Ffrwd Fawr, which can be seen from the by-road on the way to Dylife. Today Dylife is bleak, windswept and almost deserted, but a century ago it was a great lead mining centre and a veritable hive of industry. From Dylife a narrow, winding scenic-road with steep gradients climbs up through the hills to 1,671 feet and then descends down the Dulas valley to Machynlleth and the Afon Dyfi.

Machynlleth is separated from the rest of Powys by the mountains and consequently it has more in common with neighbouring parts of Dyfed and Gwynedd. The mountains around Machynlleth are wilder than in most other parts of Powys, but Machynlleth itself is a surprisingly open and spacious town. Maengwyn Street, long and wide enough to hold a market, leads up to a curious and elaborate clock tower, erected in 1873 to commemorate the coming of age of Lord Londonderry's heir. Plas Machynlleth, a largish house in its own grounds just behind Maengwyn Street, was the home of the Londonderry family. Although it has the date 1653 on its pediment, most of the building was built in the eighteenth and nineteenth centuries. Now it houses offices and an exhibition of Welsh crafts.

Opposite the entrance to the Plas is the Owain Glyndŵr Institute and next to that an older building known as Parliament House. It does not, however, appear old enough to be the actual building that Glyndŵr used for his parliament in 1404, but it may incorporate remains of the original building. At this and other parliaments Glyndŵr laid down his plan for an independent Wales with its own laws, universities and ambassadors. Though the dream never came to fruition the people of Machynlleth still speak the same language that they did in Glwyndŵr's day.

Penegoes, two miles east of Machynlleth, was the birthplace of the famous landscape painter Richard Wilson (1714–82). Although Wilson's paintings are now worth many thousands of pounds they were not always so well acclaimed and in his later life he became embittered by poverty. Apart from a few childhood years at Penegoes Wilson spent most of his life in London. He returned to Wales, however, to live near Mold in Clwyd during his last years.

At Cemaes Road the main road leaves the Dyfi valley behind and follows the Afon Iaen up a winding valley through Commins Coch to Llanbrynmair, a village divided into two distinct parts. The modern village is on the main road, and has a Victorian church, built in 1868, already derelict and decaying. The older village, now known simply as Llan, is two miles up the beautiful Twymyn valley. The old church here is set in a circular churchyard and inside it has a timber belfry and fine king-post roof trusses. Llan was the home of the celebrated nonconformist radical Samuel Roberts (1800–85), known simply as 'S.R.', who shared the pastorship of the local chapel with his father. Roberts founded the magazine *Y Chronicl* in 1843 and in this he expounded his humanitarian views on subjects as diverse as railways, slavery, taxation, education, toll-gates and Temperance. In 1857 'S.R.' emigrated to America hoping to find there a colony free from oppression and tyranny, but ten years later he returned to his native land, disappointed and poorer. The road continues up the narrowing valley to the watershed at Talerddig. Here in 1859 railway navvies quarried 120 feet into the solid rock to make a route for the new line to Machynlleth. At the time of construction it was the world's deepest railway cutting. Beyond Talerddig the road descends steadily down towards the Severn valley. Carno, half-way down, is on the site of a Roman fortlet and has a peculiar church (1863), an inn strangely named the Aleppo Merchant and a surprisingly large and modern dress and fabrics factory.

East of Llanidloes the character of the Severn valley changes to a more open aspect. The road swings north to follow the river scurrying along below the steep, bare-backed slopes of Allt-y-moch, Allt-yr-hendre and Alltgethin until at Llandinam the valley is again temporarily narrowed by the hills closing in. Llandinam, a neat and tidy village, is of note as the home of the Davies family whose fortunes were established by the ambitious and energetic David Davies – the greatest of the purely Welsh industrialists – in the nineteenth century. Davies started working at the age of eleven on his father's farm and at 20, when his father died, was able to support his mother and eight younger brothers and sisters. His career is said to have started when he bought an oak tree for £5 and sold it for £80 after sawing it up into planks. With the proceeds he went into the contracting business, his first contract being the construction of foundations and an approach road for the elegant cast-iron bridge (designed by Thomas Penson of Welshpool) in his home town. From road and bridge-building he ventured into the railway business, constructing the line between Llanidloes and Newtown and advising on the railway system in Sardinia. After railways Davies turned to the coal industry, starting with the development of the Rhondda coalfield in southern Wales. This in turn led him to the construction of the great dock system at Barry, in order that he could export coal from the Rhondda without using the docks at Cardiff. Davies died in 1890 at the age of 72 and is commemorated at both Llandinam and Barry by identical bronze statues sculptured by Alfred Gilbert.

Caersws lies on the northern bank of the Severn near an important road junction. It has a grid-iron street plan reflecting the Roman fort that lies under the surface just north of the village. Nothing is to be seen of the fort now and a bath house discovered in 1854 is concealed by the railway station. From the station a railway once ran westwards to the lead mines at Fan, near Llyn Clywedog. The station's manager was the accomplished nineteenth-century lyric poet John Ceiriog Hughes (better known by his bardic title *Ceiriog*), whose house just beyond the church at the level-crossing bears a plaque to his memory. Of more architectural interest is Llanwnnog Church with its early sixteenth-century rood-screen with lace-like frills of carpentry, to the north, and Maesmawr Hall, standing in the open countryside between the Severn and the road to Newtown. The latter is a very fine, picturesque seventeenth-century example of a timber-framed house with decorative black and white panelling. It is now a hotel. Beyond Caersws the Severn valley appears wide and open. Fields extend to the tops of the hills, softening the landscape, while the lower valley is decorated with a scattering of black-and-white houses and farms.

Newtown (Y Drenewydd) was first planned as a new town in the thirteenth century, developed rapidly as an industrial town in the nineteenth century and was given a rebirth as a planned new town in 1965. The origin of Newtown was a political one and stemmed from Prince Llywelyn's abortive attempt in 1273 to build a new castle at Dolforwyn which would have protected a town that he intended establishing at Abermule. The English king argued that another 'new' town in this part of the Severn valley would be a threat to his own town at Montgomery and as a result of this intimidation Dolforwyn became a main cause of the first war of Independence. After the war Edward I forgot his own argument and founded Newtown in 1280 four miles west of Abermule and in sight of Llywelyn's uncompleted castle.

Comparatively little is left of early Newtown, but its wide and straight main street (appropriately called Broad Street) together with High Street, set at right angles, still recalls the town's medieval planning. More recently, Newtown has become the 'new town' of the Mid-Wales Development Corporation and, like Edward I's venture, was the offspring of an earlier proposal to build another (and larger) new town at Caersws a few miles upstream. Whereas the Caersws plan was intended to create a town of 70,000 inhabitants, the Newtown venture contents itself with merely doubling the size of the town from 5,500 to 11,000 people. Despite the new housing and industrial development (which is mainly on the outskirts) Newtown still retains its rural market town atmosphere. The Severn, which is here quite wide, sweeps around in a giant loop under the main bridge, its banks neatly trimmed and lined with a raised walkway on the town side. On the bank of the river stands old St Mary's Church, a ruined shell except for the west tower with its latern-belfry. The medieval church was replaced in 1847 by St David's – a Gothic Revival building in yellow brick and an elaborately decorated interior – at the southern end of the town. Across the road from St David's, and in complete contrast, is Zion Baptist Chapel (1881) built in grand style with a Classical portico. The interior is unusually lavish.

Newtown's heyday was the latter part of the eighteenth century and the beginning of the nineteenth century, when it became the centre of a flourishing flannel industry. The flannel was manufactured on hand-looms which were housed on the specially designed and lighted top floors of three-storey terrace houses. Most of these domestic weaving factories have disappeared, but three at Llanllwchaiarn, on the opposite side of the river, have been restored as a Textile Museum. Here, behind the large windows of the high-level factory, floorboards bearing the marks of the heavy looms and exhibits of tools and machinery tell the story of the woollen industry in the Severn valley. A large Flannel Exchange (now the cinema) was built in 1832 at the side of the river, but by the middle of the nineteenth century hand-loom weaving had already started to decline because of the competition from the steam mechanized flannel industry in Lancashire. Though an attempt was made to stem the tide by erecting massive new mills with steam-powered looms in the 1860s and 1870s Newtown never regained the position it had once held in the woollen industry.

It's an ill-wind that blows no good, however, and what had been the woollen industry's loss became the mail order's gain, for in 1859 a certain Mr Pryce-Jones started selling Welsh flannels through the post. The business prospered to such an extent that the great red-brick Royal Welsh Warehouse was opened opposite the station in 1875 and then was followed by another warehouse selling everything from furniture to fancy goods. The Royal Welsh still houses the largest departmental store in mid-Wales while the mail order side of the business is now run under the name of Kay and Co Ltd. It was the same Mr Pryce-Jones who in 1885 bought Owain Glyndŵr's little stone and timber parliament house at Dolgellau and had it transported by a special 32 truck train to Llanllwchaiarn to be re-erected at Dolerw. The erstwhile senate building now stands, rather forlornly and somewhat altered in appearance, at the side of the road and is used as a Quaker meeting house.

Newtown's most famous hero was undoubtedly the great social reformer and visionary, Robert Owen. Born in 1771 and brought up in the traditions of the local weaving industry he left Newtown at the age of ten to go first to London and then to Stamford. At 18 he moved to Manchester and with money borrowed from his brother he opened a factory there to make textile machinery. Later he settled in Scotland where he became renowned for his pioneering establishment of a model industrial village at New Lanark, near Glasgow. Owen never forgot the conditions of workers in the weaving industry and in attempting to improve the labourers' conditions he devoted much of his life to educating and reforming society. His social ideal of co-operation was formulated in *A New View of Society* (published in 1813) in which he proposed setting up villages of co-operation. In 1825 Owen managed to establish a co-operative settlement at New Harmony in the United States and in 1841 he began the development of another in Hampshire. Although these experiments in living were only partially successful, they gave rise to hundreds of smaller societies with broadly similar aims and also to the Co-operative Movement of today. Towards the end of his life, Owen returned to Newtown. He died in 1858 and was buried in the old churchyard of St Mary's. A museum dedicated to his memory is housed on the floor above the Midland Bank, on the site of the house where Owen was born in Broad Street.

A few miles north of Newtown is the little village of Tregynon where about 1870, Henry Hanbury-Tracy of Gregynog built a series of cottages and a village school entirely of concrete, then a daring and novel form of construction. Not only were the walls and floors of concrete but so also were the roof slabs, stairs and chimneys. Some of the detailing was based on traditional construction, such as Victorian Gothic porches and some pseudo-black-and-white timber-work, but generally the buildings are straightforwardly simple and in keeping with the new material. Not so, however, Gregynog Hall itself which was altered into a great rambling mansion of many gables with imitation concrete half-timbering. Buried inside the house there is a room with elaborate and genuine timber panelling dating from 1636. Outside, in the grounds, there is a wide concrete bridge spanning a dry ravine. Eventually the money ran out and the Hanbury-Tracys, despite their example to other landowners in cottage building, were forced to sell the estate as a result of over-spending on various industrial and commercial experiments.

In 1920 Gregynog was bought by Gwendoline and Margaret Davies, grand-daughters of the industrialist David Davies of Llandinam, partly as a home for themselves and partly as a conference centre for Welsh cultural organizations. The sisters were patrons of the arts in the best sense and together they built up a rich collection of paintings, founded an annual Festival of Music and Poetry, established a private printing press and generally helped and stimulated living artists, musicians and craftsmen in many ways. The printing press became famous in its day as the Gregynog Press, producing limited editions of books with magnificent bindings, immaculate typography and splendid illustrations. The collection of paintings, ranging from Botticelli to Augustus John but particularly fine in works of the French Impressionists and Post-Impressionists, was of world fame and eventually became one of the most treasured possessions of the

National Museum in Cardiff. Gregynog Hall itself and the surrounding park was bequeathed by the Davies sisters to the University of Wales in 1960 and it is now used as a residential study and conference centre.

Abermule, three miles north-east of Newtown, dozes on the banks of the Severn where the hills begin to close in on either side. Strategically it was an important site both as a river crossing and as the entrance, from the east, to the upper Severn Valley. In legend it was the supposed site where Hafren (Sabrina in Latin), the daughter of King Locrinus, was drowned by her stepmother. It is from this folk tale that the longest river in Britain gets both its Welsh and English names. The remains of Llywelyn ap Gruffydd's fateful Castell Dolforwyn stand on the prominent hill opposite Abermule, but the site is difficult of access and has not yet been fully excavated. The castle was built in 1273 and captured by the English four years later. Now all that remains is a rectangular walled enclosure with part of a round tower and the earthwork foundations of Llywelyn's new town. Abermule has two bridges – one a modern road bridge and the other a fine cast-iron single arch structure designed by Thomas Penson of Welshpool and erected in 1852. Across the bridge the main road leads directly to Welshpool, thus by-passing the picturesque little riverside village of Berriew with its rows of black and white cottages ('improved' in the nineteenth century with 'Jacobean' chimneys) and timber-framed vicarage with jettied first floor.

The secondary road on the north side of the Severn also leads to Welshpool but by way of Montgomery. Approaching Montgomery the view is dominated by the magnificently sited castle standing on a great lump of rock above the valley and town. The tiny town itself, though chartered as long ago as 1227 by Henry III, is little larger than a village and still retains a seventeenth-century appearance, unvisited by trunk road, railway or canal or, for that matter, twentieth-century commercialism. Though the walls which surrounded the town have long gone, there has been little expansion and the original rectangular layout can still be made out. Compact and neat, with a distinctly Georgian flavour and cobbled pavements, the town nestles below the east side of a steep hill. In the centre there is a tidy square with a whimsical little red-brick Town Hall, dating from 1748, at one end. The thirteenth-century parish church, with a tower rebuilt in the early nineteenth-century, has a splendid part-panelled roof over the nave. The church has two rood-screens; one, facing west, was made for the building and the other, facing east, came from Chirbury Priory.

The ruins of Montgomery Castle lie spread out along a long, rocky ridge above the town and can be reached by a steep, winding path behind the Town Hall. The ridge was artificially divided by a ditch into a lower part, containing the outer ward, and a higher part, where the ground falls away most steeply, on which was sited the keep. There are now only a few bare walls of the castle, but what is lacking in material remains is more than compensated for by the splendid views north-east across a vast patchwork of fields to the marchlands and England and north-west across the Vale of Severn to the Berwyn Mountains and beyond. The earliest castle at Montgomery was erected about 1070 a mile to the north-west at Hen Domen and became the property of Baldwin de Boulers, after whom the town got its Welsh name, Trefaldwyn ('Baldwin's Town'). The second castle was erected by Henry III between 1223 and 1227 on the ridge above the town and though attacked and damaged by both Llywelyn Fawr and Owain Glyndŵr it remained in English hands. Later it passed to the powerful Herbert family of whom the best remembered is the poet George Herbert (1593–1633). Though writing in English, George Herbert exploited the Welsh love of *dyfalu* – heaping up of comparisons – in many of his poems to obtain a colourful and memorable effect. He had made a study of foreign languages hoping to become Secretary of State in the Tudor administration, but after being passed over he took holy orders. His brother Lord Edward Herbert also had a religious bent and wrote a number of controversial treatises on the subject.

A mile to the east of Montgomery, where once stood the magnificent three-storey half-timbered mansion of Lymore, Offa's Dyke still forms the political boundary between Wales and England. North of Montgomery, on the way to Welshpool, the bank of Offa's eighth-century boundary can be clearly seen alongside the road while the modern border line veers to the north-east. It was here, on the Long Mountain to the east of Welshpool, that Henry Tudor, after landing at Milford Haven and travelling through mid-Wales, gathered his forces before marching to the English Midlands to meet and defeat King Richard at the Battle of Bosworth in 1485.

Just outside Welshpool, and on either side of the Severn, are two great estates. The nearer is Leighton Park which, together with its great 'Gothic' mansion and church, was laid out and developed from 1851 onwards by John Naylor, a Liverpool banker. The church was also built on an elaborate scale with flying buttresses and has a tall stone spire which forms a prominent landmark at the northern entrance to the park. The nearby Home Farm was built on an ambitious scale in the 1850s and designed to be as self-sufficient as possible. All waste material and sludge was drained via channels to a large circular building in the centre of the group and then pumped up to a reservoir at the top of the hill where it was mixed with other materials (brought up by a funicular railway) and then piped back down to the fields as liquid fertilizer.

Powis Castle on the opposite side of the Severn has a much longer history than Leighton being at one time both the fortress and administrative centre of the princes of Powys. In those far off days it was known as Castell Coch (Red Castle) from the colour of its stone and was a much smaller building than the present castle. It was destroyed in 1275 by Llywelyn ap Gruffydd in order to thwart Gwenwynwyn's alliance with Edward I. The English king was victorious, however, and after first persuading Gwenwynwyn's son Owain to relinquish his title of Prince of Powys, he awarded his Welsh supporter with a barony out of which Owain (who now adopted the Norman style 'de la Pole') was able to rebuild the castle on a more sumptuous scale. Below the castle, a series of terraces and gardens were laid out and beautifully landscaped during the eighteenth century and are now maintained in impeccable order. Looking up from the gardens the red sandstone castle stands high and dignified on its long ridge, forming a view of magnificent splendour unsurpassed by any other inland castle in Wales. From the late thirteenth-century onwards the castle has been continually altered and extended. Of the medieval features that remain the most impressive is the fourteenth-century twin-towered gateway between the outer bailey and the inner castle. Sir Edward Herbert bought the castle in 1587 and added a strikingly attractive Long Gallery with superbly decorated plaster ceilings and also had fashionable Elizabethan windows inserted into the walls. In 1784 Henrietta Herbert married Edward Clive, the son of Clive of India, who later became Earl of Powis. As a result of this marriage many relics and mementos connected with the victor of Plassey were brought to the castle. The castle has been subject to almost continuous alteration and improvement since the sixteenth century and has, as a result, a number of interesting rooms of varying styles. The most recent alterations, by G. F. Bodley in 1902, include some fine linenfold panelling in the Oak Drawing Room. The castle and grounds are in the care of the National Trust and are open to the public during the summer months.

Welshpool (Y Trallwng) itself lies at the northern end of the ridge on which Powis Castle stands. Pool, the original name, like its Welsh counterpart, refers to the marshy and waterlogged land alongside the Severn near which the town was sited. The appendage 'Welsh' was added in order to distinguish it from Poole in Dorset. The town is busy and bustling, especially on market day, and fortunately still retains a homely architectural character belonging to the eighteenth and nineteenth centuries. The main shopping area, High Street and Broad Street, curves gently around the foot of Powis Castle park with little to interrupt the continuous line of terraces save the projecting façade of the proud and brash nineteenth-century Town Hall. At the cross-roads Church Street drops down the hill towards the solid pile of St Mary's Church. Mostly an eighteenth-century rebuild, it still retains its massive thirteenth-century tower and fourteenth-century chancel. Nearby is a small half-timbered cottage known as Grace Evans' Cottage. Grace Evans helped Lord Nithsdale to escape, disguised as a woman, from the Tower of London on the eve of his planned execution for a part in the 1715 Jacobite rising. The story seems to vary as to whether Grace Evans was actually born in the cottage or whether she was given it by Lady Nithsdale for her help.

Just beyond the church is the yellow-brick Powysland Museum, erected in 1874 by the Powysland Club, the oldest archaeological society in Wales. Its exhibits are mostly local material and include a remnant of an Iron Age chieftain's shield found at Moel Hiraddug, oddments from the medieval abbey of Ystrad Marchell and relics from the Roman camp at Forden.

Following Severn Street from the cross-road one goes over the Shropshire Union Canal, passing on the way the Smithfield Market and a large earthen mound (once the fortress of Welshpool), ending at the grandiose French Renaissance-style railway station. The station was intended to be the headquarters of the Cambrian Railway, but in fact it was Oswestry in Shropshire that became the main centre. The railway reached Welshpool in 1860 and it was hoped that the line could be continued west to the mountainous interior and the little market town of Llanfair Caereinion. Nothing happened immediately, however, and it was not until 1903 that Llanfair got its own narrow-gauge branch line. Passing through the centre of Welshpool and then up-hill and down-dale along the pretty Sylfaen and Banwy valleys the little trains chugged their way until 1931 with passengers and until 1956 with goods. In 1963 the Welshpool and Llanfair Light Railway was re-opened by a preservation society, at first from Llanfair to Castle Caereinion, and then, in 1972, as far as Sylfaen.

Llanfair Caereinion is a grey little town, built on the hillside above the Banwy. At one time it had its own flannel industry. The church is a nineteenth-century rebuilding and the half-timbered Institute is even more recent. On the hills immediately to the south is the site of a well-preserved Roman fortlet.

From Llanfair the Afon Banwy runs down to join the larger Afon Fyrnwy at Mathrafal, after making a detour around Llangynyw with its little white-washed church. Castell Mathrafal, once a palace of the princes of Powys, lay on the east bank of the Banwy just above its confluence with the Fyrnwy, but nothing now remains of the site save a tree-covered mound and some banks and ditches. Dolobran Hall, a mile upstream, was the home of the Lloyd family who founded Lloyds Bank in 1765. The Lloyds became Quakers in the seventeenth century. The tiny Quaker Meeting House where they attended lies a quarter of a mile west of Dolobran and is now bereft of its original furnishings which were taken to the United States.

Downstream the Fyrnwy flows more sedately through trough-like Dyffryn Meifod with the village of Meifod lying near the upper end of the flat-floored, glaciated valley. Meifod was once of great importance due to its association with the Powys princes, some of whom were buried in its historic churchyard. There were once three separate churches within the very large churchyard, but only St Mary's survived beyond the eighteenth century. Inside the church there is a good Early Christian ornamental wheel-cross slab dating from the late ninth-century. Meifod is the headquarters of the Council for the Protection of Rural Wales and it is ironical that the site chosen for the largest radio telescope in the world was to have been on the hill overlooking the village; for Meifod's sake, it was fortunate that the project had to be abandoned because of rising costs.

Llanfyllin, lying amongst the hills at the confluence of the strangely named Cain and Abel rivers, is a charming little eighteenth-century town mostly built in brick. It is a good centre from which to explore the northernmost parts of Powys. The parish church is unusually plain and built in red brick with a mixture of round-headed and pointed windows. Erected in 1706 it represents architecturally not only the last survival of the Gothic tradition but also the first church in Wales in the watered-down Renaissance style known as Georgian. Pendref Chapel, also in red brick, was built two years later, then destroyed in 1715 by the Jacobites, rebuilt in 1717 and altered in 1829. It was in this chapel, at the Easter service in 1796, that Ann Griffiths – one of the best-loved hymnists in the Welsh language – was converted at the age of 20. She died nine years later, but in her brief life she composed 76 hymns of passionate joy. Surprisingly, only a single verse remains in her handwriting – all the rest were remembered by her servant Ruth who later recited them to her husband, the Rev John Hughes, to write down. The little old Town Hall – another eighteenth-century brick building, with an arched street-level market – was, sadly, taken down in 1960 to make way for a pedestrian precinct, but the handsome, brick Manor House (1737) and the Hall (erected in 1599, but remodelled in early nineteenth-century 'Gothic' dress) still stand around the little square.

Westwards from Llanfyllin a secondary road goes more or less directly alongside Nant Alan, but by-passes Llanfihangel-yng-Ngwynfa and Dolwar Fach (where Ann Griffiths was born in 1776), towards the Afon Fyrnwy, Llanwyddan and the Berwyn mountains. Lake Vyrnwy, the largest of the nineteenth-century reservoirs in Wales, lies in what is still one of the most attractive valleys of the

Berwyn range – dark, steep and forest clad. Four miles long and encircled by a good road which crosses the majestic dam over an arched viaduct it is now a great tourist attraction. Its construction between 1881 and 1892 unfortunately involved the destruction of a village and a thriving community, but the village of Llanwyddyn, including its school and church, were later rebuilt on a new site just below the dam. Some way along the eastern side of the reservoir a fascinating Gothic-style valve tower projects out into the water in a romantic evocation of the medieval castle of Chillon on the Lake of Geneva. Lake Vyrnwy supplies Liverpool with water which is carried first through a long tunnel under the mountain and then by aqueduct down Cwm Hirnant and along the Tanad valley to the English border.

The Tanad valley lies just north of Llanfyllin. A road from there follows the river to Llangynog, once an important lead-mining and slate-quarrying centre but now only a scattered village, in the most northerly corner of Powys. At Llangynog the valley bifurcates and the main road turns north to follow Nant Eirth through a cliff-hung valley and up to the Berwyn ridge before descending down to Bala in Gwynedd. To the west a narrower road follows the infant Tanad river through the steep sided, but softer and more wooded Cwm Pennant to the secluded and isolated church of St Melangell at Pennant Melangell. The simple twelfth-century church is full of interest and provides the setting for the story of St Monacella (Melangell), the daughter of an Irish king who lived as a hermit in the area. One day Brochwel, Prince of Powys, was out hunting a hare but the animal was saved when it sought refuge in the folds of Monacella's clothes. The hounds ran away and the Prince, much impressed, gave the princess land at Pennant to establish an abbey. The church itself is of Celtic origin, but rebuilt, and stands within a circular churchyard approached through a massive stone lychgate. The squat tower with its lantern belfry was restored in 1894 along with the rest of the church. Inside a fifteenth-century rood-screen, now forming part of the west gallery, is carved with scenes from the legend of St Monacella. The shrine of the saint, in the *Cell y Bedd* at the east end of the church, was reconstructed in 1958 from twelfth-century fragments found in the lychgate and elsewhere.

PART TWO

Clwyd

Map 3 Clwyd

ENGLAND
GWYNEDD
POWYS
BERWYN
CHESTER
LLANDUDNO
CONWY
COLWYN BAY
ABERGELE
RHYL
PRESTATYN
HOLYWELL
FLINT
MOLD
DENBIGH
DINBYCH
RUTHIN
RHUTHUN
WREXHAM
LLANGOLLEN
BALA
OSWESTRY
MAELOR
SAESNEG
Hanmer
Bangor Is-coed
Overton
Holt
Marford
Gresford
Rossett
Marchwiel
Ruabon
Chirk
Cas.
Offa's Dyke
Wat's Dyke
R. Dee
Hawarden
Cas. Ewloe
Buckley
Northop
Caergwrle
Minera
Bersham
Rhosllanerchrugog
Cas. Dinas Bran
Valle Crucis
Froncysyllte
Horseshoe Pass
Glyndyfrdwy
Llansantffraid Glynceiriog
Llanarmon Dyffryn Ceiriog
A. Ceiriog
Llansilin
Llangedwyn
A. Tanad
Llanrhaeadr -ym-Mochnant
Pistyll Rhaeadr
Llangynog
Moel Sych 2713
Moel Fferna 2066
Llandrillo
Cynwyd
Corwen
Carrog
Llangar
A. Dyfrdwy (R. Dee)
Cerrig-y-drudion
Pentre Foelas
A. Alwen
Alwen Resr.
Brenig Resr.
MYNYDD HIRAETHOG
CLOCAENOG FOREST
Clocaenog
Derwen
A. Clwyd
Llanfair Dyffryn Clwyd
Llanferres
Nerquis
Moel Famau 1817
CLWYDIAN RANGE
Cilcain
Pen-y-Cloddiau
Llanynys
Llanrhaeadr -yn-Cinmerch
Nantglyn
Llansannan
Henllan
Llanefydd
Cefn
A. Elwy
St. Asaph Llanelwy
Tremeirchion
Rhuddlan
Diserth
Gwaenysgor
Mostyn
Whitford
Offa's D.
Caerwys
Ysgeifiog
Greenfield
Basingwerk Abbey
A. Alun
Bodelwyddan
Towyn
Gwrych Cas.
Llanelian -yn-Rhos
Llanfair Talhaearn
Llangernyw
Gwytherin
A. Aled
Llanrwst
A. Conwy
Betws y Coed
10m
16k
JBH

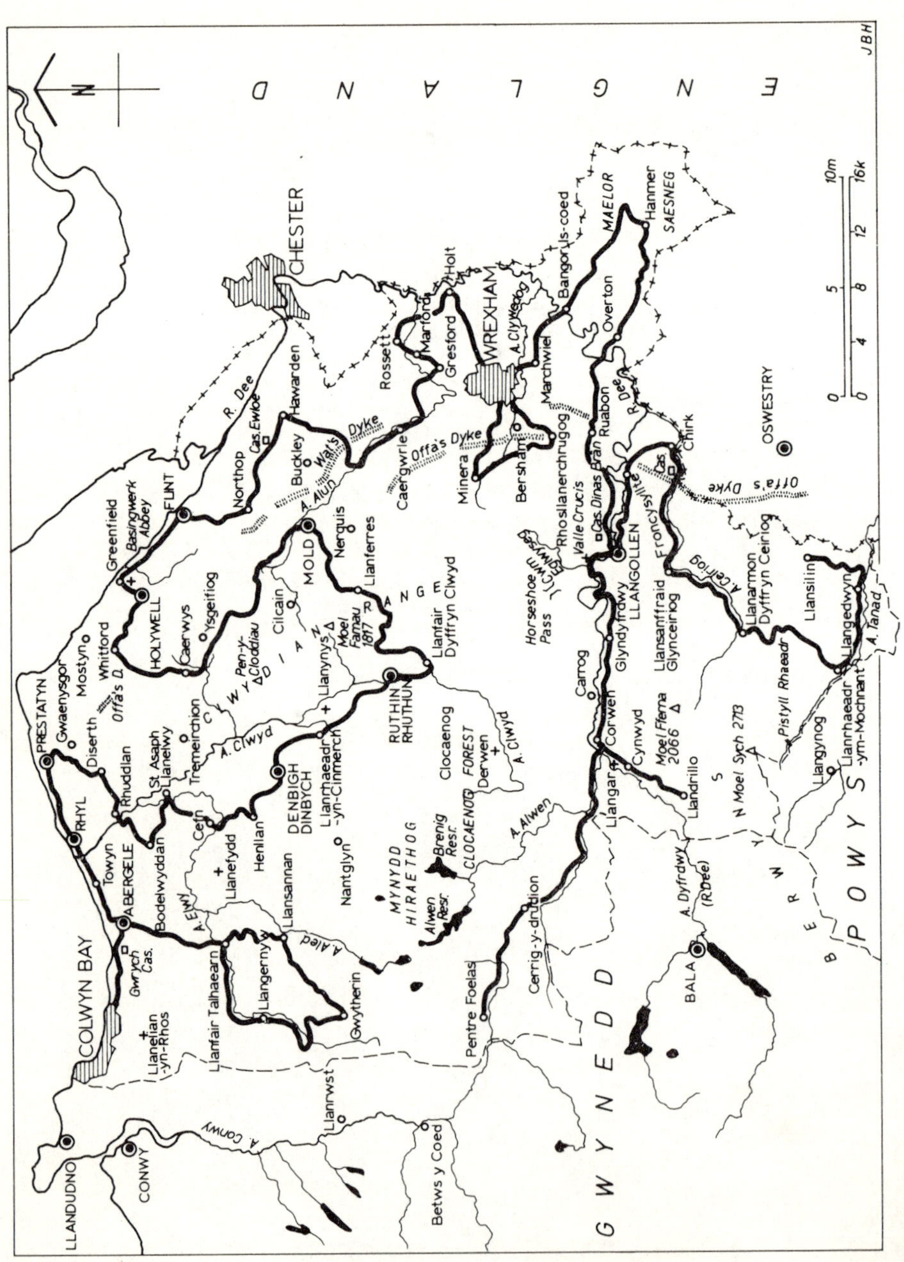

FIVE

Clwyd

Clwyd occupies the north-eastern corner of Wales. Wedged in between the rocky mountains of Gwynedd to the west, the pastoral hills of Powys to the south and the English plains of Cheshire and Merseyside to the east, this part of Wales is something of a mixture and perhaps for that reason, one of the most under-rated regions of the Principality. Clwyd is an amalgam of vast rural landscapes west of the Clwydian Hills and intense industry around Wrexham, the largest town in northern Wales. In places, such as the entrance to the Vale of Llangollen, unsightly industrialization and splendid scenery rub heads together. Industry is not new in Clwyd, for even the Romans had brick factories here, but it is limited in area and makes a wonderful hunting ground for the industrial archaeologist.

The riches of industry in the hills and of agriculture in the vales made Clwyd one of the more prosperous parts of Wales and for many centuries this was reflected in the county's architecture and its men of learning. The list of leaders and men of letters from Clwyd is a long one and includes among the more famous, Owain Glyndŵr, Dafydd ab Edmwnd, William Salesbury, Huw Morus, Humphrey Llwyd, Twm o'r Nant, Talhaiarn, Ceiriog, Thomas Gee and Daniel Owen. They were all thorough Welshmen and spoke and wrote in Welsh just as many people in Clwyd still do. Curiously, although some parts of Clwyd, such as Maelor, are now almost entirely English in speech, other parts, such as the Tanad valley, are predominantly Welsh right up to the English border.

A chain of hills and mountains formed by the Clwydian Range and Berwyn Range and composed of old and hard Silurian rock crosses the county from south-west to north, dividing Clwyd into its component regions. The eastern foothills of the Clwydian Range are mostly composed of coal measures which extend in a narrow curving band from the Dee estuary, through industrial Wrexham and Ruabon to the English border. Underlying the coal measures there is a limestone strip which ends in a striking cliff escarpment above Llangollen and the Dee valley. Further east, and jutting out as a wedge into the Cheshire plain, are the flat fields of Maelor Saesneg with villages more English in character than Welsh. The Clwydian Range itself is subdivided by many little valleys into rounded hills, often topped by prehistoric earthworks, but always steeper on the western side where they border the vale of Dyffryn Clwyd. Through the centre of this rich and broad vale flows the Afon Clwyd, passing the older towns of Ruthin, Denbigh and St Asaph before entering the sea near the holiday resort of Rhyl. To the west of Dyffryn Clwyd the landscape becomes more and more sombre as moorlands take over and homely fields succumb to dark pine forests. The moors, however, are indented by many streams hastily dropping down to the lowlands in deep and attractive valleys.

Where the River Dee gouges its way through the mountain chain in the southern part of Clwyd the scenery takes on a different appearance. Here the mountains are wilder and higher and the valleys deeper and more luxuriant. South of the Dee, the Berwyns form a barrier between the main part of Clwyd and the lovely Ceiriog and Tanad valleys flowing eastwards towards the Shropshire border.

This southern part of Clwyd had comparatively populous settlements in prehistoric times and the remains of bronze Age burial tombs are scattered along the hilltops of the Berwyns. Sometimes remains, such as the small stone circle on the hill above Llandrillo or the Rhos-y-beddau stone circle and avenue a few miles upstream of Llanrhaeadr-ym-Mochnant, indicate religious sites, but they are difficult to find amongst the bracken. Easier to locate are the ancient trackways of the Bronze Age and Iron Age travellers which cross the Berwyns from the Dee valley to the Severn valley. They are usually high up the sides of the tributary valleys just above the natural tree line.

In the northern part of the county relics found at a number of places east of the Clwydian Range give tangible clues to the richness and sophistication attained by chieftains of the Bronze Age. At Mold, for instance, a superb cape of embossed gold was found by workmen in 1883 under Bryn yr Ellyllon ('Mound of the Fairies') and a great golden torc, 2,000 years old, was unearthed in 1813 at Caerwys. Further south a beautifully carved wooden bowl discovered in a bog near Caergwrle, shaped like a boat and inset with gold leaf, suggests that there were artistic links with Scandinavia long before Vikings threatened these shores.

The hills and mountains of Clwyd are littered with remains of the Iron Age, mostly in the form of hill-forts. They are particularly prominent on the Clwydian Range where their multiple-earth banks and ditches are engraved on the summits of the hills overlooking

Dyffryn Clwyd. At some of these hill-forts, the remains of a few stone hut circles and excavated platforms (where wooden huts may have been erected) can still be seen. They were first constructed up to three or four centuries before the Romans came and were occupied throughout the Roman period.

The native tribes of Clwyd, known as the Deceangli, were the first in Wales to be conquered by the Romans, well before the massacre of the Druids of Anglesey or the defeat of the Silures of southern Wales. Soon the Romans were employing the native people to work their lead-mines in the hills near Flint, as a bar of lead found near Holywell and stamped DECEANGL and dated AD74 shows. In addition to lead the Romans also mined copper near Abergele and had a large tile and pottery factory at Holt a few miles from their legionary fortress of Deva (Chester). The Roman occupation appears to have been reasonably peaceful and there are few signs of any forts in the area although presumably there were some along the lines of the main roads radiating westwards from Deva.

For a century or so after the departure of the Romans there was a lull during which period Christianity developed rapidly in Wales. In Clwyd Celtic monasteries were established at Bangor Is-coed and at St Asaph at an early date during this 'Age of Saints'. Soon, however, Clwyd was to become aware of the Anglo-Saxons pressing forward from the east against the northern borders of Powys. In the early seventh-century the north-eastern corner of Wales and also Chester were within the domain of Powys. As Aethelfrith, the Anglican ruler of Northumbria, advanced towards Chester, Selyf, the Prince of Powys, collected an army together to defend the city. In 615 Selyf and his army were defeated in a great battle and Chester fell into the hands of Northumbria. With this defeat the Welsh in Wales were cut off forever from their fellow Celts in Cumbria and Scotland. At the Battle of Chester the monks of Bangor Is-coed accompanied Selyf and his army to pray for success, but victory was to be with the heathen Aethelfrith, who slaughtered the monks and triumphantly razed their monastery to the ground.

A century and a half later Offa, king of Mercia, ordered the great bank and ditch known as Offa's Dyke to be built as a boundary between his kingdom and the Welsh. Part of the Dyke was built within the boundaries of the present county of Clwyd, showing that the Saxons had already settled along both sides of the Dee estuary. The Dyke was not in a continuous line and in places was so poorly constructed that it appears never to have been finished. The land west of the Clwydian Range formed part of the kingdom of Gwynedd, but by the time of the Norman conquest Gwynedd and Powys had become united under Gruffyd ap Llywelyn and the territory between Offa's

Dyke and the River Dee had been regained by the Welsh.

The union of Powys and Gwynedd was short-lived, however, and the Normans, profiting by civil war in Gwynedd, made swift gains. By 1086 all of Clwyd, apart from a small area at the upper end of Dyffryn Clwyd, had fallen into Norman hands. During the twelfth century the Normans were ousted from northern Wales and Clwyd fell once more under the domination of Gwynedd. In the second half of the thirteenth century the territories making up Clwyd were constantly changing hands between rival Welsh princes and the English. After the Treaty of Aberconwy in 1277, following the first war of independence, Llywelyn ap Gruffydd remained as prince of a reduced Gwynedd and David his brother, was given the lands east of the Afon Conwy as a reward for his support of the English king. Ironically it was David who, discontented and upset by continual interference in his lands by Crown officials, rose in revolt and prepared the way for the fateful second war of independence and the end of Welsh sovereignty. After Llywelyn's assassination in 1282 David carried on the war until June 1283, but he was finally captured and executed and with him died Welsh independence.

Another son of Clwyd attempted to restore Welsh independence during the fifteenth century. At first Owain Glyndŵr seems to have been an unlikely person to start a revolution for, though he was descended from the princess of Powys on his father's side and the princes of Deheubarth (Dyfed) on his mother's side, he lived the life of a wealthy and cultured country gentleman with estates at Glyndyfrdwy on the Dee and at Sycharth on the Cynllaith. Owain had also studied law in England and had even fought with the English, under Richard II, against the Scots at the battle of Berwick in 1385. There was, however, much poverty amongst the peasants at this period and discontent was in the air. The spark that lit the fire in 1400 was a boundary dispute between Glyndŵr and Lord Grey of Ruthin. Failing to get just satisfaction Glyndŵr decided to take up the cudgels on behalf of his fellow countrymen and put an end to despotism and alien oppression.

In September Glwyndŵr was proclaimed Prince of Wales at Glyndyfrdwy. Hearing of the proclamation Henry IV panicked, marched to Anglesey and then forced violent anti-Welsh legislation through Parliament. The effect of this was to fan the flickering flames of independence in Wales with the result that soon Welshmen everywhere flocked to the Prince's cause urged on by the bard's echoes of ancient prophecies. In 1401 Glyndŵr and his followers captured the castle at Conwy and then fought and won a great battle on the slopes of Pumlumon south of Machynlleth. There were some set-backs in the early years, such as the sweeping incursion by an English army under

Prince Henry (later to become Henry V) in 1403 when Glyndŵr's courts at Sycharth and Glyndyfrdwy were burnt to the ground. Elsewhere the English army floundered in mud and rain while Glyndŵr took over the Edwardian castle at Harlech and made it his home and headquarters. Soon the whole of Wales was under Glyndŵr's control and in 1404 he called together a Welsh parliament at Machynlleth followed by others at Dolgellau, Harlech and Pennal. At these parliaments he outlined his plans for Wales which included an independent Church and two universities as well as courts of law. In 1405 Glwyndŵr, Sir Edmund Mortimer and the Earl of Northumberland drew up a plan, known as the Tripartite Indenture, for dividing England into two kingdoms and extending the boundaries of Wales to the rivers Severn and Mersey. At about the same time Glyndŵr also entered into a formal alliance with Charles IV of France. These alliances were, however, short-lived.

After 1408 Glwyndŵr's power and influence weakened as English pressure increased. The loss of Aberystwyth was followed by that of Harlech and by 1410 the Prince of Wales was being hunted as an outlaw. About the year 1412 he disappeared into the mists of time, lost to history. It is not known what happened to Owain Glyndŵr, but there has remained a strong tradition that he retired to his daughter's estate on the Herefordshire side of the Black Mountains and lived there for another four years. Although Owain's rebellion had failed it altered the course of Welsh history and made Welshmen aware, as never before, of their nationality – an awareness that has persisted for nearly six centuries down to the present. Glyndŵr remained a symbol of nationhood, yet after his death no memorials were erected and no elegies were written to commemorate the last Welsh prince of Wales for the poets refused to believe that he had died.

During the Wars of the Roses in the second half of the fifteenth century Clwyd was divided in its sympathies. The western part of the county, including Denbigh and Ruthin, generally supported the Yorkist cause while the eastern part was either in the hands of Lancastrian supporters or of the Crown. As the fortunes of the Houses of York and Lancaster ebbed and flowed so the sympathies of the Marcher lords changed. The Stanleys of Mold were unerringly foresighted in following the changing tide and so rose to high honour and had become, by the end of the century, one of the most important families in Wales. At first they supported the Lancastrian cause and then became firm Yorkists, but during the reign of Richard III they changed sides again and played an important part in bringing Henry Tudor to the throne. More consistent in his support of the Lancastrian cause was Ieuan Fychan and his son Howel of Mostyn Hall who helped both Jasper Tudor and Henry Tudor to escape from the clutches of Yorkist soldiers.

During the Civil War Clwyd was, like most of the rest of Wales, strongly Royalist and provided valuable recruits to the king's cause. Attacks were directed at Wrexham, Mold and other towns in the early stages of the war, but the region remained firmly Royalist until the final campaign in 1646 during which Denbigh underwent a year-long siege before surrendering.

More rewarding, perhaps, for the tourist than the battles of the past are the buildings that were erected down the centuries and have survived. Clwyd is probably richer in architecture than most other parts of Wales. This is especially the case with domestic architecture and from the end of the sixteenth century onwards Clwyd led the field with its country houses. Sir Richard Clough built the first Renaissance house in Wales at Bachegraig and introduced brick (for the first time since the Romans) and crow-stepped gables to Duffryn Clwyd. Other great houses, such as Plas Têg, Nerquis Hall and Erddig, near Wrexham, were the result of mineral wealth and peaceful prosperity. In the eighteenth century outstanding wrought-iron gates and screens were produced by the Davies brothers of Bersham to adorn the entrances of estates and churches and in the nineteenth century the romantics built their 'castles' at Hawarden and Gwrych. Genuine medieval castles, both English and Welsh, abound. Most such as Dinas Brân, Denbigh and Flint, have long since been in ruins, but others such as Chirk and Ruthin have been adapted, altered and extended or rebuilt and are still in use. Clwyd is also rich in late-medieval churches resulting from the relative prosperity that followed the Tudor accession; the Perpendicular churches of Wrexham, Gresford and Holywell and the double-aisled churches of Dyffryn Clwyd are some of the more outstanding examples.

Although the industrial development of Clwyd started early it has always remained confined to the eastern part of the county. Lead was mined in Roman times and in the Middle Ages it became an important source of wealth, being sold in large quantities in market and border towns for flat roofs to the towers of churches and castles. By the seventeenth century coal and iron were also being mined in the hills of the Clwydian Range and in the next century an important iron industry, with works at Bersham, Brymbo and Ruabon, had been established near Wrexham by John Wilkinson. When the local iron ore ran out the industry declined until new works could be built along the shores of the Dee estuary using imported ore. For a time too, Clwyd had an important cotton industry centred on Holywell, where there were four large mills alongside the stream that flowed from the miracle well below the town. Other industries, based on zinc, chemicals, woollens and silk, have come and gone, leaving behind them the ruins loved by industrial archaeologists. Although the kinds of industry have changed the area around Wrexham and the Dee estuary is still largely industrial and the most densely inhabited part of Clwyd. These, however, are relatively small areas of the county which for the most part still remains rural and full of delightful surprises.

SIX

Dyffryn Ceiriog and the Vale of Llangollen

The lower part of the Tanad valley lies just within Clwyd. Here the boundary between the new counties still follow the dividing line between the old counties of Montgomeryshire and Denbighshire and the still earlier division between the old Welsh princedoms of Powys Wenwynwyn and Powys Fadog. Although anglicization is creeping in the area is still, in the main, Welsh-speaking, a fact which would have delighted its two most famous inhabitants – William Morgan, translator of the Bible into Welsh, and Owain Glyndŵr, the national leader. The Tanad valley is, in addition, almost the last stronghold of the Welsh custom of unaccompanied carol-singing known as *plygeiniau*. The carol service, or *plygain*, is usually a very informal occasion, held just before or after Christmas, when up to a dozen parties of trios and quartettes from different chapels and churches in the district meet to sing folk-carols long since forgotten in most other parts of Wales.

Llansilin lies just above the Afon Cynllaith, a small tributory of the Tanad, half a mile from the English border. Its mainly fourteenth-century church has an early nineteenth-century pinnacled tower. Inside there are good fifteenth-century roofs over the two naves and a fine, panelled barrel roof over the chancel as well as some good monuments and a handsome brass chandelier. Huw Morus, the seventeenth-century poet and political satirist from Dyffryn Ceiriog, is buried in the churchyard. A little to the south of the village and almost within a stone's throw of the English border, is the site of Owain Glyndŵr's chief residence, Llys Sycharth. Nothing now remains of the wooden hall and fort, for it was burnt to the ground by the English forces under Prince Henry in 1403, but the flat-topped mound on which it stood and encircling ditch can still be clearly seen near the bridge across the Cynllaith. Although the *llys* ('court') has gone it is still possible to get some impression of life at Glyndŵr's court, from the evocative description written by the poet Iolo Goch in 1390. The poem was written before Glyndŵr had started his rebellion and praises both the architecture of the place and the generosity of its host:

Couplings secure the rooftree,
each rafter safely coupled in,
like Patrick's belfry, fruit of France,
or the fine-linked cloister of Westminster . . .
Four sweet lofts joined together,
where travelling poets sleep . . .
Spirits and finest bragget,
all liquors, white bread and wine,
with meat and fire in the kitchen . . .
There'll be no lack of gifts,
no fault, no famine, no shame,
*no thirst ever in Sycharth!**

It might be difficult to accept such extravagant descriptions from the visual evidence but recent excavations have confirmed that there was a timber hall such as the poem depicts on top of the mound *mewn eurgylch dwfr mewn argau* ('in a fine circle of water within an embankment').

Llangedwyn is in the flat-bottomed and well-wooded Tanad valley. The much altered Hall, built in Elizabethan times and seen at the end of an avenue of tall lime-trees, belonged to Sir Watkin Williams-Wynn and was the home of Charles Williams-Wynn, member of Parliament and friend of Robert Southey. While staying at the Hall, Southey wrote *Madoc*.

Llanrhaeadr-ym-Mochnant, a small and attractive stone-built village, sits loosely clustered along the banks of the Afon Rhaeadr, a short distance north of the Tanad. The village is just within Clwyd and below the county's highest point, Moel Sych (2,713 feet) in the Berwyn mountains. For centuries the Berwyns have been a barrier between the lower Tanad valley and the rest of the county to which it belongs. There is no direct way over the mountains to the rest of Clwyd except by walking along the ancient trackway (Ffordd Gam Elin) at the side of Cwm Twrch and up to the shallow pass between Cadair Berwyn and Cadair Fronwen. A large prehistoric standing stone at the highest point of the track stands like a sentinel as a guide for wayfarers, as it has been for thousands of years.

It was to the church at Llanrhaeadr that Dr William Morgan came, as vicar, in 1572 from his former parish in Nant Conwy. He stayed for 23 years during which he carried to fruition his great work of translating the complete Bible into Welsh. Unfortunately, it was not an

* (Translated by Gwyn Williams, *An Introduction to Welsh Poetry*, 1953)

entirely happy time for the new vicar for he was resented by one of the wealthy landowning families in the neighbourhood and despite his endeavours he never earned their friendship or respect. Nevertheless, the translation was completed and published in 1588, only 50-odd years after Henry VIII had banned Welsh from all official usage. The translation had a far-reaching effect and as a result the Welsh Bible became, perhaps, the most important single influence in the history of the nation's language and literature, as well as of its religion; by its very existence it did much to save the ancient tongue of Britain from oblivion and extinction. After his sojourn at Llanrhaeadr William Morgan became Bishop of Llandaf for a short while and then, later, Bishop of St Asaph.

Both Llanrhaeadr and the river on which it stands take their name from the extraordinary Pistyll Rhaeadr which flows over the rocks in narrow, rushing skeins of water at the head of the valley four miles away. With a total drop of 240 feet, this is the highest waterfall in Wales. Two-thirds of the way down the fall is interrupted by a natural arch of rock. At the bottom of the cleft there is a small pavilion erected in the nineteenth century by Sir Watkin Williams-Wynn. Although the waterfall is isolated and hidden away at the end of a narrow valley it has always been well known and visited, attracting such veteran travellers as George Borrow. Long ago it earned its place amongst the 'Seven Wonders of Wales'; in fact it heads the list in the old rhyme:

Pistyll Rhaeadr and Wrexham Steeple,
Snowdon's mountain, without its people;
Overton yew trees, St. Winifred's wells,
Llangollen bridge and Gresford bells.

Curiously, all of the 'wonders' except Snowdon are in Clwyd.

From Llanrhaeadr-ym-Mochnant a narrow, crooked road winds slowly up the lower side of the hills and then crosses the saddle between Mynydd Mawr and Cefn Hir-fynydd into Dyffryn Ceiriog at Llanarmon. Llanarmon Dyffryn Ceiriog, as it is known to avoid confusion with other Llanarmons, is pleasantly situated near a bend in the river where the valley widens into a bowl. A couple of stone-built inns, a simple church with a steeple, a few stone cottages and a bridge comprise the quiet little village. Left of the bridge a lane continues up to the narrow end of the valley to Swch Cae-rhiw where there are some pretty waterfalls. From here one can follow on foot some of the trackways used by the drovers across the Berwyns to Corwen and Cynwyd in the Dee Valley. It was this route that Henry II attempted to follow unsuccessfully in 1169 on his way to attack Owain Gwynedd. At that time Dyffryn Ceiriog was thickly wooded and while trying to clear a way through the valley and across the mountains, Henry's army was constantly harassed by Owain's guerillas so that in the end the Anglo-Norman army was forced to make an ignominious retreat.

Across the Llanarmon bridge the road follows the Afon Ceiriog down the valley to Glynceiriog. After Trergeiriog the narrower, middle section of Dyffryn Ceiriog becomes steep sided and bold and on the opposite bank there is an enormous gash marking the position of an old granite quarry. Alongside the river a pleasant stretch of the tramway track from Glynceiriog to the quarries has been preserved by the National Trust. Near one end of the tramway is Pont-y-meibion, the farm where Huw Morus (Eos Ceiriog – 'Nightingale of Ceiriog') the poet lived in the seventeenth century.

Llansanffraid Glynceiriog is a sprawling place and hardly seems to belong in this delectable valley. It is situated on a great curve of the river backed by the foothills of the Berwyns. It was the main centre for Dyffryn Ceiriog and was economically supported by numerous slate quarries and woollen mills in the vicinity, all of which eventually succumbed to economic pressures and closed. The oldest part of the church, at the side of the steep road over to Llangollen, is the tower which was built in 1790.

Below Glynceiriog the valley is heavily wooded with deciduous trees while brick buildings gradually begin to replace the stone farms and cottages. Tan-y-garth Hall, a large house near Pontfadog, is exceptional and is constructed of dark rubble-stone in 'Arts and Crafts' style with a projecting verandah at first floor and many gables.

A mile further, at Castle Mill, one crosses the line of Offa's Dyke. On the opposite side of the valley the Dyke still forms the boundary between Wales and England; on the hills north of the road the Dyke goes across the deer park of Chirk Castle as it makes one of its occasional incursions into Wales. For the next mile or so the Afon Ceiriog itself is the national boundary and the road winds closely alongside as far as Chirk at the entrance to the northern part of Clwyd. At the outskirts of Chirk, the Llangollen Canal (a branch of the Shropshire Union Canal) emerges from a quarter-mile long tunnel under the hill between the Ceiriog and the Dee and a ten-arch aqueduct carries the canal across the Ceiriog 70 feet below. The aqueduct, built in 1801 to the design of Thomas Telford is paralleled by a fine railway viaduct built alongside, but at a higher level, by Henry Robertson 47 years later.

Chirk is situated on a ridge north of the Ceiriog. At the top of the hill is the site of the old motte-and-bailey castle (Castell y Waun) built to guard the important river crossing below. The parish church lies within the bailey of the castle; it was originally built in the twelfth century and a north aisle and tower were added three centuries later. Inside there are seventeenth- and eighteenth-century monuments to the Myddelton family of Chirk Castle and to the Trevor family of the nearby estate of Bryn-kinallt. One of the Trevor daughters was the mother of the Duke of Wellington. The war memorial (1920) at the cross-roads is by the sculptor Eric Gill.

The very fine Chirk Castle, bold and massive and continuously lived in since the early fourteenth-century, lies a short distance west of the village. It is approached through beautiful wrought-iron gates and screens made by the master craftsmen Robert and John Davies of Bersham. Chirk Castle was one of a series of powerful border castles built by various Marcher lords – in this case by Roger Mortimer – during Edward I's reign to supplement the royal castles built along the northern coast. The earliest part of this forbidding structure, with drum towers at each of the four corners, was completed about 1310. Subsequently, the castle was extended and completely refurbished internally. Interior decoration at its most stately can be seen inside in a series of impressive rooms which in appearance are completely at variance with the exterior character of the building. The Ionic entrance hall with its graceful staircase and the staterooms with their fine stuccoed ceilings were built into the existing medieval structure between 1763 and 1773 to designs by Joseph Turner of Hawarden. The magnificent ceilings are either coffered or coved and are elaborately, but delicately, decorated with shallow, carved floral mouldings and painted panels while the walls have carved timber panels and richly moulded door casings. In the early nineteenth-century the castle was given a neo-Gothic touch by A. W. Pugin when he replaced part of the eastern range with another fine suite of rooms and re-vamped the entrance hall with oak-panelled walls and an ornate stone chimney piece.

A couple of miles north of Chirk the main A5 road enters the Vale of Llangollen near Froncysyllte. At the lower end of the Vale the River Dee contorts itself into two great loops around projecting spurs of land which provide springing platforms for routes crossing the river. At the first horseshoe loop the A483 road crosses over the Cefn Mawr and a short distance upstream the railway is carried across the mouth of the Vale on a great stone viaduct. A mile further upstream, at the second loop, a minor road crosses to Pont Cysyllte, while alongside, but high up, a splendid aqueduct (carrying the Llangollen Canal) strides majestically across the Dee, 127 feet above the river. This aqueduct, like the shorter one at Chirk, was designed by Thomas Telford and completed in 1805. The canal, together with its cantilevered towpath, is carried on 19 cast-iron arches supported on tall, hollow stone piers – a pioneering and economical form of construction which at the time of its erection caused the canal committee considerable concern. It has, however, withstood the test of time remarkably well.

Perhaps Telford's chief claim to fame in Wales is the Holyhead Turnpike Road which he built between 1815 and 1829 to improve the stagecoach route from London to Dublin. This is now the A5 road which passes near the end of the Pont Cysyllte aqueduct on its way to Llangollen. The road hugs the southern side of the flat-bottomed Vale, neatly accommodated between a steep outlier of the Berwyns and the winding Dee. Across the Vale, which is here at its widest, can be seen the limestone crags of Creigiau Eglwyseg and, to the left of these, outlined against the sky and standing guard over Llangollen, the craggy remains of Castell Dinas Brân.

At the time of the Holyhead Turnpike's construction Llangollen was already something of a tourist centre, but its narrow and crooked streets were by-passed by Telford when he drove his road straight through the southern edge of the little town in the manner of the railway builders yet to come. This was fortunate for later visitors, for it meant that the older part of Llangollen around the parish church was preserved and it still retains the flavour of an old coaching town. Despite the beautiful situation of Llangollen not all writers in the nineteenth century were agreed on the merits of the town. Edward Mogg, who wrote the 1822 edition of *Paterson's Roads* – the 'Baedaeker' of the stage coach era – dismissed the town as containing 'nothing really worthy of notice except the bridge . . . a very curious structure' and Cliffe in 1851 reported that 'the town of Llangollen contains but little to interest the tourist'. Other writers were more complimentary for even the caustic Ruskin commented that 'the village of Llangollen is one of the most beautiful and delightful in Wales or anywhere else', while Robert Browning recorded that 'I received an impression of the beauty around one which continued ineffaceable during all subsequent experience of varied foreign scenery, mountains, valley and river'. And this was before the coming of the International Eisteddfod which brought thousands in their colourful costumes from foreign lands and made the name Llangollen internationally known.

Llangollen owes its development to its position at a point where the River Dee could be crossed. The Trefor Bridge – one of the 'Seven Wonders of Wales' – which here spans the swirling rapids of the Dee, is named after Bishop Trefor who is reputed to have built the first stone bridge in the common practice of the church in those days to improve communications. The present arched and buttressed bridge, however, is probably of Tudor vintage and has been widened several times since, fortunately without impairing its handsome appearance.

Llangollen was once a thriving wool-manufacturing centre, specializing in flannel, and had a number of mills some of which still survive. Where the river erupted into rapids over the rocky bed the woollen manufacturers constructed weirs, above and below the bridge, to control the water used in their mills. An attractive old Corn Mill stands wedged between the Dee and a lane west of the Bridge. The lane leads to the Victoria Promenade alongside the river and beyond that to the Riverside Park; from these there are views upstream to Cwm Eglwyseg and, across the river, to the silhouetted outline of Castell Dinas Brân perched on the hill above the town.

The main shopping street, Castle Street, is in a direct line with the Trefor Bridge and this together with the rectilinear network of streets to the west marks the development which took place in the nineteenth century after Telford's Turnpike road had been constructed. The older part of the town lies east of Castle Street. Here, along the irregular line of Bridge Street and Church Street, were all the coaching inns which were such a feature of the town before the coming of the railway. Some, such as the Sun Inn, Hand Hotel and Royal Oak are still there; others such as the King's Head Inn and Eagles Inn have changed their names (to Royal Hotel and Wynnstay Arms) or have become shops or simply reverted back to dwellings.

St Collen's Church lies in the centre of the older part of the town. It is a typical double-naved church with fine fifteenth-century carved roofs, one of which is reputed to have been taken from Valle Crucis Abbey after the Dissolution of the Monasteries. The aisle was added in 1865 when the church was restored. Inside there is a memorial to the eccentric and indefatigable 'Ladies of Llangollen' who are buried in the churchyard.

The famous 'Ladies' – Lady Eleanor Butler and Miss Sarah Ponsonby – lived at Plas Newydd, a picturesque black-and-white timbered mansion halfway up Butler Hill on the outskirts of the town. The elaborately carved and richly decorated house is set in a public park which also contains a Gorsedd Circle and the remains of a medieval cross. The 'Ladies' moved to Plas Newydd in 1780 and for nearly half a century these gossipy busy-bodies became part of the life of Llangollen and entertained almost everyone of repute who passed through the town, including Wellington, Burke and Byron. Visitors were expected to contribute gifts, particularly curios of carved wood, but William Wordsworth proffered instead a sonnet describing the mansion as a 'low-roofed cottage' and was never invited back.

At the bottom of Hill Street on the way back into town, there is another old coaching inn (now the Grapes Hotel) and opposite this is the Old Armoury. This was once the Town Hall, but has now become the administrative headquarters of the Llangollen International Music Eisteddfod.

The International Eisteddfod, which is held every July, takes place in grounds alongside the canal on the far side of the river. It was started from small beginnings in 1947 but soon became so popular that would-be competitors had to be turned away. Nevertheless, each year about 200 choirs from between 30 and 40 countries from all over the world come together here to compete in the giant marquee and perform all kinds of music from folk-singing to operatic arias. In addition there are instrumental and folk-dance competitions. The latter, in particular, have done much to give the International Eisteddfod its colourful flavour and promote its popularity. During Eisteddfod week one is as likely to see the competitors proudly wearing their resplendent folk costumes in the streets of Llangollen as on the competition field. The costumes emphasize the variety of nations taking part and the individuality of their traditions, but the International Eisteddfod itself reflects their common interests and the universality of people. The Eisteddfod motto 'Blessed is a world that sings, Gentle are its songs' is, for once, something more than just another empty slogan.

Not far from the Eisteddfod field is the Canal Exhibition Centre, housed in a nineteenth-century warehouse at the side of the canal. In the Canal Centre the growth of the canal system from its early days to its heyday can be followed in displays and films while preserved features and working models give some idea of the life of those who built and worked the canals.

From near the Canal Centre a footpath climbs steeply up to Castell Dinas Brân – an eerie ruin supposedly the scene of supernatural events and once the nesting place of eagles – high up on the hill overlooking Llangollen. The castle was built by the Welsh princes in the mid-thirteenth century on the site of an isolated Iron Age hill-fort overlooking the Dee valley to guard the eastern entrance into Wales. Despite the immense natural strength of its position Dinas Brân was not defended in the war of 1277 but was burnt by the garrison when the hopelessness of their resistance had become apparent. The ruins follow the lines of a large rectangular courtyard with a square keep tower at one end and a typically Welsh apsidal tower on one of the long sides overlooking a formidable ditch excavated out of the rock. The apparently simple plan is misleading for in reality the castle was remarkably well-fitted to its towering site and provided, at one and the same time, the basis for an enormously powerful fortress and an opulent residence.

The mountain behind Dinas Brân terminates against a spectacular rim of near-precipitous limestone cliffs curving north-westwards for three miles towards the source of the Afon Eglwyseg. On the upper parts of these cliffs, known as Creigiau Eglwyseg, horizontal bands of stratified rocks can be clearly seen, but the base of the escarpment is buried in mounds of fallen scree produced by the weathering and erosion of the limestone. For a closer look at the cliffs one can follow a narrow, twisting lane which runs from Llangollen alongside the foot of the scree to the end of Cwm Eglwyseg and up onto the moorlands at World's End. Near the extremity of the valley is Plas Uchaf, a Tudor farmhouse which was once the home of Colonel John Jones, a signatory of Charles I's death warrant. Legend has it that this is the farm to which Elizabeth I is supposed to have secretly retired to give birth to a baby which was immediately and unceremoniously thrown in the fire.

Further west the main road crosses the lower part of Cwm Eglwyseg and sidles up the flank of Maesyrychen Mountain before curling round the head of a secondary valley to travers the Horseshoe Pass. From the pass there are excellent views across to Creigiau Eglwyseg and back down the valley towards Llangollen. In the lower part of Cwm Eglwyseg, there are two interesting monuments from the past. The nearest to the road is Eliseg's Pillar, a remnant of a ninth-century pillar-cross inscribed with possibly the oldest surviving record of a Welsh pedigree. It was wantonly broken up by the Puritans during the Civil War and although the main part was re-set in 1779 it is now more of antiquarian than visual interest. A long, and now almost illegible, Latin inscription on the shaft records that Prince Cyngen erected the cross as a memorial to his great-grandfather King Eliseg of Powys, who had recovered his inheritance from the English.

A short way down the lane to the right are the ruins of the Cistercian abbey of Valle Crucis or Glyn-y-groes ('Valley of the Cross', i.e. Eliseg's Cross) as it is otherwise known. Founded in 1201 by Madog ap Gruffydd, Prince of Powys and cousin of Llywelyn Fawr, it was one of the more important religious houses in northern Wales and became well known for its patronage of the bards. Both Iolo Goch, a famous fourteenth-century poet from Dyffryn Clwyd, and Guto'r Glyn, a fifteenth-century poet from Glynceiriog, were buried here. Most of the buildings that remain, including the ruined abbey church, were built in the thirteenth century. The lovely vaulted and ribbed chapter house under the monk's dormitory was completed in the following century and is still intact.

West of Llangollen the Dee Valley can be explored from roads on either side of the river. The narrow, minor road on the northern side of the valley is a leisurely route that hugs the interlooping bends of the Dee as the river cuts a swathe through the hills. The placid-looking horseshoe falls across the Dee at Llantysilio is really a curving weir constructed by Telford to divert water from the river into the Llangollen Canal which starts at this point. From here this is a pleasant walk alongside the canal back to Llangollen. Llantysilio Church stands slightly back from the river in the lee of wooded hills.

Although restored in 1876 the church is mainly a late fifteenth-century building and still retains some glass of that period and also incorporates fragments of a twelfth-century edifice. The north chapel, which was formerly detached from the rest of the church and used as a school, was built in 1718.

On the south side of the Dee Telford's A5 road runs in a more-or-less straight line through Glyndyfrdwy to Corwen, slicing off bends wherever possible on the flank of the Berwyn mountains except where at one point the hills sweep down to deflect the river's course into a giant horseshoe bend.

All the lanes south of the main road peter out into disused tracks amongst the steep side valleys and now there are no roads across the Berwyns. In the fifteenth century, however, the tracks were well used for this was the domain of the Glyndŵr family and in all probability Owain Glyndŵr himself would often have crossed the Berwyns on his way to and from his estates at Sycharth near the English border and Glyndyfrdwy in the Dee Valley. The family name Glyndŵr ('Glen of the Water') is a shortened version of the Glyndyfrdwy ('Glen of the Water of Dee') Lordship. Appropriately the administrative district which covers the area included in this chapter has now been given the name Glyndŵr.

The site of Owain's residence is no longer known with certainty – it may have been either the farmhouse known as Carrog Uchaf near the main road or an old castle motte overlooking the Dee to the west of the village. The motte is still called Owain Glyndŵr's Mount. It was at Glyndyfrdwy that Glyndŵr was proclaimed Prince of Wales on 16 September 1400 by a gathering of relatives and Welsh nobility. Three years later Owain's court at Glyndyfrdwy was burnt by the English king and the Prince took up residence at Harlech Castle. For a further four years Glyndŵr controlled the fortunes of Wales, but it was not to last and after years of being hunted in the wilderness he retired from the field of politics and battle to end his days in mysterious silence on the borders of Gwent.

The little village of Carrog on the other side of the valley rests on a natural ledge between the Dee and Afon Morwynion and is reached across an ancient five-arch bridge with cutwaters. The present church, built in 1852 and extended with a large chancel in 1867, replaced another church which had been erected on the spot in 1611 after the original medieval building near the river had been swept away by floods. Beyond Carrog the secondary road on the northern side of the Dee runs beneath Caer Drewyn, a large Iron Age hill fort with a stone rampart. The main road on the southern side of the valley continues beyond Glyndyfrdwy below the steep forested slopes of the Berwyns to Corwen.

The little town lies near the confluence of the Dee and Afon Alwen at a point where the main valley begins to widen out into the rich vale of Edeirnion. Though small and straggling, with only two winding streets, Corwen is an important market centre for the area. Its chief claim to fame is that in 1789 it was the venue of an eisteddfod which became the forerunner of the modern National Eisteddfod which is now held each year in a different town. The Corwen Eisteddfod was held in the Owain Glyndŵr Hotel and was the first eisteddfod to which the general public were admitted instead of, as formerly had been the case, only the competitors and judges. The parish church, though in the centre of the little town, is almost hidden behind the terraced houses and shops. It stands, plain and sombre with a thirteenth-century tower, in the middle of a trimly-kept sloping churchyard. The old Corwen College, behind the church, is a low two-storeyed row of almshouses built in long slabs of stone-slate by William Eyton of Salop for 'the support of six widows of clergymen of the county of Merionedd only'. The most striking of Corwen's building, also known as The College, but in fact erected as a workhouse in 1830, is a long, cruciform building with columned and pedimented entrance standing near the Telford Road at the entrance to the town.

From Corwen one can make for Gwynedd and Snowdonia, the historic bastion of 'Wild Wales', by following Telford's road directly to Betws-y-Coed (see Chapter Ten). After crossing the Dee the road passes alongside the Rug estate with its park landscaped by Humphry Repton in 1793. The mansion itself was built in neo-Classical style with a portico of giant Ionic columns about 1800. Within the grounds is a lovely little chapel built in 1634 by William Salusbury of Denbigh.

At Cerrig-y-drudion Telford's road crosses the open moorlands in an arrow-straight line. The village itself has now been by-passed by a modern road. Long before Telford drove his new road across the moors this was one of the many routes taken by the cattle drovers on their way from the north-west to England. There was a shoeing station at Cerrig-y-drudion and one of the most famous drovers was Edward Morus who lived near the village during the seventeenth century. He was still droving in his eighties and eventually died in Essex in 1689 probably at the end of one of his journeys. Morus was better known as a poet, however, and composed many carols in both 'strict' and 'free' metres. His profession as a drover enabled him to make accurate and lively descriptions of animals and birds. Another poet from Cerrig-y-drudion was John Jones, better known as Jac Glanygors, who was born in a nearby farm in 1766. At 23 he left for London where he took a leading part in London-Welsh affairs. After coming under the influence of the French Revolution, he turned to writing poetic satire and political pamphlets.

On the way to Pentre Foelas, near the head of the Conwy valley, there are two old houses of interest. Plas Iolyn, near Rhyd-lydan, was the home of yet another poet, Tomos Prys. Before retiring to Plas Iolyn (where he had been born in 1564) Prys led the life of an adventurer and pirate, waging war against Spanish treasure ships on the high seas and travelling across the Continent. The other house is Gilar, owned by another member of the Prys family. The solid-looking gatehouse at Gilar, dating from 1623, is built over a wide archway and is entered at first floor level from external steps.

An alternative route from Corwen to Gwynedd goes south-west towards Bala and its lake (see Chapter Thirteen). Of the two roads to Bala the southern route following the Dee is the more interesting. It passes the old church of Llangar standing isolated above the river. Inside the church there are original seventeenth- and eighteenth-century fittings, including wall paintings, a three-decker pulpit and box pews. The old church fell into decay and was replaced by a new church at Cynwyd in 1856. Cynwyd itself is a pleasantly grouped village at the entrance to Cwm Trystion. A lane follows the Afon Trystion, passing near its waterfall and lakes, and up into the Cynwyd Forest. Across the Dee there is an ancient four-arched bridge. A mile or so further on is Plas Uchaf, a carefully restored hall-house (*c.* 1400) small in size but still containing a delightfully ornamented spere-truss dividing the screen passage from the spacious hall.

The last village in this part of Clwyd is Llandrillo, situated at the lower end of the lovely Cwm Pennant. Another pleasantly neat village with low terraces of eighteenth-century houses, it has a lofty church (rebuilt in 1877 with a spire) and a prominent chapel of about the same date. Around Llandrillo there are remains of a number of prehistoric burial chambers at Rhydyglafes, Tyfes and Branas Uchaf. The most interesting prehistoric monument is, perhaps, the Bronze Age stone circle of 41 stones sited high up on the hills beside the ancient trackway Ffordd Gam Elin. The trackway starts as a tarmac lane near the main road north of Llandrillo but soon becomes a grass track climbing up to the top of Cadair Bronwen and back over to Llanrhaeadr-ym-Mochnant.

SEVEN

Maelor and the Dee Estuary

Maelor Saesneg ('English Maelor', to distinguish it from Maelor Cymraeg or 'Welsh Maelor' around Wrexham) is the rural wedge that lies on the east side of the Dee and juts out towards England between Cheshire and Salop. Although more English in character than the hillier parts of Clwyd, Maelor Saesneg has always been, despite its name, an integral part of Wales except during the couple of centuries before the coming of the Normans when it was held as part of the Saxon kingdoms of Mercia. When Saxon influence waned the district became part of the Welsh kingdom of Powys again, although some of the Saxon names, such as Overton, Hanmer and Worthenbury, remained side by side with even older Welsh names like Bangor Is-coed. As part of Powys the *cwmwd* of Maelor was a single district, but when the first Welsh counties were created on the English model in 1284 under the Statute of Wales, it was divided into two parts; Maelor Saesneg was annexed to Flintshire and Maelor Cymraeg became an integral part of Denbighshire. It remained thus until the most recent reorganization of Welsh counties when the two halves of Maelor were united again as part of Clwyd.

Overton lies just across the Dee. It was once a borough and had a castle, but suffered badly during the Black Death plague and also at the time of Owain Glyndŵr's rebellion so that by the sixteenth century it was a mere shadow of its former self. Leland visited the place in 1533 and wrote that 'Overton hath had burgesses but now there is not 20 houses. One part of the ditch and hill of the castle yet remaineth; the residue is at the bottom of the river'. Today it is a neat village almost entirely built in red brick. The yew trees which gained fame as one of the 'Seven Wonders of Wales' still stand around the church although they appear, in fact, to be no different to any other church-yard yews.

Hanmer lies in the furthest corner of Maelor Saesneg near an attractive mere after which it gets its name. The Hanmer family, though of English descent, had by the fourteenth century become thoroughly

Welsh as a result of marrying local heiresses. In 1383 Margaret Hanmer married Owain Glyndŵr in the local parish church (rebuilt in the eighteenth and nineteenth centuries) and during the subsequent War of Independence her three brothers supported Glyndŵr; one of them John, acted as the Prince's envoy in Paris. Dafydd ab Edmwnd, one of the greatest Welsh poets of the fifteenth century, was also a native of Hanmer. His poems – more often than not in praise of feminine beauty – are masterpieces of technical skill and he was acknowledged in his day as the final authority on all matters concerned with poetic language and metre.

On the way to Wrexham the road passes through the village of Bangor Is-coed (or Bangor-on-Dee as it is now more commonly known). The church, pleasantly sited by the side of the Dee, is near the site of a large and important Celtic monastery. At one time the monastery was reputed to have more than 2,000 monks, but the life of the great monastery was suddenly brought to an abrupt end in 615 after the fatal Battle of Chester. At that time Selyf, Prince of Powys, was defending Chester from the heathen Northumbrians approaching from the east. Supporting Selyf and praying for a Welsh victory over the pagans were a thousand or more monks from the monastery. Unfortunately for the Christians, the Welsh soldiers were heavily defeated and the monks themselves massacred by order of Aethelfrith, the victorious Northumbrian king. The famous monastery was destroyed without trace.

From the flat river plain where the Dee seems to wind endlessly towards its estuary, the land gradually rises in gentle undulations towards Wrexham. Marchwiel, on the outskirts of Wrexham, is distinguished by a prominent church rebuilt in 1778 in a rather crude Classical style; the tallish tower was added ten years later by James Wyatt. Erddig, one of the many large houses that once dotted the countryside around Wrexham, stands to the west of the village in a beautiful wooded park bordering the line of Wat's Dyke. The house was originally built in 1684 for Joshua Edisbury, but after becoming bankrupt he sold it to John Mellor who added two wings in 1723. A decade later the estate was inherited by Simon Yorke and then remained in the Yorke family until it was bequeathed to the National Trust in 1973. Although suffering badly from subsidence due to coal mining the mansion has now been very carefully restored and saved for posterity. The interior of the house is lavishly furnished almost entirely with furniture and fittings belonging to the Yorke family and includes a majestic four-poster bed. The formal gardens centred on a long, ornamental canal have also been restored to their former splendour. North of the house the remains of a medieval castle motte stands on a hillock overlooking the Afon Clywedog and the suburbs of Wrexham.

Wrexham, by far the largest town in northern Wales, lies just a few miles from the English border on a rising shelf of land above the Clywedog River. Seen from the south-west the valley of the Clywedog looks like a great dry-moat protecting the prosperous town. Wrexham's prosperity is due to its border position between hills of profitable coal on one side and the rich agricultural plain of the lower Dee on the other side. Since Tudor times this has been one of the wealthiest and most populous regions of Wales and this in turn accounts for the unusually large number of great houses and the richly decorated churches found in eastern Clwyd. Indeed, during the seventeenth century Wrexham appears to have been the largest town in Wales and it is not surprising therefore to find that its church is the greatest and most splendid parish church in the principality, as well as being one of the 'Seven Wonders of Wales'.

The parish church of St Giles is the finest of a group of Perpendicular Gothic churches, all within a few miles of each other, built during the fifteenth century by Margaret Beaufort, widow of Edmund Tudor and mother of Henry VII. The six-bay nave of St Giles' was started in 1463 after a disastrous fire had destroyed an earlier church; at the same time an octagonal chancel was added at the east end. The interior is lit by five-light windows to the aisles and clerestory windows above the nave arcades. The nave has a beautiful flat, timber panelled roof. But the glory of St Giles' and its master-mason architect John Hart is the superb five-stage tower (built in 1506) which rises up majestically at the west end to a height of 136 feet. The whole surface of the tower is richly ornamented with mouldings, sculpture and 29 statues (including one of St Giles, with a hind at his feet, over the north porch) and is crowned by octagonal turrets at each of the four corners.

The adjacent churchyard houses the tomb of Elihu Yale (1649–1721), the famous benefactor of St Giles' (he gave the iron screen in the chancel) and New Haven College (renamed Yale University in his honour in 1745) in the United States of America. Although 'born in America, in Europe bred, in Afric travell'd, and in Asia wed . . .' as his epitaph states, Elihu Yale's family hailed from Clwyd with seats at Plas yn Iâl (hence the name Yale), near Llanelidan and Plas Grono on the outskirts of Wrexham. Elihu returned to Britain with his parents when he was only two years old and then went to London to be educated, after which he travelled to India in the service of the East India Company and eventually became governor of Madras. The last 21 years of his life were spent in Britain living alternately at Plas Grono and in London. Another of the many mansions that were built near Wrexham during the fifteenth and sixteenth centuries was Acton Park on the northern edge of the town.

The house was partly rebuilt by James Wyatt in the late eighteenth century and in the early nineteenth century. Thomas Harrison added a grand entrance screen in Greek Doric style. The house has since been demolished and all that remains is the screen. It now forms an entrance to Garden Village, an early Welsh example of garden city planning which was unfortunately interrupted by the First World War and never completed.

The centre of Wrexham still contains, despite continuous redevelopment, a number of interesting eighteenth-century buildings, such as the Jacobean Crest Hotel (formerly the Wynnstay Arms), as well as some good nineteenth-century buildings, such as Ebenezer and Seion Chapels and the Market. In between the buildings there are narrow alleyways, while footpaths form pleasant walks and help to create the atmosphere of a cathedral close in the area around St Giles'.

Development has grown out from Wrexham westwards to the industrial villages of Brymbo, Coedpoeth, Gwersyllt and Minera (once known as 'the El Dorado of North Wales' because of its rich deposits of minerals) hidden away in their little valleys. On the more open land to the east and south, development has extended to Gresford and Rhosllanerchrugog. Although they now appear to be red-brick suburbs of the larger town each, however, still retains its own individuality although perhaps not to the same extent as the coal mining valleys of southern Wales. Rhosllanerchrugog, in particular, is renowned for its choirs and retained its Welsh language long after most places twice or three times further away from the border had succumbed to English speech.

Nearby are two places of interest to industrial archaeologists. At Croes Foel, near the junction of the main road and the Wrexham bypass, a plaque commemorates the talents of Robert and John Davies who had a smithy here in the eighteenth century. Together the Davies brothers produced marvellous wrought-iron gates and screens to ornament the entrances of numerous parks and churches in the region. Robert Davies (1675–1748) is reputed to have been a pupil of Tijou, the famous French wrought-iron smith. The art of the Davies brothers can be seen at its most magnificent at Leeswood Hall, near Mold, where they provided two sets of gates and screens. Other gates manufactured by the two brothers can still be seen at St Giles' Church in Wrexham, St Peter's Church in Ruthin, Erddig Park and Chirk Castle, as well as at Eaton Hall just across the border in Cheshire.

Bersham, a mile to the north, once had an ironworks which became famous in disputes and for supplying munitions to each and any country, whether friend or foe, that would pay for them. The site of the ironworks is now rural countryside again and apart from a farm barn which was once the works' mill, there is little evidence on the ground of their former importance. Yet here was one of the first ironworks in the world to use coal instead of charcoal for smelting. That was as far back as 1721, but the new-fangled methods seem to have been unprofitable for within five years the works were closed. In 1753 Isaac Wilkinson of Furness in Lancashire took over the ironworks, but he too failed and eight years later a new company was founded by his two sons, John and William. John, the elder brother, was the moving spirit and under him new and improved methods were used during the 1780s which were to revolutionize the iron industry generally. Cannon, grenades and large shells were turned out in unheard quantities and sold to both sides during the Russian-Turkish war of 1768 and, according to rumour, to the Americans during their war of independence. In addition the Bersham works supplied most of the special castings for the new steam-engines then being made by James Watt and Matthew Boulton in the English Midlands. It was this last venture which brought about the downfall of the Wilkinsons when William, the younger brother, discovered that John had been fraudulently infringing the Boulton and Watt patent by making steam engines for other buyers. The brothers quarrelled with each other violently – reputedly to such an extent that they both hired gangs of thugs to smash up the machinery in the works. As a result of the bitter dispute the ironworks were wrecked and the brothers ruined, at least temporarily. Within a few years, however, the ironworks were rebuilt, but on a new site. A mid-nineteenth century Cornish style Beam Engine House at Minera is a feature of the newly developed Bersham Industrial Trail.

Five miles to the east of Wrexham is Holt where the Romans had a large tile-factory worked by the Twentieth Legion stationed at Chester. The remains of the kilns have been excavated and tiles made there have been recorded in Roman forts as far afield as Caernarfon and Caerhun in Gwynedd and at Caersws in the Severn Valley. In the late thirteenth-century Edward I built a new castle on the Welsh bank of the River Dee to guard the important river crossing into Wales. Most of the castle was demolished at the end of the seventeenth century in order to provide building stone for Sir Thomas Grosvenor's Eaton Hall near Chester and very little is now left to be seen. The lovely old eight-arch bridge across the Dee, dating from the early fifteenth century, is fortunately still intact.

Rossett, a few miles to the north, has an interesting railway station built in the local sandstone, a squat and bold nineteenth-century church and two lovely old corn mills by the side of the Alun river. The older mill, with brickwork painted in the local black-and-white tradition, was mainly built in 1661, although it is reputed to have been a mill site since Saxon times. It was powered by water from the river until 1961. The other mill was built in 1791 and is now powered by electricity. A mile further on the main road passes through the model village of Marford sited at the bottom of an outlying hill. The two houses with low semi-circular towers on the Rossett side of the village provide a kind of formal entrance to this curious collection of cottages. The fanciful 'Gothick' cottages (originally thatched) with their ogee arches, cross 'arrow slits' and eye-shaped windows were built in 1805 by a Mr Boscawen with money inherited by his wife ten years earlier.

At the top of the long hill up from Marford is Gresford, a small town with little of visual interest apart from its fine parish church. The church is certainly worth looking at, however, being another of the group of Perpendicular Gothic edifices built by Margaret Beaufort at the end of the fifteenth century. The tower, pinnacled and buttressed, is similar to that at Wrexham, but more restrained in its decoration. Splendid windows, with stained glass dating back to 1498, make the interior light and spacious and show the carved woodwork in the screen, stalls and ceiling to advantage. The bells of the church figured as one of the 'Seven Wonders of Wales'. A few low, country cottages, the remnants of the old village centre, still stand around the church while a nearby duckpond contributes to the rural atmosphere. Industry, when it came to Gresford, came with a vengeance, causing much suffering and adding nothing to the attractions of the place. It was here, in 1934, that tragedy struck the local colliery when an explosion started a fire underground, causing the death of 261 miners, making it one of the worst disasters in coal-mining history.

West of Gresford the Alun river turns sharply north towards Caergwrle and marks a notable change in the landscape. On the west bank the land rises steeply to the foothills of the Clwydian Range. The east bank is distinguished by the line of Wat's Dyke, a double ditch and embankment constructed between Basingwerk on the Dee estuary and Welshpool on the Severn to mark the earliest boundary of the Mercian kings. It was probably built by King Ethelbald, who reigned between 725 and 750, and was a much smaller structure than the more famous Offa's Dyke built a few decades later on a more westerly line. Beyond Caergwrle, where the river valley is wider, Wat's Dyke was built half a mile east of the river. Offa's Dyke was built on a parallel course two miles to the west and can be clearly seen at Llanfynydd where the modern road runs along the top of the bank.

At Caergwrle the river runs in a deep, narrow valley between two hilly spurs of sandstone. Both spurs were once topped by Iron Age forts guarding the narrow pass into the upland regions. In the late thirteenth century Caergwrle Castle was built within the ramparts of the western fort by Dafydd ap Gruffydd, the son of Llywelyn Fawr, to guard his princedom. Although very little remains of the castle, and even what is left is obscured by the trees, it is interesting because of its peculiar mixture of English and Welsh features – features perhaps recalling the maverick character of the ambitious Dafydd who, though Welsh by birth and upbringing, was not above allying himself to the English side in order to outsmart his fellow Welsh princes. It was one of the first of the Welsh castles to fall to the English in 1282 at the beginning of the second war of independence. A reconstruction was put in hand immediately by Edward I and in the following February he granted the castle and the surrounding lands to his consort Queen Eleanor. Within a few months, however, the newly repaired building was destroyed by an accidental fire. The ravages of time in succeeding centuries have now made it virtually impossible to distinguish which parts were built by Dafydd and which by Edward.

If the castle has been largely forgotten by historians, that is not the case with the famous coracle-shaped bowl of oak found in a bog (possibly a former sacred pool) near the castle, in the early nineteenth century. The bowl, now kept in the National Museum at Cardiff, is less than eight inches long, yet probably at least 2,500 years old. It is richly decorated with incised gold leaf in patterns representing eyes at one end and oars and waves along the sides. The decoration suggests Scandinavian influence, possibly even the work of ancestors of the Vikings who, during the same period, were carving similar 'long-ships' on the rocks of Norway as ritualistic symbols.

Just north of Caergwrle is Plas Têg, a proud looking mansion standing dark and grey in its hilly park near the main road. Built in 1610 by an admiralty official, Sir John Trevor, Surveyor of the Queen's Ships, it has a very formal appearance with none of the rural simplicity and naïvity found in other local buildings of the period. Four-square on plan, it has tall, square towers at the corners, each roofed by leaded cupolas. Although traditionally attributed, like many other houses in Wales, to Inigo Jones, it is more likely to have been the work of the Court Surveyor, Robert Smythson.

The road to Hawarden passes close to Buckley, an industrial town noted in earlier days for its bricks and pottery made from the local clay. Pottery had been made at Buckley since late medieval times, but for the most part it was produced on a small scale; some family groups, however, were producing ware of high quality during the eighteenth century which exhibited some of the most sophisticated techniques of the period. In the nineteenth century the potteries became industrialized and there was a general lowering of standards following the mass production of coarse black-glazed kitchen ware. At the beginning of the twentieth century the decline in quality was halted for a while when Powell's Pottery, trading under the name of the North Walian Art Pottery, introduced new forms and designs. Some of these were influenced by the Art Nouveau movement, but it was a short-lived revival and in 1929 the pottery closed.

St Matthew's Church at Buckley dates from 1821, although parts of it look much older. Its strange appearance reflects its mixed history. In 1845 it was first altered and then 20 years later, it was altered again by James Harrison only to be changed yet again at the beginning of the twentieth century by John Douglas, who added a chancel, lengthened the tower and rebuilt the nave with a curious half-timbered clerestory.

Hawarden, once the gateway to Wales, lies on a gentle ridge above the mouth of the Dee and looks down to the mini-conurbation of Connah's Quay, Shotton and Queensferry. Where once there was flat marshland on either side of the river there is now a fast-growing development of houses and industry and Hawarden has now become almost part of the Deeside sprawl. In the Middle Ages the marshland was a real obstacle to movement between England and Wales and Hawarden was sited on the nearest piece of dry land west of Chester. Having succeeded in crossing the marshlands the Normans built a castle at Hawarden to defend their gateway to the west and this ancient redoubt has survived as a picturesque ruin on the wooded mound behind the main road. It was here that the second War of Independence started in 1282 when David (brother of the Prince of Wales, Llywelyn ap Gruffydd) attacked the castle on Palm Sunday in 1282.

Below the old castle and near the Chester road is the new 'castle' built in 1752 as Broadlane Hall and then Gothicized in 1810 and renamed Hawarden Castle. It was here that William Gladstone, four times Liberal Prime Minister under Queen Victoria, came to live after marrying Catherine Glynne, the heiress to the Hawarden estate. Two other buildings in Hawarden also commemorate the 'Grand Old Man' of British politics. First there is St Deiniol's Library, an institution founded by Gladstone as a library for divine learning and for which he left some 32,000 books from his own collection. The attractive, sandstone library, built between 1899 and 1906, is now a National Memorial to Gladstone. Nearby is the parish church, rebuilt by Sir Giles Scott after a fire, with its Gladstone Memorial Chapel designed by John Douglas. The vast monument in the chapel, depicting the Gladstones in a marble ship, is by Sir William Richmond. Gladstone and his wife were, however, buried in Westminster Abbey.

Just two miles from the Norman castle at Hawarden the Welsh princes built their own fortress at Ewloe to fend off the Earls of Chester. The castle is not visible from the road, but a signpost directs the visitor across a couple of fields to substantial and impressive ruins magnificently sited above the confluence of two deep, tree-filled valleys. In this situation, it is not difficult to imagine the medieval atmosphere of Ewloe and the fighting that took place there. The formidable strength of the castle is emphasized by the great encircling ditch and embankment and by the fact that, even in ruins, the main part of the citadel built by Llywelyn Fawr seven centuries ago is inaccessible except by climbing the walls (which apart from being dangerous, is also forbidden by notices).

Northop, although at the cross-roads of two important through routes, still has the air of a quiet and pleasant village. Its glory is the Perpendicular style church rebuilt by Margaret Beaufort in the fifteenth century. Built in the warm, local yellow-brown sandstone, it has a lowish nave (with a good flat panelled timber ceiling) and a massive, but comparatively simple tower over the entrance. Alongside the churchyard is the old school (now restored) dating from 1609.

One of the main roads from Northop runs down to Flint on the edge of the Dee estuary. Flint was one of the chain of new towns that Edward I established along the northern perimeter of his new Principality at the end of the thirteenth century. They were planned as bases to control and administer the king's recently acquired territories and were designed to withstand all-out warfare when necessary. Each town was surrounded by a strong defensive wall and guarded at one end by a powerful castle. Flint was the first of the new towns to be built in this way and had a rigidly regular street layout, with its main thoroughfare centrally aligned to link the church and market with the castle. Flint Town Hall, which stands in the main street, is a pleasant example of Victorian Gothic Revival architecture. It was built in 1840 in the local brown sandstone to designs by John Welch. Although the general plan of Flint has been retained over the centuries it is difficult now to appreciate it on the ground, for in the nineteenth century the railway sliced the town into two parts and the spaces have now been infilled with industrial and post-war red-brick terraces; the edge of the town is dominated by enormous multi-storey blocks of flats. The castle too, although bounded on one side by the marshy estuary, has unsympathetic groups of tall factory chimneys alongside. It is now in a very ruinous condition and small in size when compared to other Edwardian castles. It is worth visiting in order to see the great circular Donjon tower which was built in an unusual manner as an external adjunct to the rest of the fortress. The tower is the best preserved part and has enormously thick walls threaded by vaulted tunnels and passages.

The main road to Holywell continues parallel to the coast, passing through Bagillt and Pentre Bach, and then suddenly turns inland up the first of two valleys towards Holywell. For those interested in medieval ruins, carry straight on at Pentre Bach and continue past the textile works to Greenfield and the second valley where, in surprisingly rural surroundings, one will find the remains of Basingwerk Abbey. The remains are rather bare, but there are enough pieces of walling and stone arcading (and even some timber windows and bits of cruck-trusses) to show that at one time this was a large monastery. It was founded as a house of the Savignac Order of France in 1131 and subsequently transferred to the Cistercians. By the thirteenth century, the monks of Basingwerk had come into the possession of the famous Well of St Winifred, further along the valley, and did exceedingly well out of the donations of pilgrims. In return the abbey was noted for its lavish hospitality.

The second valley leading to Holywell is filled with small reservoirs which once provided power for the numerous wool and flannel mills and metal works which thrived here. One of the textile mills is still in production and can be visited. Nearby, at the top end of the valley, is St Winifred's Well, the sacred well after which the town gets its name. According to legend, Winifred (or more correctly Gwenffrewi), the daughter of a local prince, was attacked by a neighbouring chieftain called Caradoc who unceremoniously chopped her head off after attempting to seduce her; Caradoc was naturally swallowed up by the earth as a punishment and Winifred had her head restored to place by her uncle (the great Saint Beuno) who happened to have a church nearby. Only a thin white line showed where Winifred's head had been severed from her neck and at the place where the unfortunate incident took place a spring of healing water suddenly gushed up. All this is supposed to have happened in the seventh century and ever since then the site has been a place of pilgrimage. The well soon became one of the 'Seven Wonders of Wales' and fittingly so, for there is nothing quite like it anywhere else in the land. The star-shaped well is now part of the elegant crypt of the beautiful Perpendicular style well-chapel, the fan-vaulted ceiling of which culminates in a carved central boss depicting scenes from the life of St Winifred. The upper chapel is itself a remarkable little building with an apsidal chancel and is full of delightful wood carvings. The well-chapel replaced an earlier and simpler building and was donated by Henry VII's mother, Margaret Beaufort, soon after her son's victory at Bosworth. As if in piety, Henry VIII spared St Winifred's Well when he caused other popular shrines to be closed or destroyed. Above the well is the handsome Roman Catholic Church for which Frederick Rolfe, under the assumed name of Father Austin (but better known as the self-styled Baron Corvo) painted ten banners at the request of Father Beauclerk. Rolfe also wrote scathing articles for the *Holywell Record*, causing chaos within the social circles of the little town. To restore peace, Beauclerk was moved to another parish and Rolfe ended up in the local workhouse.

Holywell seems to have more places of religious interest than any other town in Wales except, perhaps, St David's in the south. A short way west of the town is Pantasaph, a nineteenth-century monastery originally run by the Capuchin Franciscans. The church was started in 1849 by the Earl of Denbigh as an Anglican church, but before it and the adjoining rectory were completed the Earl was converted to Roman Catholicism and called in the architect Pugin to adjust the designs to meet his new requirements. The change of heart gave rise to a lawsuit and also to an appeal for money to build a new church. The Church of England lost the legal battle but collected enough money to build two churches (at Brynford and Gorsedd) instead. The poet Francis Thompson lived at Pantasaph for a number of years during the 1890s.

The pleasant village of Whitford lies a couple of miles to the north in rolling pastoral scenery. At the crossroads to the west of the village is Maen Achwyfan, a superbly carved wheel-cross from the eleventh century. Nearby, on the hill behind the village, is a large ruined tower of uncertain age and use. It is now almost surrounded by forests but once commanded extensive views over much of northern Wales and parts of England. Thomas Pennant, the eighteenth-century naturalist and author, thought it to be the remains of a Roman lighthouse, but recent research suggests that it is one of a line of beacons between Whitford and Anglesey and the Llŷn peninsula erected in the seventeenth century, probably by Lord Mostyn, to forewarn shipping of the presence of pirates. Pennant was born locally, at a house called Downing in the valley just below Whitford. He is best known for his *Tours in Wales*, published in 1778 and 1781 with illustrations by the self-taught artist Moses Griffiths. Pennant also wrote a 'Tours' of London, Scotland and the Continent as well as a 22 volume work entitled *Outlines of the Globe*, only part of which was published.

Alongside the Downing estate, and connected to it by a castellated lodge and arch over the public road, is the Mostyn estate. Mostyn Hall, partly medieval and partly Victorian, was one of the treasure houses of Welsh literature and culture. The Mostyn family, who were related to the royal line of Tudor, played an important part in both Welsh and English politics. In particular they conspired with other Lancastrian sympathizers in helping Henry VII to obtain the English crown and on two occasions helped the Tudors to hide from the king's men. The first time was when Howel ap Ieuan Fychan helped Jasper Tudor to escape from Mostyn to Brittany. The second occasion was when Henry Tudor was staying at Mostyn Hall and Richard ap Howel helped him to escape from Richard II's soldiers. The window from which Henry made his escape has been retained in all the subsequent alterations to the Hall.

Chief amongst the cultural possessions of Mostyn Hall were valuable manuscripts in Welsh, including the earliest known edition of *Brut y Tywysogion* ('Chronicle of the Princes') which have now been given to the National Library at Aberystwyth. During the Middle Ages the Mostyn Family did much to stimulate the flourishment of Welsh poetry. Wandering poets, known as bards, were always welcome at the house and Ieuan Fychan ap Ieuan, the grandfather of Richard ap Howel, was noted as a fine poet in his own right as well as being a proficient harpist. Richard himself kept up the family tradition and was the patron for the celebrated Caerwys Eisteddfod of 1523. It was he who presented the famous Mostyn silver harp for competition at the Eisteddfod.

Caerwys itself lies at the foot of the hills five miles south of Mostyn and has – for such a small place – a curiously urban feeling. Three streets running north to south are bisected by three more running east to west with the remnants of a small market place at the central crossing. This grid layout gives it the appearance of a pocket-sized nineteenth-century model town. It is, however, much older; at least as old as 1290, when it was granted a borough charter, and possibly older still.

It was in the sixteenth century that Caerwys had its heyday for it was in 1523 that the first of the famous Caerwys Eisteddfodau were held. It was proclaimed in accordance with a Statute of Gruffudd ap Cynan, Prince of Gwynedd, to certify and confirm master craftsmen in the arts of poetry and was thus different to the modern eisteddfod which is entirely competitive. The next Caerwys Eisteddfod, proclaimed by royal commission of Queen Elizabeth I, was not held until 1567, more than 40 years later. It too had the same aim, namely to safeguard the privileges of the craftsmen poets and to get rid of the vagabonds that roamed the countryside begging at the houses of the gentry. Poets who were judged worthy received a degree confirming them in their status and were therefore free to wander around the countryside, practice their craft in an orderly manner and get paid for their work. Those who did not qualify were treated as vagrants and put to other work. Despite the Caerwys Eisteddfodau there was little improvement in the lot of the poet and during the next century the traditional craft of poetry was on the decline. Occasionally, a poet would be well paid, but there were few who could support themselves by writing verse. In the seventeenth century, there were hardly any true eisteddfodau or poet-assemblies of the Caerwys type and in the following century the eisteddfod had degenerated into feeble localized affairs usually held in a tavern. By the end of the eighteenth century the old type of eisteddfod was virtually finished. Instead the organization of holding an eisteddfod passed into the hands of regional cultural societies and it is from these that the modern competitive eisteddfod, culminating in the massive National Eisteddfod with competitions in nearly all the arts, developed.

From near Caerwys the main road follows first the Wheeler river and then the Alun river on a winding journey, between the gentle backs of the Clwydian Range on one side and the low-lying Halkyn Mountain on the other side, to Mold. Ysgeifiog, with its lake and fish hatchery, lies up on a hill to the north while Nannerch, with its nineteenth-century church containing a 1693 monument by Grinling Gibbons, is pleasantly situated on sloping ground on the opposite side. Further south the valley opens out and the countryside around Cilcain is dotted with many tiny cottages and farms. Cilcain itself is a delightful, close-knit village of stone and whitewashed buildings. There is a fairly large double-aisled church standing in a traditionally oval-shaped Celtic churchyard at the higher end of the village. Inside the church there is a fine hammerbeam roof-truss (said to have come from Basingwerk Abbey) carved with angels.

Mold, originally the administrative centre of the old county of Flintshire and now the county town of Clwyd, is a pleasantly open and clean-looking town, busy on Saturdays with its market stalls lining the High Street. There are some good chapels, such as the pedimented Bethesda and the Gothic Revival Wesleyan, and a fine sixteenth-century parish church (built in local sandstone in Perpendicular style) proudly standing on a slight hill just north of the centre.

Mold was the home of a number of important literary people. Daniel Owen (1836–95), the novelist, has his statue in front of the library in the new shopping centre behind the High Street. Owen was brought up in poverty after his father and two brothers were killed in a mining accident and he therefore had only a sketchy education. He was apprenticed to a tailor and later took up preaching, but although he contributed to various newspapers he did not turn to writing novels until 40 years old. Then, with the life around him as his raw material, he wrote four books which quickly became very popular and broke through, almost for the first time, the old Welsh prejudice against any kind of fiction writing. In his best known novel, *Enoc Huws*, Owen portrayed the threatened break-up of Welsh society at the hands of the new industrialism and thus laid the foundation for many latter-day novels such as Richard Llywelyn's *How Green was my Valley.* The hymn writer John Ambrose Lloyd (1814–74) and the poetess Jane Bereton (1685–1740) were also born in Mold.

Bailey Hill, just beyond the parish church, was the site of Mold Castle in the eleventh century. Now it is a public park and contains a modern stone circle erected for the National Eisteddfod in 1922. In complete contrast, on the hill on the opposite side of the river, are the new County Council offices built since 1967. For a town the size of Mold it is an enormous complex; and however well designed the individual parts are, it appears as something of an officious affront amidst the semi-rural scene. The feeling of 'big brother is watching you' is fortunately compensated for by the very fine landscaping around the buildings. The most interesting of the group is Theatr Clwyd at the top of the hill. Its irregularly shaped outline in conjunction with red-brick walls and lead roof gives it a slightly Scandinavian appearance. Inside, its spacious entrance hall, restaurant, exhibition gallery, three theatres, radio and television studios – all lavishly equipped with every technical facility – makes it the most advanced music and drama ensemble in Wales.

The countryside immediately south of Mold has a fair sprinkling of interesting mansions and country houses. Leeswood Hall dates from the eighteenth century and has ornamental gardens by Stephen Switzer. The most outstanding feature of the estate, however, are the profusely decorated gate-screens made by the local iron-smiths Robert and John Davies of Croes Foel; the Black Gates stand between a pair of lodges alongside the main road and the White Gates (really a grand screen and not an entrance) can be seen from a lane to the south. The White Gates (100-feet-long including the screens) are superbly executed with elaborate crestings and delicate tracery and must surely be amongst the finest in Europe.

Nerquis Hall was built in 1640 and had wings added on in 1797; the wings were later removed. After years of dereliction the house had now been lovingly restored to its original state complete with panelled rooms, moulded ceilings and a long gallery on the top floor. In the grounds there is a Gothick Orangery built in 1813 with pinnacled buttresses. Of the smaller houses the most important are: The Tower, which was built in the fifteenth century as a defensive tower-house and considerably altered by the Victorians; Pentrehobyn, a seventeenth-century house with projecting wings; and the lovely but more modest Fferm with its splendidly carved timber-work fittings.

West of Mold the main road follows the Afon Alun as far as Llanferres before crossing over the Clwydian Range and down to Ruthin and Dyffryn Clwyd. Llanferres has associations with the landscape painter Richard Wilson. Although Wilson himself was born near Machynlleth in 1717, his mother came from Leeswood and it was to here that he often came on holiday as a child. Later, when Wilson had become well established as a painter and was living in London, he would return to the area to stay with his cousin Catherine Jones who lived at Colomendy near Llanferres. While staying there Wilson painted a sign for the local inn. The inn, near where the Alun has gouged out a miniature gorge amongst the limestone rocks opposite

Colomendy, is known as 'We Three Loggerheads', the name loggerhead being a variation of 'blockhead'. Wilson, however, painted only two heads on the signboard (now restored), it being assumed that the onlooker was the third! During the last year of his life and with his health rapidly deteriorating Wilson came to live at Colomendy. He was buried in the churchyard of Mold parish church.

The gentle slopes of the Clwydian Range form a continuous chain of hills from north to south guarding the way between Mold and Ruthin. From Llanferres it is a comparatively easy walk, partly along the old road through Bwlch Pen Barras, to the highest point (1,820 feet) of the range at Moel Famau. The rounded summit is distinguished by a pile of rubble which is the collapsed remains of the Jubilee Tower erected in 1810 to commemorate the fiftieth year of George III's reign. Originally in the shape of a squat Egyptian-looking obelisk, the tower was partly blown down in 1862 during a gale (or, as a local policeman who saw the disaster described it, a 'strong breeze'). Most of the subsidiary peaks of the Clwydian Range are crowned by massive hill-forts; Foel Fenlli (1,676 feet) and Moel y Gaer (1,092 feet) to the south, and Moel Arthur (1,494 feet) and Pen y Cloddiau (1,400 feet) to the north. Each fort has multiple protective ramparts and all appear to have been constructed 2,000 or more years ago during the Early Iron Age or the Late Bronze Age.

EIGHT

Dyffryn Clwyd

The heart of north-eastern Wales is the broad, fertile vale known as Dyffryn Clwyd which runs diagonally north-westwards from the base of the hills around Ruthin to the sea at Rhyl. The eastern limits of the vale are clearly defined by the abrupt slopes of the Clwydian Range, but the western side dissolves into a rolling landscape of wooded hills enclosing quiet, secluded valleys; beyond are the moorlands of Mynydd Hiraethog. The Afon Clwyd rises to the south of Mynydd Hiraethog in the midst of the vast coniferous dome of Clocaenog Forest, one of the largest and earliest man-made plantations in northern Wales. A monument sited conspicuously on an outlying hill near the village of Clocaenog identifies itself with the following inscription:

> *As a memorial of his having completed the large range of mountain plantations which in part skirt the base of this hill, William, Second Lord Bagot, erected this pile of stones in the year 1830.'*

The young river flows to the south for a few miles and then, after tumbling past the old mill at Melin-y-wig, takes a sharp turn north-east to follow a deep valley below the multiple ramparts of Dinas hill-fort and the hillside village of Derwen. Derwen is off the main road and can be reached by a short detour across a narrow bridge at Bryn Saith Marchog ('Hill of the Seven Knights' – a reference to the knights who, in one of the Mabinogi stories, were left to govern Britain in the absence of King Bendigeidfran) and up a very steep hill. At the top of the hill there is a lovely little church with a double belfry and buttressed gable at one end. Inside there is a fine sixteenth-century rood-screen and rood-loft. The loft is double-sided and faces both the nave and the chancel, spanning the width of the church like a bridge beneath massive roof trusses. In the churchyard, in front of the restored church house, is the decorated shaft of a late fifteenth-century cross.

The main road continues alongside the tree-bordered estate of Nantclwyd Hall and the Afon Clwyd, until now a mountain stream, then drops down quickly to the level fields of Dyffryn Clwyd and turns north again towards Ruthin. The tiny village of Llanfair Dyffryn Clwyd, dominated by its double-naved Perpendicular church, stands near the head of the vale. In the background the skyline is formed by the hills of the Clwydian Range which, until relatively recent times, were a physical barrier to communication between east and west. The silhouette of a massive castle a mile and half to the north marks the position of Ruthin.

After crossing the Afon Clwyd the main road enters Ruthin (Rhuthun) alongside the grounds of the castle. The ruined walls of the original thirteenth-century fortress stand near the entrance to the grounds and other ancient remnants are incorporated in the dark red, sandstone walls of a vast nineteenth-century Gothic pile which now houses a hotel. 'Medieval' banquets are regularly held within the resurrected halls of the hotel; outside, the extensive grounds offer splendid views across the lower part of the vale.

Ruthin itself is situated along the ridge which spreads out behind the castle. From near the river winding streets lead up the hill towards St Peter's Square in the centre. A charming mixture of architectural styles and the use of a wide range of building materials such as stone, brick, stucco and a good sprinkling of half-timbered houses give the town its own special character. The three banks in the centre are each Tudor-bethan; Barclays is a restoration of the Exemewe Hall built in 1517. The nearby Old Court House, however, is probably the oldest of the secular buildings; it was erected in 1401 and still has part of the old town gibbet on display.

St Peter's Church, at the lower end of the square, dates mainly from the fourteenth century. The heavy broach spire was added to the tower when it was restored in 1856–9. The interior of the church is embellished by magnificent sixteenth-century oak panelled roofs over both aisles. That over the north aisle is the earlier and more decorative of the two; its 480 carved panels are reputed to have been given to the church by King Henry VII in gratitude to the Welshmen who supported him at the Battle of Bosworth Field in 1485. St Peter's was originally a monastic foundation and the very pleasant precinct around the church still has the air of a small cathedral close. Christ's Hospital (founded 1590, reconstructed 1865), on the east side, is a low, single-storey building; to the north is the old Grammar School (1700) and Headmaster's House. Adjoining the church are the Old Cloisters, a fourteenth-century two-storey structure originally intended as dwelling and workrooms for resident priests.

Other notable buildings in St Peter's Square are the eighteenth-century Castle Hotel and, alongside it, Sir Richard Clough's town house, an unusual sixteenth-century structure with a high roof and tiers of dormer windows in Dutch style. Nantclwyd House, in Stryd-y-Castell, is another sixteenth-century building, but of a more traditional design with a half-timbered porch carried on pillars. From later centuries, the Old Gaol (built in 1775 and now converted into a library) in Heol Clwyd, the County Hall (1785) in Record Street and bow-fronted Pendref Chapel (1827) in Well Street are well worth looking out for.

The vale north of Ruthin can be explored from the roads on both sides of the river. The lonely church of Llanynys lies in the flat, low lying lands between the two roads. The name Llanynys means 'island church' and is a reference to its situation between the parallel rivers of Clwyd and Clywedog which has always been a wet and marshy spot. The church, though Celtic in foundation, dates from the thirteenth century and was considerably restored in 1770 when the central arcade of arches was replaced by closely spaced fluted columns of oak. In 1968 a fine fifteenth-century mural painting of St Christopher was discovered on the north wall of the church under thick layers of whitewash.

Llanrhaeadr-yn-Cinmerch at the side of the Denbigh road is a pretty village with a large double-nave church. The entrance to the church is through a finely carved timber porch. Inside there is an elegant barrel-shaped roof over the chancel. The excellent Jesse window, dating from 1533, was taken out during the Civil War and hidden in the wooden chest (carved out of a single piece of oak) which now stands below it.

Approaching Denbigh from the east, one's eye is automatically drawn to the distant view of the hill-top castle and it is all too easy to miss the parish church of St Marcella and the meagre remains of the Friary, hidden away on the fringes of the town. The church, also known as Eglwys Wen or Whitchurch, stands in a side road and is a typical Clwydian double-nave edifice with corbelled hammer-beam roof trusses. The remains of the thirteenth-century Carmelite Friary, largely destroyed by fire in 1898, are hidden away behind a petrol-filling station on the road to Mold. Denbigh (Dinbych) is huddled around a long, undistinguished street which climbs up to the market place at the top of High Street. Facing proudly onto the market place is the old County Hall. High Street is a lively, bustling place, full of character and lined with buildings (some with arcaded fronts) of all periods. Around the market place there is a network of interesting side streets and narrow lanes, two of which (Broomhill Lane and Bull Lane) lead steeply uphill to Denbigh Castle.

The castle, though very much ruined, overlooks the town and

dominates it from its high point. In its heyday, Denbigh Castle formed one of the links in the mighty chain of Edwardian fortresses encircling the highland redoubt of northern Wales. It was not, however, one of Edward I's own castles, but was built by the Earl of Lincoln, Henry de Lacy, between 1282 and 1322 after he had been given the lordship of Denbigh as a reward for his support during the king's campaigns. Denbigh Castle, like the other Edwardian castles, was built on a formidable scale and in conjunction with the establishment of a new town. The walls of the town were intended to form the outer defences of the castle. The castle gatehouse is an immensely powerful structure, consisting of three great octagonal towers surrounding an inner hall and linked together in a triangular plan. The twin-towered Burgess Gate, at the foot of Tower Hill, is now the only remaining gate into the medieval town, although most of the town walls are still standing. Of the old town virtually nothing remains – the streets and houses have all disappeared over the centuries and all that is left, apart from the Town Walls, is a large sloping grass field and the ruins of two churches. St Hilary's Church, near the Castle gatehouse, was formerly the garrison chapel, but only its square tower now stands. Leicester's Church, with its long range of round-headed windows, was never completed. It was originally started in 1579 by the Earl of Leicester as a replacement for the cathedral at St Asaph – hence its great size – but the plan was abandoned.

Henry Morton Stanley (originator of the famous greeting 'Dr. Livingstone, I presume') was born in a cottage, now demolished, just below the castle. Stanley, whose real name was John Rowlands, was brought up in the workhouse at St Asaph, but before long he rebelled against the onerous conditions and ran away to sea. He eventually became a newspaper correspondent for the *New York Herald* and while working for the newspaper, was sent out to the interior of Africa to lead an expedition in search of the Scottish explorer, Dr Livingstone.

Other natives of Denbigh were Humphrey Llwyd (1527–68), the antiquary, and Thomas Gee (1815–98), the Welsh patriot and forerunner of the nationalists. Humphrey Llwyd studied medicine at Oxford and became the private physician to Lord Arundel for a number of years. He returned to Denbigh in 1563 to devote himself to writing. Amongst his published works were *An Almanack and Kalender containing the Day, Hour and Minute of the Change of the Moon for ever* and *The Treasury of Health*, but he is now chiefly remembered as being the author of the first individual map of Wales. The map, with its place-names in Welsh, English and Latin, was used in the famous world atlas *Theatrum Orbis Terrarum* published in Holland by Abraham Ortelius in 1573. Llwyd was introduced to

Ortelius by his friend Sir Richard Clough of Bachegraig, who lived for a time in Antwerp, and as a result was commissioned to provide manuscripts for a map of England and Wales, as well as the map of Wales.

Thomas Gee, a printer and publisher by trade, was a staunch Radical and Nonconformist who did much to influence and enlighten Welsh public opinion in the nineteenth century by the establishment of the Welsh-language weekly newspaper, *Baner ac Amserau Cymru* ('The Banner and Welsh Times'). Known simply as *Y Faner*, it is still published and widely read throughout Wales. Another of Gee's ventures was the publication, between 1854 and 1878, of a Welsh Encyclopaedia in ten volumes.

West of Denbigh, and beyond the little white-washed village of Nantglyn, are the moorlands of Mynydd Hiraethog. The monotony of these bleak hills is being transformed by reservoirs and coniferous forests into a new landscape and the area of primeval heather moor is gradually being reduced. The narrow Alwen reservoir with its lofty, Victorian dam has long been a picturesque landmark, but now the shallow Brenig valley has also been dammed to provide a new reservoir to quench the ever-growing thirst of industry.

Henllan, to the north-west of Denbigh, is situated in a more varied landscape of wooded hills and delectable little valleys. Pretty stone cottages vie for interest with the tall, detached church tower standing isolated on a tump of rock. Just below the village an infant river descends rapidly through a miniature valley to join its parent, the Afon Elwy, in a heavily wooded limestone gorge at Cefn. Here, amongst the trees and reached by a steep zig-zag footpath, are caves that were known to Stone Age man. Excavations have unearthed neolithic implements as well as the bones of prehistoric animals. At the lower end of the gorge there are some forlorn remnants of Ffynnon Fair, a Perpendicular style well-chapel. Higher up, on the ridge, there is a small nineteenth-century church with an apsidal end by Benjamin Ferrey.

Beyond Henllan, amongst the folded hills above the Elwy, is the quiet little village of Llanefydd where Twm o'r Nant (Thomas Edwards), the poet and interlude writer, was born in 1739 in a farm nearby. The eldest of ten children in a poor family, Twm was largely self taught. By the time he was nine years old he had begun both to work on the farm and write verses. He led a troubled life and was nearly always battling against poverty – for misfortune seemed to pursue him – and in order to clear his debts Twm was forced to compose interludes (rhyming folk-plays) and take them on tour while trying his hand, at the same time, on various jobs he could get. Interludes were the most popular form of entertainment in Wales during the eighteenth century and they were usually performed from an open waggon at local fairs. Twm o'r Nant's interludes were particularly successful because he was writing with feeling born of poverty. As a result, his are of more than passing interest as social commentaries on the conditions of the poor in Wales during the period.

Another famous person from the same parish was Catrin o'r Berain (Katheryn of Berain), born in 1534. She became known as 'Mam Cymru' ('mother of Wales') because, as a result of four marriages, she was the ancestress of several important Welsh families. Katheryn's first marriage was to John Salusbury of Llewenni. Ten years later she married Sir Richard Clough and then after another six years she married Maurice Wynn. Apparently Wynn had first proposed to Katheryn on the way back from her first husband's funeral, but she had had to refuse, as she had already accepted Sir Richard Gough's proposition on the way to the funeral! She promised Wynn, however, that in case she performed the same sad duty to the knight, he might depend upon being the third. The fourth marriage was to Edward Thelwell in 1583. Amongst Katheryn's descendants were Hester Lynch Piozzi (the friend of Dr Samuel Johnson and a gifted writer herself) and Sir Watkin Williams-Wynn of Wynnstay. Katheryn herself was descended from Henry VII and before she died in 1591 she was able to buy Penmynydd in Anglesey, the old ancestral home of the Tudors. Another view of Katheryn's marriages is that some were arranged by Queen Elizabeth I, who preferred not to take chances with anyone who might have a claim to royal blood and therefore the throne. Berain, a sixteenth-century hall-house with hammer-beam roof trusses, which Catrin probably had built for herself, still stands (though considerably altered internally) in the rolling farmland midway between Llanefydd and Henllan.

Of Katheryn's four husbands, the second, Sir Richard Clough was perhaps the most interesting. The son of a Denbigh glover he became a merchant and settled in Antwerp in 1552. There he became acquainted with Flemish building techniques and when he returned to Wales in 1567 to marry Catrin o'r Berain, he began introducing new architectural ideas based on Dutch Renaissance buildings. The house which he built for himself and his new wife – Bachegraig at Tremeirchion on the eastern side of the Clwyd – was the first to be built of brick in Wales since the Roman period. Reputedly the craftsmen were specially brought over from Holland and the house itself was similar to a Flemish château with a high, almost pyramidical roof containing tiers of dormer windows. Unfortunately, apart from the gatehouse, nothing now survives of this unusual building. After Bachegraig, Sir Richard Clough built Plas Clough at Henllan. He also had plans to improve the Afon Clwyd and make it navigable for small ships as far as Rhuddlan, but before this could be accomplished he had to return to the Continent and died there at an early age.

St Asaph (Llanelwy), the smallest cathedral city in Britain after St David's in Dyfed, stands on a narrow ridge between the Afon Clwyd and the Afon Elwy. A new by-pass fortunately diverts motor traffic away from the little cathedral which stands four-square in a neat lawn at the upper end of High Street. The mainly thirteenth-century building is cruciform in plan and has a low central tower. During its mixed history a number of attempts were made to demote the cathedral in favour of other churches in Denbigh, Rhuddlan and Wrexham and to subordinate the diocese to Bangor, but nothing came of any of these moves. The present pristine appearance of the cathedral is largely due to the thorough restoration carried out by Sir Gilbert Scott more than a century ago. Before that the cathedral had been burnt three times, by Edward I, Owain Glyndŵr and by the Roundheads during the Civil War, so that by the eighteenth century it had fallen into a very neglected state. Dr William Morgan, the translator of the Bible into Welsh, was bishop of St Asaph from 1601 until his death three years later. An elaborate memorial, erected in 1902, in the cathedral precinct commemorates Dr Morgan and his collaborators and a copy of his Bible is kept in the Chapter House museum alongside the cathedral.

A couple of miles west of St Asaph at Bodelwyddan, is the so-called 'Marble Church', the finest nineteenth-century church in northern Wales. It stands slightly back from the main road and from the outside appears extraordinarily neat and tidy. It was erected in 1856 to designs by John Gibson and has a perfectly symmetrical west-end dominated by a tall, slim tower with a beautiful spire, 203 feet high, all built in gleaming white limestone. On the opposite side of the road, behind a great park wall, is Bodelwyddan Castle, a mainly nineteenth-century reconstruction of a centuries' old building. It is now the home of Lowther College. Nearby at the side of the main road there is an elaborately carved Dutch-style gate lodge. This was the entrance to Kinmel Park, a magnificent nineteenth-century mansion which was partly destroyed by fire in 1975.

The ruins of Rhuddlan Castle stand out conspicuously in the distance above the flat, fen-like country to the north of St Asaph. Nearer at hand, one can see the grey-white limestone upperworks of the towers still firm and solid above their softer, crumbling bases standing on the banks of the Clwyd. Rhuddlan was the largest and most important of the strategic fortresses built by Edward I after the partial defeat of Llywelyn ap Gruffydd in 1277 in the first War of Independence. Built to a lozenge-shaped plan, with high walls and massive towers at the corners and surrounded by an outer defence wall with smaller square towers, the new castle was Edward's first essay in the construction of concentrically planned fortresses in northern Wales. A deep moat encircled the perimeter of the castle and in order to ensure that the castle would be provisioned in the event of a prolonged siege the Afon Clwyd was canalized and deepened at great expense to make it navigable for sea-going ships. It was from Rhuddlan that Edward, in 1284, issued his famous Statute of Wales proclaiming the conquered Welsh lands as a private principality of the king. A plaque at the corner of High Street and Parliament Street records the fragmentary remains of the building where Edward called his parliament to enact the Statute.

To the rear of the castle the king established a new borough, the rectilinear street-layout of which still survives in the present layout of the town. The new cathedral that was intended to replace St Asaph was, however, never built. Instead a smaller church, St Mary's, was built on the opposite side of High Street and enlarged in the fifteenth century to make it a double-nave building.

The Edwardian castle was not the first to be built at Rhuddlan. The mound of an earlier fortification, the Twthill, can be seen a little to the south overlooking the river. Both the Twthill and another castle at Diserth, on the ridge to the east, had however, been difficult to hold and since 796, when the English won the Battle of Rhuddlan, this part of Clwyd was constantly changing hands. Diserth Castle was destroyed by Llywelyn ap Gruffydd in 1263 and virtually nothing now remains of this stronghold, the result of centuries of quarrying for lead and zinc – but its site, below the sheer cliffs of Craig Fawr, makes a good viewpoint to scan the holiday coastline all the way from Prestatyn to Llandudno. At Diserth there is a fine waterfall almost in the centre of the village, near the church. An admission charge of 5p allows the visitor a fuller view and also gives access to a flight of steps between two massive walls leading to a miniature limestone gorge above the fall.

Bodrhyddan Hall, between Rhuddlan and Diserth, is a mainly nineteenth-century red-brick 'Queen Ann' style addition (by W. E. Nesfield) to a late seventeenth-century mansion. The panelled hall on the ground floor has much armour and many paintings while upstairs, in the former library, there is a good porcelain collection. Ffynnon Fair (Mary's Well) in the ornamental gardens surrounding the house has an octagonal well-house inscribed '1612: Inigo Jones'.

The steep hills behind Diserth are the northern end of the Clwydian Range. The northernmost tip, known quaintly as St Elmo's Summer House, is near the hilltop village of Gwaenysgor and is marked by a Bronze Age burial mound. Nearby Bryn-llwyd is the site of a Stone Age village overlooking the sea and the holiday resort of Prestatyn.

Modern Prestatyn, with its acres of holiday camps and caravan parks, is nearly all less than a century old, but beneath the streets and houses there lies a Roman fort, parts of which have been recently unearthed.

The lowland north of Rhuddlan was once an area of lonely marshes and grassy fields which reached out to meet the sand dunes along the sea-shore. That was before the railways came to Rhyl which, at that time, was only a little hamlet at the mouth of the Clwyd. The railways brought holiday makers by the thousand and, almost overnight, Rhyl flourished into a prosperous resort. A long, curving promenade and a golf course now border the fine stretch of sands while near the estuary of the Clwyd there is a Marine Lake, Leisure Park and Dolphinarium. The Royal Floral Hall, built in glass like a miniature Crystal Palace, and the nearby Sun Centre, are half-way along the promenade. The centre of the town itself is marked by the leaning tower of the Town Hall, a fanciful, Gothic-style structure built in 1874.

The coastal strip between Rhyl and Abergele is almost entirely built over with holiday houses, caravan sites and amusement arcades. Towyn, half-way between the two places, is now no longer recognizable as a distinct village. It has an unusual church (by G.E. Street, 1873), with a saddle-back tower. A vicarage and school by the same architect are pleasantly grouped along with the church and all are roofed with patterned slates.

Abergele still manages to retain a market town appearance despite its nearness to the sea and its inevitable holiday development. It has one of the largest double-nave churches in Clwyd. In the churchyard there are two mass graves, recalling a shipwreck in 1848 and a train crash in 1868. Nearby there is a strange-looking Roman Catholic church built in the form of a basilica with a large central dome and accompanying apses. Gwrych Castle is just outside Abergele and is one of the earliest examples of the nineteenth-century fashion for sham fortresses. The imposing structure was built in 1814 and consists mostly of long battlemented walls and frowning towers (18 in all) strung out along a wooded hillside with an eccentric disregard for cost and military logic. The tallest tower in the chain, known as the Hesketh Tower, was named after the original owner, Lloyd Bamford Hesketh, who probably collaborated with the architect C. A. Busby in designing the 'castle'. A long list of genuine and legendary historical events connected with the locality has been inscribed on the entrance gateway in an attempt to give the mock fortress an air of respectable authenticity.

On the hill, immediately south-east of Abergele, there are remains of a far earlier fortification; this is Dinorben hill-fort, which was started nearly 3000 years ago. It was successively enlarged and strengthened until eventually a series of five great banks and ditches had been built up at the southern end. The hill-fort is on a limestone outcrop, but as the rock is gradually being quarried away the site will ultimately be destroyed. Not far away on an adjoining hill there is a round tower which was probably erected as a watch tower in the seventeenth century to observe and warn of dangers from pirates.

Llanfair Talhaearn lies in the upper reaches of the narrow Elwy valley amongst the hills south of Abergele. Remote and unspoilt, it remains a pleasant, irregularly-shaped village with narrow streets climbing up from the stone bridge by the river. Besides being a good locality for fishing it is also a convenient centre to explore the upper end of the Elwy valley. The architect and poet John Jones (1810–69) was born here and is buried in the fifteenth-century church. Though an able architect (he was in charge of the construction of London's Crystal Palace in 1851), he was better known in Wales under the bardic name of 'Talhaiarn' and for the patriotic lyrics which he wrote for singing to traditional Welsh airs.

Llansannan is hidden away in the unspoilt Aled valley further south. Its chief visible feature is the double-nave church rebuilt in 1869 on the original medieval foundations. The village's main claim to fame, however, is the array of notable Welshmen born within the limits of the parish. Tudur Aled, a renowned poet and one of the foremost men at the famous Caerwys Eisteddfod, was born here about 1470; William Salesbury, the translator of the New Testament into Welsh, and William Middleton, a naval captain who translated the Psalms, both saw the first light of day here during the sixteenth century; Gwilym Hiraethog (William Rees), poet, preacher and novelist, was born in a farm on the moorland south of the village in 1802.

From Llansannan a hilly, minor road crosses back to the Elwy valley and Llangernyw where there is a restored sixteenth-century church with an attractive early nineteenth-century stained glass window. In the churchyard two standing stones with Early Christian crosses bear witness to the long religious history of this site. At Gwytherin churchyard, further up the valley, there is a line of standing stones (one of which commemorates a certain Vinnemaglus, son of Senemaglus) which may have a prehistoric origin. West of Llangernyw, is Hafodunos, one of the best of the country mansions designed by Sir Gilbert Scott in the 1860s. Returning down the Elwy valley to Llanfair Talhaearn the road passes close to Garthewin, a Georgian mansion of the Wynne family. The eighteenth-century barn at Garthewin has been converted into a theatre.

From Abergele to Colwyn Bay the road and railway share a narrow strip of land hemmed-in between the coast and the projecting hills. The first of these prominences is Cefn-yr-Ogof overlooking the deep

Dulas valley. The sides of the valley are lined with limestone cliffs and the hill itself is riddled with caves. Pen-y-corddyn Mawr is an isolated limestone hill crowned by the massive ramparts of a strong Iron Age hill-fort. At Penmaenrhos the hills come right up to the coast and the railway is forced to tunnel underneath at the entrance to Colwyn Bay. The road has to make a sharp bend around the headland, but even so it is a great improvement on the route used by early travellers, of which one tourist wrote 'the path is so narrow and unprotected that few people dare trust themselves on horses on it'.

Colwyn Bay (Bae Colwyn) is spread thickly along the coast, but is sheltered from westerly winds by the wooded hillside of Pwll-y-Crochan. A fine promenade, unfortunately separated from the rest of the town by the railway, follows the curving shore for three miles between Penmaenrhos and Rhos-on-Sea. Colwyn Bay is little more than a hundred years old. Its development began only after the Pwll-y-Crochan estate, with its large castellated mansion, was sold in 1865; thereafter development was intensive and it grew into a prosperous and rather select red-brick holiday resort. The down comprises three separate urban areas. Colwyn Bay itself occupies the central part just below Pwll-y-Crochan woods. It has a fine pier and pavilion and its shopping streets are made more attractive by glazed canopies above the pavements. Old Colwyn has managed to retain its own identity and lies east of the Nant-y-Groes valley and Eirias Park. It has a good early twentieth-century church, St Johns, by John Douglas, who also designed the slightly older St Paul's Church in Colwyn Bay. The village of Llanelian-yn-Rhos, just to the south of Old Colwyn, has an interesting little church with a medieval, painted ceiling and a tombstone of Ednyfed Fychan, ancestor of the Tudors of Penmynydd. Ffynnon Elian, just outside the village, was once a dreaded 'cursing well' where anyone wishing to get rid of an enemy could come and lay a curse.

Rhos-on-Sea, lies at the north-western end of the promenade and is separated from Colwyn Bay by the railway. Ednyfed Fychan, who lived at Llys Euryn, owned the land hereabouts in the Middle Ages and gave a fishing weir on the headland to the monks of Aberconwy. Until recently the stakes driven into the foreshore to form the Rhos Fynach weir could be clearly seen. The remains of Rhos Fynach monastery are now buried in the structure of a hotel and an open-air swimming pool. Rebuilt Capel Trillo (St Trillo's Chapel) is a tiny building lying at the edge of the shore near the site of the fishing weir. It has thick, pebble walls and a vaulted roof over a small well, but its age is unknown although it may have been first built during the 'Age of Saints'.

The village of Llandrillo-yn-Rhos, around which Rhos-on-Sea

developed, was the supposed departure point of Madoc, the explorer and reputed discoverer of America three centuries before Columbus. Unfortunately, it is impossible to know how far the story of Madoc is based on fact and how much it was a figment of the Tudor imagination. Madoc is supposed to have been the son of Owain Gwynedd. Tired of fighting with his brothers over his father's kingdom he decided to sail to the west and discovered a new land. He returned to Wales to take people back to settle there and after sailing away a second time, was never heard of again. There is supposed to be an old stone on Lundy island recording the expedition and there is a memorial at Mobile Bay, Alabama (where Madoc is thought to have landed), set up by the Daughters of the American Revolution, commemorating the explorer, but in Wales there is no monument to the enigmatic prince.

PART THREE

Gwynedd

Map 4 Gwynedd: West

Map 5 Gwynedd: East

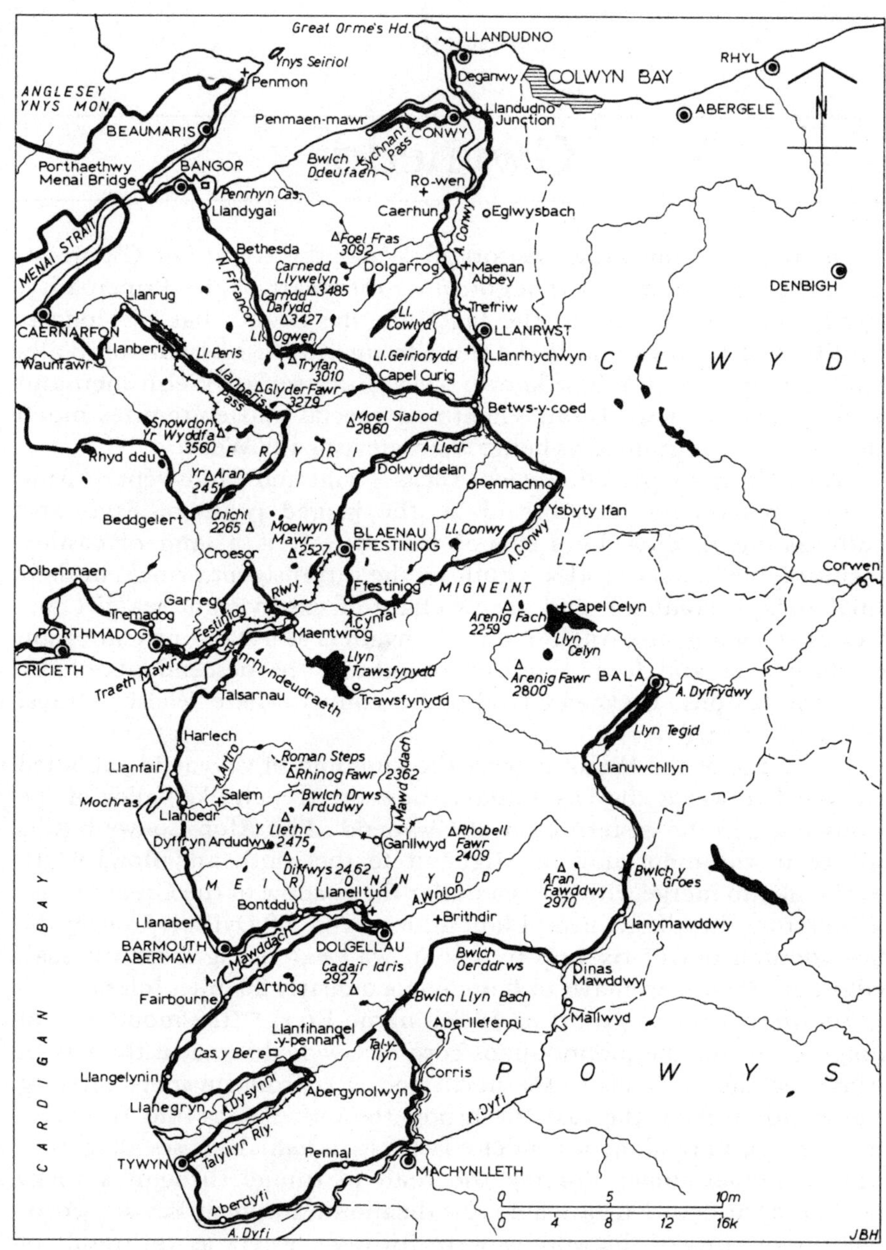

NINE

Gwynedd

For many, if not most, visitors to Wales the county of Gwynedd, including Snowdonia, is thought of as the heart of the Principality. Partly this view is due to the fact that the county has the longest tradition of tourism and is the most frequently visited part of Wales and consequently the best known area. But even to Welsh men and women Gwynedd spells out something special and epitomizes much that is taken for granted as being characteristically Welsh.

Gwynedd is a region of ancient rocks – wild and windswept – rising from a marvellous coastline up to the jagged peaks of Eryri and culminating in Snowdon's shapely summit. It is a land of castles, including defenders' castles – built by the intransigent princes in their final rocky redoubts – and also a chain of extravagant sea-girt fortresses erected by the Anglo-Norman invaders as a standing confession of the power and force required to subdue the descendants of the original Britons. Gwynedd is also the county where Welsh is most frequently heard.

In the age of the Welsh Princes the kingdom of Gwynedd extended eastwards towards the Dee estuary; now the trench-like valley of the Conwy marks the eastern limit of Gwynedd. The Afon Conwy has its source in the moorlands of Migneint to the south and flows north eventually to merge with the sea under the shadow of the Great Orme, a limestone headland near Llandudno. West of Dyffryn Conwy the Snowdonian massif rises up in a solid wall extending from the sea's edge near Penmaen-mawr to Betws-y-coed nearly 20 miles inland.

Snowdonia, or to give it its Welsh name Eryri – 'the mountains of longing', forms the mountainous core of Gwynedd and in the past it protected the lowlands to the north and west from invaders entering the kingdom from the east. Even now the only routes into Gwynedd from the east are along a slender coastal strip (which ceases altogether near Penmaen-mawr, forcing the road to tunnel through a rocky headland) or between gaps amongst the mountains near Betws-y-coed. The mountains of Snowdonia were formed largely as the result of extensive volcanic eruptions millions of years ago. They comprise three main groups (Snowdon itself, the Glyders and the Carneddau), each rising to well over 3,000 feet above sea level and separated by deep glaciated valleys, and two outer groups (Moel Hebog and Moel Siabod) of lesser height.

South of Snowdonia the high mountains continue into Meirionnydd which also forms part of the Snowdonia National Park (Parc Cenedlaethol Eryri). Meirionnydd is similar to Snowdonia in many respects but somewhat more subdued. In geological terms this region is mostly of Ordivician and Cambrian age (i.e. 450 to 550 million years old) and consists of hard mudstones and sandstones laid down in the seas then covering Wales. Amongst the intervening fissures between the two rock systems there was considerable volcanic activity which gave rise to bold ridges which were later etched into dramatically shaped mountains such as Cadair Idris and Aran Fawddwy near Dolgellau, each only just under 3,000 feet in height. Three majestic estuaries (Traeth Bach, Mawddach and Dyfi) along the coast of Meirionnydd brings the sea well inland at high tides.

Beyond Snowdonia to the west the long arm and clenched fist of the Llŷn peninsula strikes out to sea separating Cardigan Bay and Caernarfon Bay. Llŷn has an irregular back-bone of hills and mini-mountains washed by the sea on the north coast. Everywhere the sea is close at hand and the windswept peninsula seems cut off from the rest of the world, independent, unchanging and primeval in character. Much of the coast, with its secluded bays and sandy beaches, and the higher land in the Llŷn peninsula has been declared an Area of Outstanding National Beauty.

The island of Anglesey, long known as the granary of Wales because it provided Gwynedd with a ready supply of food in peace and war, is geologically the oldest part of Wales. It consists mainly of sea eroded Pre-Cambrian granites, extremely hard and a thousand million or more years old. Anglesey lies north of Snowdonia, separated from it by the broad curving water of the Menai Strait. Seen from the Snowdonian foothills the island appears low and flat. In fact Anglesey does have its hills, mostly along the northern and eastern rim of the island, but few of these are more than 500 feet high. This upland rim is Anglesey's watershed and nearly all the rivers and streams flow in shallow parallel valleys across the island to the west coast. Most of the island's coast, in parts violently rugged and other parts smooth and dune covered, is another Area of Outstanding National Beauty.

There are a number of other, smaller islands around the coasts of Gwynedd. Holy Island, the largest of these, lies off the north-west corner of Anglesey and is joined artificially to the main island both by road and rail. Puffin Island (Ynys Seiriol) and Bardsey Island (Ynys

Enlli), both rocky and difficult to land on, are famous religious sites of the Early Christian church.

Less than 10,000 years ago all the islands were joined to the Welsh mainland just as Britain itself was an extension of continental Europe. There are, however, few traces of the people who once lived in this region in those far off times probably because the lands which they occupied are those now lying under the sea. Evidence of former lowlands can be seen every now and then in the Dyfi estuary, the Menai Strait and near Llandudno when fossilized stumps of trees are bared at low tide. The remains of ancient forests gave rise to folk tales in the past and no doubt inspired the bards to recount legends of flooded territories, such as the 'Lost Hundred of Gwaelod' (Cantre'r Gwaelod) in Cardigan Bay and drowned cities and palaces like Caer Aranrhod and Llys Helig in Caernarfon Bay and Conwy Bay.

After the sea level had settled somewhere near to its present level Gwynedd became the scene of considerable new activity. Peoples of the New Stone and Bronze Ages settled there and carried on trade, via the seaways of the Irish Sea, with Ireland, Scotland and Brittany. Their most important remains, in the form of tombs built with enormous blocks of stone, are dotted around the coastal areas of Meirionnydd, Llŷn and especially in Anglesey where about 25 megalithic burial mounds have survived. It was during the New Stone Age that an important coastal and inland trade in stone axes developed. Important axe factories, using the local hard igneous rock, were located at Graig Lwyd near Penmaen-mawr and Mynydd Rhiw in the Llŷn peninsula and from these sites unpolished axes were exported to people all over Wales and England.

Almost as numerous as the earlier tombs are the great hill-forts constructed during the Iron Age. The most spectacular such as Tre'r Ceiri in Llŷn, are protected by multiple stone walls. There are also numerous groups of hut circles, some enclosed by a wall or bank and others unenclosed, and several sites of fortified farmsteads. The Celtic peoples of Iron Age Gwynedd were the direct descendants of tribes who had emigrated from their homelands on the continent due to disturbances and other pressures on living space. They brought with them fine decorative craftsmanship and a culture which had originated in the mountainous heart of Europe on the Alpine borders of Austria and Switzerland. According to classical writers the Celts were an excitable war-like race, keen drinkers, yet hospitable and fond of music and story telling. They practised a pagan religion controlled by Druids and before long Anglesey became the chief centre of the druidic cult. Druidic bards learnt their tribal lore and history by heart and thus helped to preserve fragments of age-old traditions which eventually found their way into folk tales such as the

1 A view of the Wye Valley above Hay, seen from the Black Mountains, Powys

2 Some of the thirteen arches of the seventeenth-century bridge over the River Usk at Crickhowell, Powys

3 *Top* Powis Castle, Welshpool, Powys. The oldest part of the castle was probably erected in the second half of the thirteenth century

4 The Market Hall, Llanidloes, Powys. It dates from 1609, and is now a museum

5 Part of the Elan Valley reservoirs, near Rhayader, Powys. This network of reservoirs helps supply water to Birmingham

6 Looking from the east across Llan-gors lake towards the snow-topped Brecon Beacons, Powys

7 The Vale of Clwyd near Denbigh, Clwyd, looking north

8 *Top* The River Dee about four miles below Llangollen, Clwyd, looking down from the Pont Cysyllte aqueduct

9 Flint Castle, on the estuary of the River Dee, Clwyd. The castle was built between 1277 and 1286

19 The cliffs of Cadair Idris (the chair of Idris), with Llyn Cau in the foreground; Gwynedd

20 The view from the top of Snowdon looking towards Lliwedd, the long south-east ridge; Gwynedd

21 Telford's suspension bridge across the Menai Straits, opened in 1826. The mountains of Gwynedd are in the background

22 Amlwch Harbour, on the north coast of the Isle of Anglesey

miscellany known collectively as the *Mabinogion*. When the Roman legions invaded Gwynedd they found Anglesey in the hands of the Druids who, according to the Roman Tacitus, stood with the Celtic troops on the opposite shore of the Menai Strait 'ranged in order, with hands uplifted, invoking the gods and pouring forth horrible curses'. The Romans hesitated in consternation and then, after crossing the Strait in their flat-bottomed boats, proceeded to carry out a wholesale slaughter.

The Roman occupation of Gwynedd was an entirely military affair, although some mining was carried on in the mineral rich deposits of Snowdonia and Anglesey. They constructed fortresses, of which the most important was Segontium near Caernarfon, but as far as is known built no towns. Instead the native population, known to the Romans as the Ordovices, continued to live peacefully in grouped hut circles and even continued to occupy some of the hill-forts. Some of the native farmsteads show signs of Roman influence, but by and large the Roman occupation had little lasting effect on this part of Wales.

With the departure of the Romans the land was at the mercy of Irish sea-raiders, many of whom eventually settled in the area. Their settlements in Gwynedd are recalled by the groups of stone huts known as Cyttiau'r Gwyddelod ('Irishmen's huts') found in Llŷn and Meirionydd. The Irish were also largely responsible for the introduction of Christianity in these parts and many of the churches of Gwynedd are dedicated to Irish saints.

Traditionally the principality or kingdom of Gwynedd appears to have been established during the fifth century by Cunedda Wledig, a Romanized head of a clan from southern Scotland. It is impossible now to ascertain the true facts concerning Cunedda's conquest, but it is significant that all the regions claimed to have been conquered by him bear the names of his sons who, in accordance with Celtic practice, divided the inheritance amongst themselves. Some of these names, such as Meirionnydd (after Meirion) and Ceredigion (after Ceredig) still exist as the names of local authority districts and are thus amongst the oldest regional names still in use. By the early sixth century the throne of Gwynedd was occupied by Maelgwyn Hir, the great-grandson of Cunedda; thereafter the throne descended in succession to members of the Cunedda dynasty up to the time of Rhodri Mawr.

Rhodri succeeded to the kingdom, by descent through his grandmother, in 844. Eleven years later he succeeded to the kingdom of Powys and in 871, on the death of his brother-in-law the last king of Ceredigion, he gained control of the south-western Wales. Thus, for the first time since the time of the Romans, the greater part of Wales was under the rule of a single king. After Rhodri's death the unity of

Wales was broken up. For brief periods Wales was reunited under the overlordship of kings of Dyfed, but the unity never became permanent. It was not until the eleventh century that a ruler of Gwynedd, in the person of Gruffydd ap Llywelyn, managed to gain control of the other Welsh kingdoms. Gruffydd, however, went further than any before him and, mainly by conquest, succeeded in incorporating the whole of modern Wales into his kingdom, as well as making inroads into English territories in Shropshire and Herefordshire.

Gruffydd ap Llywelyn was killed in 1063 and once more the political unity of Wales was broken and the countryside divided by civil war. Three years later the Normans landed at Hastings and within a short time were pressing against the borders of Wales. With no strong kings to oppose them the Normans achieved a lightning conquest in Gwynedd. But the conquest was a fragile affair and when a great Welsh revolt broke out in the north in 1094 the Normans were speedily ejected from Gwynedd, although they managed to retain their hold on other parts of Wales. For nearly two centuries Gwynedd remained firmly independent, protected from outside interference by the mountains of Eryri. By the end of the twelfth century Gwynedd had become the most powerful of the independent Welsh kingdoms and henceforth it became the guardian of Wales' heritage. Llywelyn ab Iorwerth, better known as Llywelyn Fawr or Llywelyn the Great, seized the power of Gwynedd back from his uncles between 1194 and 1199 and then continued to push eastwards, driving the Normans out of northern Wales and back to Chester. At a great council of Welsh rulers in 1216 Llywelyn was acknowledged as the undisputed overlord and leader of independent Wales. After Llywelyn's death in 1240 war broke out once again and the English king was able to force Llywelyn's successors to accept humiliating peace terms in 1247.

In 1255 Llywelyn ap Gruffydd, grandson of Llywelyn Fawr, became the sole ruler of Gwynedd and once again began to rebuild the shattered kingdom. Taking advantage of King Henry III's weak position, due to shortage of money and constant troubles and disputes with his barons, the last Llywelyn quickly regained all the former possessions of Gwynedd and more besides, so that within a decade he had become overlord of all Wales except for the southern coastal strip. Llywelyn was acclaimed 'Prince of Wales' by his fellow nobles and his rights and possessions were confirmed in 1267, in the presence of the Pope's legate, by a treaty with Henry III.

The reconciliation was not, however, to last for when Henry died his successor, the ambitious Edward I, determined to rule with absolute power over an undivided empire. Before tackling Scotland, Edward decided to reduce the Welsh prince's position by force of arms. According to the *Brut y Tywysogion* ('Chronicles of the Princes')

'Llywelyn sent frequent messages to the king's court to arrange a peace between them, but it availed him nothing . . . . the king held a council at Worcester . . . and thence he sent three hosts to war against Wales'. In the first war of independence Llywelyn lost of much of his territories to the English, but though forced to submit to terms it was not an unconditional surrender. Llywelyn retained his title of Prince of Wales and retired to the mountains to lick his wounds and live to fight another day.

After the first war of independence discontent became widespread throughout northern Wales. This was as much the result of injustices by crown officials as of petty disputes between the Welsh nobles. Gradually, the troubles boiled over into yet another full-scale war. The indirect cause of the calamitous second war of independence had its source in a long-standing dispute between Llywelyn and the English king. Although Edward was overlord to the Prince of Wales it had, nonetheless, been customary to settle disputes within the Principality in accordance with Welsh law. But when Llywelyn deprived the lord of Powys (Gruffydd ap Gwenwynwyn) of the territory of Arwystli in the Severn valley, the king interfered and demanded that the matter be settled according to English law. Incensed, but patient, Llywelyn tried continually to make the king see reason, but each time he was fobbed off with unjustifiable excuses. Eventually, after four years of protracted negotiations the prince's patience turned to exasperation and in concert with his brother David, hitherto an adherent of the king, he declared war on the English in 1282 by attacking Hawarden, Oswestry and Llanbadarn.

After further successes at Llandovery and Carreg Cennen and at Llandeilo in June and in Anglesey in November the prince marched south to Builth Wells to rouse his southern compatriots to the cause. There, on Friday 11 December, Llywelyn the Last met his death at the hands of an assassin. His brother David assumed the leadership and held out for a further six months. In June 1283 David was captured and taken to Shrewsbury for execution and the lesser Welsh rulers were thrown into prison. With the execution of David the independence of Gwynedd and Wales was lost.

In order to secure his newly-won principality Edward I erected a chain of monumental castles around the coast of Gwynedd and settled the towns with non-Welsh merchants and officials. The Welsh were excluded and they withdrew into sullen silence. There were occasional outbursts, such as the burning of Caernarfon Castle before its completion, and for a few brief years in the early fifteenth century Gwynedd was the cornerstone and last bastion of Owain Glyndŵr's independent Wales.

Welsh discontent was partially mollified by the arrival of Henry

Tudor on the scene and by his eventual enthronement in 1485 as king of England. Henry VII's capture of the throne seemed to bring true an ancient prophecy, attributed to the legendary Myrddin (Merlin), that 'there shall a king come to England from a princely race, with his noble descent from Anglesey'. Henry, although born at Pembroke in Dyfed, was the grandson of Owain Tudor of Plas Penmynydd, a lonely farmhouse near the centre of Anglesey. Owain Tudor had been a servant at Henry V's court and then became the lover of Catherine de Valois, Henry's widow. Owain and Catherine had a son, Edmund Tudor and it is from this liaison that Henry Tudor claimed his inheritance. In Wales Henry VII was regarded as a Welsh king and now, for the first time the Welsh people could identify themselves with the crown. Under Henry's influence Welshmen received promotions at court, churches were built and rebuilt and a new era of comparative prosperity emerged, but politically Wales was still administered in a piecemeal manner. Gwynedd remained part of the king's private principality and other parts of Wales were governed by Marcher lords. In 1536 Henry Tudor's son Henry VIII annexed the whole of Wales and divided it into 13 counties on the English pattern.

Gwynedd remained a remote land, isolated from the rest of the kingdom by its mountains. It became a region mainly of crofters and shepherds with only a few large estates owned, as often as not, by absentee landlords. Until the latter part of the eighteenth century most parts of Gwynedd remained virtually unknown and unvisited by outsiders. All this changed when, firstly, the mountains were quarried for their precious minerals and rocks, and secondly, the mountains and lakes became favourite places for tourists in search of the sublime.

The mineral wealth of the mountains had been known to the Romans and was worked spasmodically up to the eighteenth century. Then Gwynedd became involved in the industrial revolution as copper was sought after in ever growing quantities, and slate was quarried to roof expanding towns throughout the world. Fortunately, for the tourists, quarrying was localized and never came to dominate the landscape as coal-mining and iron-making did in the valleys of southern Wales. Copper, lead and gold were mined in a number of places, but most extensively in Anglesey where, after 1768, Mynydd Parys became the greatest copper mine in Europe. Slate quarrying, the 'most Welsh of Welsh industries', was almost entirely developed by local people; at first by small groups who did their own quarrying and selling and then later by local landlords like the Pennants of Penrhyn. New ports and railways were constructed to transport the slate to the coast and new towns, villages and barracks were built to house the workers. Most of the quarries were open to the sky, but in Meirionnydd vast caverns were excavated in the bowels of the earth to extract the slate more easily. Due to competition from man-made roofing materials slate quarrying has been declining for a generation or more and only a few quarries here and there are still in active production.

With the decline of extractive industries other industries have come to take their place. There are many new small-scale factories and a few larger ones, like the brake-lining factory near Caernarfon, but the industrial sights now are the nuclear-fuelled power stations and the hydro-electric schemes which feed electricity into the national grid to serve townships far beyond the Welsh border.

Gwynedd has a long history of tourism going back to 1778 when the dauntless Thomas Pennant of Downing wrote his pioneering *Tour in Wales*. Pennant, who was an antiquary and naturalist, was followed by others of less studious but more romantic nature who found the scenes of rocky waterfalls and glaciated mountains both 'aweful' and 'picturesque'. Painters, such as Moses Griffiths (working for Thomas Pennant), Ibbetson, Rowlandson and Turner visited the mountains, painted them and made a widespread audience aware of the beauties of Eryri. With the Napoleonic Wars travel in Europe became difficult, and northern Wales was an obvious alternative for tours and holidays and has remained so ever since.

In the second half of the nineteenth century railways made Gwynedd ever more accessible for seaside holidays and mountaineering expeditions. The motor car and road improvements in the twentieth century has made the region a favourite for second homes and retirement. While superb mountain and lake scenery and handsome sandy bays are still the main attractions there are numerous other allurements for tourists; ancient history, for instance, in the form of megalithic monuments and magnificent medieval castles, natural history within the national parks and nature reserves and industrial history exemplified by cavernous quarries and mines and a host of narrow-gauge railways that once served the slate industry.

Despite all the invaders, past and present, Gwynedd still retains its essential Welshness. The eyrie of Glyndŵr and the last princes is still the linguistic redoubt of Wales. Here two-thirds of the population are Welsh-speaking (though all inevitably speak English as well) and the 'language of heaven', as the bards described their own tongue, is still the language of classroom, kitchen, quarry and even council chamber. The Welsh language, however, like Snowdon, is under constant threat of erosion and also requires to be treated with respect. It may still be true that modern Welsh poetry can reach a larger audience than most modern English poetry, but a language cannot survive by poetry alone, and in the face of television and commercial economics it is little short of a miracle that about half-a-million people in Wales still speak Welsh. Bi-lingual signs and notices in Welsh only are not intended to deter visitors, but are there to be helpful to local inhabitants. They also help to confer an identity to the area – an historic, Welsh identity which has survived for countless long centuries. Indeed, in Gwynedd history, legend, poetry and fine scenery keep company with modern life more acutely than perhaps anywhere else in Wales.

TEN

Vale of Conwy and Nant Ffrancon

The Conwy, rising in the moorlands of Migneint, flows due north in a trough-like vale for nearly 30 miles before entering the sea in a placid estuary between two widely spaced headlands, Great Orme's Head and Penmaen-bach. Each headland shelters a town of unusual interest; Llandudno behind the former headland and Conwy at the rear of the latter. Llandudno, the largest town in Gwynedd, is the main seaside resort of the north and in its scenic setting is comparable, although entirely different in appearance, to Tenby in the south. The town is situated on a neck of low-lying land between the Conwy estuary and the sea facing north across a wide, sandy bay between the rocky outcrops of the Great Orme and Little Orme's Head.

Today Llandudno has a settled, established look based on a generous grid of broad streets and a gracious promenade, adjusted to follow the crescent-shaped curve of the beach. Until the opening of the Chester to Holyhead railway in 1849, which brought the place within easy reach of holiday makers, Llandudno as a town did not exist; in its place there was only a scattered cluster of cottages belonging to miners and fishermen. Like its sister town, Colwyn Bay, Llandudno was developed as a resort by a local landlord, in this case Lord Mostyn, out of land belonging to his country estate. The town that took shape prospered and, though it has few individual buildings of architectural interest, its generally unified appearance and its wide shopping streets lined with iron and glass canopies has earned it the reputation of being the best preserved Victorian town in Wales. The town has an enviable position situated between two seafronts, each with their own beach, and has, as a backcloth to the street vistas, the rocky slopes of the Great Orme peninsula.

The west shore, though facing the sun, is the less developed of the two beaches. Here at the northern end of the West Promenade, at the foot of the Great Orme, there is a large model yachting pool and nearby a white rabbit memorial erected to commemorate Llandudno's association with *Alice in Wonderland*. Alice was Alice

Liddell, the daughter of Dean Liddell who had bought a house (Penmorfa) facing the west shore in 1862. The family visited Llandudno regularly for their summer holidays and one summer the Dean invited a young don named Charles Dodgson to stay with them. Dodgson, much to the delight of Alice and her sister, was a great storyteller and here he began to develop verbally the story which he wrote down later and published under the pen-name Lewis Carroll.

Along the north shore four-storey stucco terraces and hotels built in the grand manner follow the gentle curve of the promenade ending with a splendid iron pier (1876) at the foot of the hills. The pier is the fulcrum of Llandudno's activities. The Pier Head Pavilion stands a third of a mile out to sea at the end of the pier while near the landward side is the Pier Pavilion. Just beyond the pier is Happy Valley, with its rock gardens, open air theatre and Alice in Wonderland playground, and the gateway to the Great Orme's Head.

The Great Orme's Head is partly encircled by a four mile long marine drive which has been carved out of the cliffs in places. At Pen-y-Gogarth one can look down from the drive to a lighthouse and nearby caves before continuing to the western side of the headland, passing on the way some scant remains of a fourteenth-century Bishop's Palace. Back at Happy Valley a mile-long cabin lift carries four-seater cabins through the air to the summit of the headland. Not far away, at Victoria Station, is the start of the Great Orme Railway, a funicular tramway opened in 1902. Passengers can reach the headland summit more leisurely by tramcar, with a change of trams halfway up. There is also a very steep lane up to the top, or one can follow a five-mile nature trail which, starting at Happy Valley, passes the tiny windswept church of St Tudno's (after which Llandudno got its name), a Stone Age burial chamber, remains of ancient dwellings and old copper mines used by the Romans. The headland – mainly heathland with expanses of bare limestone rock – rises to nearly 700 feet above sea level. At the summit there are memorable views all around; south to the Conwy estuary and the Carneddau mountains; west to Puffin Island and Anglesey; north to the Isle of Man; east to the Lancashire coast.

South of Llandudno two fine old mansions, which once belonged to the Mostyn family, have now found other uses. Gloddaeth is a girls' school, but its sixteenth-century hall with open timber roof, elaborate chimney pieces and wall paintings remain intact. Bodysgallen, dating from the seventeenth century, is now a hotel. Both estates have wooded areas with public walks.

Further south the rocky hill at Deganwy overlooks the entrance to Conwy estuary and has fragments of a castle built by Welsh princes. It occupies an ancient fortified site straddling two volcanic outcrops.

The castle has remains of three small round towers and a larger D-shaped tower. Many Anglo-Norman expeditions came to grief at the castle but eventually the Welsh were overthrown; then Llywelyn ap Gruffydd burnt it during his battle with Henry III and it was ultimately destroyed by Edward I as the final affirmation of his triumph over the last of the Welsh princes. Today Castell Deganwy is surrounded by residential suburbs which threaten to become a continuous urban belt joining Llandudno to Llandudno Junction. From the hilltop there is a fine view across the estuary towards the walled town of Conwy and its castle.

Taken together Conwy's castle and town walls form the most perfect surviving example in Britain of a medieval fortified town. Three parallel bridges link Llandudno Junction to Conwy. Stephenson's railway bridge was constructed in 1846–8 as a tubular bridge with brash stone towers to match the castle. Telford's suspension bridge, built in 1822 to carry the London to Holyhead road, is dainty by comparison and also has castellated towers; unfortunately, it is crowded between the railway bridge and a modern, no-nonsense road bridge and is now relegated to foot traffic only.

Conwy is dominated by the elephantine castle splendidly sited on a promontory at the junction of the Afon Gyffin and the Conwy river. Both castle and town were started by Edward I immediately after his defeat of the last Welsh prince in 1283. The castle, built on an enormous scale to a roughly rectangular plan, has eight bold circular towers punctuating the perimeter curtain walls and, at either end, fortified barbicans to defend the approaches from town and river. Even so a castle is only as good as its defenders, a point which Owain Glyndŵr discovered when he captured it by surprise in 1401 while the castle's garrison were attending a Good Friday service in St Mary's Church. The interior of the castle is divided by a cross-wall into an outer and inner ward. The Great Hall in the outer, or upper, ward is now ruined and open to the sky but still retains one of its great roof arches as a reminder of former splendour.

The new town of Conwy which Edward built next to the castle has the usual chequerboard street pattern of military towns, but due to its hilly location alongside the estuary it is shaped in plan like an irregular triangle. The castle is at one of the base corners and from there the many towered walls run north alongside the river and west up the hillside to encircle the older part of the town. Both the walls and the towers of Conwy are remarkably complete and surprisingly unmodified by later additions or alterations. Altogether there are 21 powerful round towers together with three twin-towered gateways of which Porth Isaf (Lower Gate) is at the quayside end of High Street, Porth Uchaf (Upper Gate) is near the station and Porth-y-Felin (Mill

Gate) is near the church. Halfway between the last two gateways is Llywelyn's Tower and the site of Llywelyn's Hall. The Hall was originally the town residence of the last Welsh prince, but was subsequently altered and modified to provide accommodation for the new English Prince of Wales, Edward I's son. With the death of Edward I in 1307 the younger Edward ascended the throne and was able to use the castle itself as his royal palace, Llywelyn's Hall consequently became redundant and was dismantled and ignominiously shipped to Caernarfon for re-erection as a store house.

St Mary's Parish Church, although lying within the town walls, is hidden behind the shopping streets to which it is linked by footpaths. The earliest parts of the church, the east and west walls, are a century older than the town itself for before Edward I's conquest this had been the abbey of Aberconwy. It was established in 1186 by the Cistercians who had been granted a charter and rich endowments by Llywelyn Fawr. After the conquest Edward I persuaded the monks to re-settle at Maenan, five miles upriver, and St Mary's was largely rebuilt as the town church. The best part of the church is the south transept, added in the early fourteenth century, and a moulded door at the base of the tower. Inside there is a fine fifteenth-century rood-screen with elegant fan-vaulting. Of the many memorials the most interesting is a bust of the famous classicist sculptor John Gibson carved by his pupil W. Theed. Gibson was born in 1790 at the little village of Gyffin on the outskirts of the town, and although at an early age he had showed an aptitude for drawing and painting he was first employed with a firm of cabinet makers. At the age of 27 he went to Rome to study sculpture and became so accomplished in the art that he was able to stay there for the rest of his life.

Conwy has a number of old houses, but none finer than Plas Mawr in High Street. Built by Robert Wynn of Gwydir between 1576 and 1580 it is the best preserved town house of the Elizabethan period in Wales and is now the headquarters of the Royal Cambrian Academy of Art. The entrance is through a gatehouse leading into a courtyard from which a flight of steps leads to a terrace in front of the H-plan house. Elaborate crow-stepped gables and stone mullioned windows adorned with pediments give the house a rich appearance externally. Inside, the most notable features are the grand Italianate fireplaces and boldly decorated plaster ceilings. At the rear of the house two spiral staircases, medieval in feeling, lead to a watch-tower looking out on to an upper courtyard.

Also in the High Street is Aberconwy, an earlier house built at the beginning of the sixteenth century. Its lower stone floors carry an oversailing upper floor constructed of timber and plaster. High Street leads down to the quay through Porth Isaf. Here the estuary seems as crowded with fishing boats and yachts as the roads into Conwy are with traffic. A tiny dwelling at the castle end of the quay is reputed to be the smallest house in Great Britain.

Two roads lead west from Conwy to Penmaen-mawr. The main road skirts the northern side of Conwy Mountain but at the first headland the coastal strip disappears and both road and railway are forced to squeeze through tunnels below the 700-foot-high Penmaen-bach. The old road follows a route south of Conwy Mountain and over the bare Sychnant pass into a deep valley between Allt Wen and Foel Lus.

Penmaen-mawr lies beyond Foel Lus, hemmed in between steep sided hills and the sea. The little holiday resort was originally a quarrying town and takes its name from the bold headland further along the coast, which until a road was built in 1772, was virtually impassable for travellers. The way around the mountainous headland was notoriously dangerous for early travellers who were required to descend at this point while their coaches were taken to pieces and laboriously man-handled along the ledge skirting the headland. Over the years the upper stages of the headland have been quarried away for roadstone and with it the large Iron Age hill-fort of Braich-y-dinas.

The surrounding hills are scattered with prehistoric remains, the most famous of which is the Graig Lwyd Axe Factory lying at the eastern end of the quarries. Here, amongst the natural outcrops and screes, was the material which neolithic man used for his stone axes which he fashioned by flaking off the outer surfaces to provide sharp cutting edges. The stone axes were roughly shaped at Graig Lwyd and then sent all over southern Britain for final grinding and polishing locally. On the slopes of Moelfre above Graig Lwyd there is a group of four burial chambers and a number of Bronze Age stone circles. The best of the stone circles, known as the Druid's Circle, has ten upright pillars standing on a low circular bank with an entrance on one side.

From Conwy the main road south to Llanrwst follows the east bank of the river and passes close to Bodnant Gardens with its beautifully landscaped grounds. The entrance to the gardens is on a side road to Eglwysbach. The grounds were laid out from 1875 onwards by Henry Pochin for Lord Aberconway and presented to the National Trust by his son in 1949. The rambling Victorian house, built in 1881, is near the entrance and from here a great series of terraces laid out in the Italian style sweep down towards a small valley. The Canal Terrace has an open air stage at one end and an eighteenth-century Pin Mill, brought from Gloucestershire, at the other end. From the terraces there are superb views across the miniature valley to the Conwy and the Carneddau mountains beyond. Below the terraces a narrow path drops down through rock gardens to an old mill beside the stream; after following the valley for some way the path returns steeply up the hillside towards the house past a dramatically sited Mausoleum.

Six miles beyond Bodnant the main road passes Maenan Abbey Hotel, which has some remnants of the former Cistercian monastery preserved within its grounds. These remains are part of the religious house which Edward I had transferred from Conwy in 1283 to provide room to build his new town.

A detour to Caerhun and Dolgarrog on the west bank of the Conwy can be made at Tal-y-cafn. Caerhun has an interesting thirteenth-century church, long and narrow, standing on a raised platform within the ramparts of the Roman fort of Canovium. The fort, covered over after its excavation in 1926–9 but still clearly visible in outline, was built by Agricola probably in 78 AD, at a strategic crossing point of the Conwy between Chester and Caernarfon. The Roman road west of Caerhun crosses the hills through Bwlch y Ddeufaen ('Pass of Two Stones') following a prehistoric trackway already ancient when the Romans came. Unfortunately, this lonely windswept route has been violated in modern times by the demands of modern living and industry which have resulted in a clutter of three lines of tall electricity pylons.

The valley between Caerhun and Bwlch y Ddeufaen is scattered with ancient relics and full of interest. Amongst these are standing stones, a Bronze Age burial cairn in the pass itself, Maen-y-bardd cromlech and an Iron Age settlement near Ro-wen, another Iron Age (or Bronze Age) settlement with ancient field enclosures below Llyn Dulyn, Caer Bach hill-fort near Ro-wen and the much larger Pen-y-gaer hill-fort above Llanbedr-y-cennin. This last camp is stone walled and has groups of sharply pointed stones, known as *chevaux de frise*, set upright into the ground immediately outside the entrance to deter attackers. Apart from a couple of hill-forts in Wales, the use of *chevaux de frise* is almost unknown outside Spain and suggest that the hill-fort builders in the Conwy valley may have been refugees from the Iberian peninsula. North of Ro-wen, in the empty moorland, is the isolated little church of St Celynin. The church is sparse and primitive in appearance, but still retains a saint's well and a roughly circular churchyard wall indicating a continuous history since the Early Christians first discovered the site in the Dark Ages.

At Dolgarrog there are large aluminium works using hydro-electric power generated from the waters of Llyn Cowlyd and Llyn Eigiau. The plateau above and behind Dolgarrog is wild and bare save for showers of stones and boulders scattered everywhere. Where the rolling plateau meets the craggy outliers of the Carneddau range a series of tarns, since transformed into larger reservoirs, nestle at the foot of the mountains: Llyn Cowlyd, long and narrow and over 200 feet deep, squeezed into a canyon-like valley; Llyn Eigiau wrapped around the base of thousand-foot-high cliffs; the roughly circular twin lakes of Llyn Dulyn and Melynllyn seated in their ice-gouged Alpine cwms. In 1923 the dam of Llyn Eigiau burst, causing torrents of water and boulders to crash down on Dolgarrog, drowning 16 people, destroying a terrace of houses and ruining the aluminium works.

Llyn Crafnant and Llyn Geirionydd, to the south east, are accessible by car. Both lakes have delightful settings amidst forest-clad hills. At the head of Llyn Geirionydd there is a monument to the sixth-century poet Taliesin. The narrow, twisting road between Llyn Geirionydd and Trefriw passes near Llanrhychwyn old church, a simple double nave building almost square in plan. Traditionally known as Llywelyn's church, after Llywelyn ap Iorwerth, it was originally built in the twelfth century and the second aisle or nave was added in the sixteenth century. Llanrhychwyn lies on the hills above the Conwy valley and in order to avoid the long journey up to the church Llywelyn built a new church at Trefriw nearer the river about 1230. This in turn was replaced in the fifteenth century by the existing church of St Mary's.

Trefriw is now better known for the large woollen mill in the centre of the village. It is the last of a number of mills of all kinds which once used water from the fast flowing streams dropping down suddenly from the hills to the main valley. In the nineteenth century Trefriw was famed for its healing waters which erupted in two springs (iron oxide and sulphur) a mile north of the village. A spa was established in 1833 and the crow-stepped well building at the side of the road was built in 1873, but now all is forgotten and disused.

Two miles further south Gwydir Castle stands in its own grounds near the road to Llanrwst. It is not in fact a castle but a large fortified mansion started by John Wynn ap Maredudd in the sixteenth century and added to and rebuilt over a long period, largely with materials brought from Maenan Abbey. It was gutted by fire on two occasions early in the present century and is now mostly a reconstruction. During most of its life Gwydir Castle was the seat of the great Wynn family. The most famous member of the family was Sir John Wynn (1553–1627), a selfish and ruthless acquirer of property who, nevertheless, brought benefits to the district and Llanrwst in particular, where he was responsible for establishing a free school, almshouses, a fine chapel and a splendid bridge. Sir John introduced the making of Welsh frieze – a woollen cloth – to the Conwy valley and also proposed damming the Traeth Mawr estuary near Porthmadog to reclaim land two centuries before the project was actually carried out by Madocks. He also continued the tradition by the older Welsh families of artistic patronage. He supported Thomos Wiliems, compiler of the Welsh-Latin dictionary, and in 1594 petitioned for an eisteddfod to be held in northern Wales similar to the famous Caerwys Eisteddfod. In his biographical account of the *History of the Gwydir Family* Sir John Wynn graphically portrayed life in northern Wales at the beginning of the seventeenth century when family feuds, banditry and lawlessness were, as often as not, the norm and 'everye man stood upon his guarde and went not abroade but in sorte and soe armed as yf he went to the field to encounter with his enimies'.

Less historic, but perhaps more architecturally interesting, is Gwydir Uchaf Chapel in the woods overlooking Gwydir Castle. It was built in 1673 as a private chapel for Sir Richard Wynn and is notable for its remarkable four-bay ceiling boldly painted with primitive-looking cherubs and scrolls. The small chapel, a very late example of the Gothic style, also has some well executed carvings and panelling and a timber gallery at the west end.

Llanrwst lies on the east bank of the Conwy and is entered across the finest bridge in Wales. Pont Fawr, built in 1636, is beautifully proportioned and gradually rises to a point at the centre which is marked by armorial tablets on the parapet walls. The three wide arches spanning the Afon Conwy rest on narrow hexagonal piers which, together with its low parapets, give the bridge an unusually slender appearance. It is reputed to have been designed by Inigo Jones (1573–1652), the first Renaissance architect in Britain, whose forbears may well have hailed from the Llanrwst district. Jones visited Italy twice to study the work of Palladio and, as a result, brought back to Britain a genuine Italian Renaissance style quite different from anything else that had been built in these islands. His first major work, the Queen's House at Greenwich, was an absolute break with tradition and it does not seem unreasonable therefore to credit Jones with the design of Pont Fawr, the first bridge to break away from the medieval vernacular. Next to the bridge on the west bank is Tu-hwnt-i'r-bont, a charming vernacular style seventeenth-century house with roof dormers added in the following century. It once served as a courthouse but is now run by the National Trust as a restaurant.

Llanrwst, unlike most country towns in Wales, never had any castle, much less one built by the Normans. Unfortified though it was the town suffered desperately in the Glyndŵr War of Independance and became virtually deserted so that grass grew in the streets and deer grazed in the churchyard. Today it is a lively little stone-built town which is also the market centre of the Conwy valley and its surroundings. The parish church, although partly rebuilt in the nineteenth century, still retains an excellent rood-screen and loft (elaborately carved with vine leaves, birds and pigs) brought here from Maenan

Abbey at the Dissolution of the Monasteries. The fine late-Gothic Gwydir Chapel, built by Sir Richard Wynn in 1633, is attached to the south side of the church and overlooks the river. Most of the memorials are of the Wynn family, but pride of place goes to a large stone coffin transferred from the abbey of Aberconwy in Conwy via Maenan to Llanrwst. It is said to be the tomb of Llywelyn Fawr who founded Aberconwy and was buried there in 1240. Near the church are the Jesus Hospital Almshouses established by Sir John Wynne in 1610. The little Town Hall at one end of Ancaster Square is nineteenth century and replaces an earlier building which fell into disrepair.

Betws-y-coed, long famous as a tourist centre and the entrance to the mountains of Snowdonia, has a fine valley setting between the confluences of the Afon Llugwy and Afon Lledr with the Conwy. The surrounding rocky hills are luxuriantly clad in coniferous forests. The place itself, however, is little more than scattered groups of individual grey-stone houses, cottages, hotels and tourist shops strung out along the main road. To avoid the crowds of tourists, spring and autumn are the best times to visit Betws-y-coed. Visitors are nothing new here, however, for as long ago as 1848 a government surveyor posted to the area complained that 'every house is crammed full of amateurs of scenery and salmon fishing and I had to wait two months for lodgings the year before last'. Amongst the many visitors who came to paint the scenery were the artists Henry Gastineau and David Cox. Cox stayed for some time and while here painted the original inn sign of the Royal Oak Hotel which is now preserved within under glass. Apart from the humble little fourteenth- or fifteenth-century parish church, with its well preserved effigy of Gruffydd ap Dafydd Goch (great nephew of Llywelyn ap Gruffydd), the most interesting man-made things in Betws-y-coed are its numerous bridges. One of these, a relatively modern iron suspension bridge for foot traffic, spans the river alongside the old church. Half a mile up the Conwy is Thomas Telford's Waterloo Bridge decorated with leeks, roses, thistles and shamrocks. Telford himself was very proud of this work and is quoted as saying 'it is the best cast-iron bridge yet constructed'. Pont yr Afanc, half a mile further up-river, although built only 15 years earlier, is a traditional stone bridge comprising a lovely semi-circular arch which leaps from one rocky bank across to the other. The oldest bridge is the curved, five-arch Pont y Pair which spans the Llugwy in the centre of Betws-y-coed and is reputed to have been built by a certain Howell Saer in the fifteenth century.

The main attractions of Betws-y-coed are its waterfalls and its forest walks. The Swallow Falls (Rhaeadr Wennol), the best known, if not the loveliest waterfall in Wales, lies two miles upstream on the Llugwy and is well worth viewing, especially after heavy rain, though entry to the falls is by ticket only. On both sides of the Llugwy valley there are delightful walks across the hills through the Gwydir Forest where rocks and boulders intermingle with coniferous trees. In amongst the clearings are pools and lakes and remains of abandoned lead mines and quarries. There are more waterfalls on the Conwy at the end of a wild stretch of river south of Pont yr Afanc known as the Fairy Glen. Nearby, on a tributary of the Conwy, are the splendid Machno Falls and beyond these, on the road to Penmachno is Hannah Jones Mill, a woollen mill still in use and open to the public. Almost alongside the mill is an ancient, parapetless single-arch bridge known as the Roman Bridge.

Penmachno, a doleful, stone and slate village, is reminiscent of the valley townships of southern Wales and looks as though it had escaped from the Rhondda. Situated alongside the Machno in a cul-de-sac valley, Penmachno's main road leads only to the disused slate quarries from which its inhabitants once scratched a living. Apart from some good farms in the surrounding district there is little to indicate that the village has had a long history. There were, however, once two medieval churches in the extra large churchyard and some early Christian inscribed stones (dating from the fifth or sixth century). Now only a mid-nineteenth-century church remains and the ancient stones have been removed to the National Museum in Cardiff. A rough five-arch bridge crosses the river in the centre of the village. It was constructed in 1785 and has a stone on the south parapet inscribed with a Welsh poem and drawings of its builders, I. Hughes and Harry Parry of Caernarfon.

The moorland ridge north of Penmachno is mostly covered in forest. A road, climbing steeply up the hillside, crosses over to the Lledr valley and in a clearing on the far side of the ridge is Tŷ-mawr, the birthplace of Bishop William Morgan, translator of the Bible into Welsh. William Morgan's Bible gave written Welsh a new lease of life when it was published in 1578 and profoundly influenced the pattern of spoken Welsh throughout Wales. The seventeenth-century cottage where Morgan was born is now cared for by the National Trust.

Returning to the upper Conwy valley the landscape is noticeably more subdued as the A5 road, following Telford's route, climbs gradually upwards and twists and turns as it tries to follow the river. Northwards a by-road leads to Capel Garmon with its burial tomb dating from the New Stone and Bronze Ages. The dumb-bell-shaped chamber has been restored, but only one of the great capstones which covered the tomb now remains in place.

Ysbyty Ifan stands on a secondary road alongside the upland stage of the young Conwy. Although now a small village Ysbyty Ifan once had a Hospice of St John, presumably for the use of medieval pilgrims on their long trek to the sacred isle of Bardsey at the extreme tip of the Llŷn peninsula. After the suppression of the order the hospitaller's church became the parish church and was rebuilt in 1861. South of the village the road continues to climb for a few miles up to the boggy moorlands of Migneint. Away to the right, near the summit of the road, is Llyn Conwy, an attractive little lake and source of the river of the same name. From here there are excellent views north-westwards to the outer bastions of Snowdonia with the central peak of Yr Wyddfa showing up in the gap between Cnicht and Moel Siabod.

The road sweeps down to Ffestiniog passing close to the Afon Cynfal where Rhaeadr-y-cwm breaks out of the peat-covered moorland in a series of spectacular cascades. Two miles further on the Cynfal enters a deep gorge and there are more waterfalls (Rhaeadr Cynfal) almost within a stone's throw of Ffestiniog. A rock in the Afon Cynfal is known as Pulpud Huw Llwyd ('Huw Llwyd's Pulpit') after the poet who used to stand on it and declaim his verses. Huw Llwyd's grandson, Morgan Llwyd (1619–59), was also an accomplished poet, both in Welsh and English, as well as being a religious leader and Parliamentarian. He was born at Cynfal Fawr nearby. Ffestioniog, or more correctly Llan Ffestiniog, is the original village and centre of a parish more famed for its slate mines and industry than for scenery. The little village seems hardly to have been affected by the hectic activity which went on a couple of miles further north at Blaenau Ffestiniog and it still retains a rural atmosphere amidst glorious countryside.

The slate town of Blaenau Ffestiniog is an entirely different kind of place. Depending on the visitor's inclination and the weather (for with up to 100 inches of rain a year, and sometimes more, this is the wettest town in Wales) Blaenau can be either depressingly sombre or grandly dramatic. Its setting is a giant bowl scooped out of the earth and rimmed by a jagged and serrated skyline of craggy hills and rocky mountains formed by volcanic eruptions in the time before pre-history. Dark and grey with rugged, rough stone and slate slabbed buildings Blaenau Ffestiniog is as unique and individual in its own way as is Dolgellau further south. Rocky cliffs stand precipitously behind the winding terraces of houses and slate dominates everything. Slate is everywhere; slate fashioned for use in the roofs and walls of the terraced houses and numerous chapels; waste slate piled up into gigantic tips like mountains of scree that seem to threaten the very existence of the town. Normally slate is quarried from the sides of hills where the beds meet the surface at a convenient angle, but at Blaenau the strata are at such a steep pitch that the slate has to be mined far below the surface. Blaenau Ffestiniog is worth seeing for the natural grandeur of its setting alone, but there is also – perhaps surprisingly – much of interest as a result of human endeavour and achievement. Immediately north of the town, on the Betws-y-coed road, the two largest mines, after being run down almost to extinction, have now opened their caverns to the public and the slate industry, if not prosperous, is at least surviving. Llechwedd, on the east side, has been worked continuously since 1849 when John Greaves (after spending £25,000 and three years blasting and searching) eventually discovered a thick bed of slate running at a thirty degree angle into the mountain. Later other parallel beds of slate were discovered and each was opened up until finally the slate-miners had excavated 16 separate floors of underground caverns. One of these floors in the heart of the mountain has been developed as a tourist attraction and is reached by a chilly, bone-shaking tram ride through underground tunnels skirting vast 200-foot-deep chambers. Life-size models of miners and period equipment help to recreate the scene of a century ago, but it is not until the main electric lights – a modern innovation – are switched off that one can really appreciate the awesome and almost totally dark conditions that the early miners had to face with only small candles to help them. In fact, until candles were replaced by battery lamps in 1947 the magnificence of the underground caverns was virtually unknown even to the miners.

Gloddfa Canol Mountain Tourist Centre on the opposite side of the main road is the site of the world's largest slate mine. The Oakely Slate Quarry, as it was known until its closure in 1971, was re-opened in 1974 for small-scale quarrying and as a tourist amenity. Besides conducted tours up the side of the hill to a vantage point (with superb views across the Vale of Ffestiniog to Trawsfynydd and the mountains of Ardudwy) there are quarrymen's cottages to visit and a slate museum overlooking a 350-foot-deep artificial valley which once, until a disastrous collapse of rock in 1883, comprised an immense series of interconnected underground slate caverns.

The mountains on either side of Blaenau Ffestiniog are strewn with slate waste and the hollows and building remains of old quarry workings while the intervening cwms are filled with innumerable lakes and pools. The largest lake, at Tanygrisiau, is an artificial reservoir which was formed by damming the Ystradau stream. A thousand feet above, in a glaciated cwm at the foot of Moelwyn Mawr (2,527 feet), is a smaller reservoir formed by enlarging Llyn Stwlan. The reservoirs are part of a hydro-electric pumped storage scheme in which electricity is generated at peak periods at a power station on the shores of the lower lake by water cascading down to it, via underground pipes, from Llyn Stwlan. In off-peak periods the system is reversed and water is pumped back up the mountain to fill the upper lake. The power station is open to the public and a special coach takes visitors along the winding road to Llyn Stwlan high up in the cwm.

From Blaenau Ffestiniog the main road climbs to the crest of the watershed at the Crimea Pass before entering the Lledr valley. At the crest there is a fine view down to Dolwyddelan and across the valley to the great bulk of Moel Siabod. The railway to Betws-y-coed passes under the ridge in a two-mile-long tunnel before it too enters the Lledr valley just above Roman Bridge Station, where there is a primitive bridge of unknown date comprising eight great stone slabs supported on angular piers.

Dolwyddelan is a sizeable village where once soldiers of the Legionary army following the Roman highway dipped down momentarily from the foothills of Moel Siabod before crossing the river to march up the steep side of forest-clad Cwm Penamen on their way southwards. The sombrely expressive remains of Castell Dolwyddelan, standing lonely as a sentinel, crown a rocky outcrop just to the west of the village. The castle was built to guard the eastern entry into the mountains of Eryri, last stronghold of the Princes. A medieval track west of the castle which linked it with the Princes' other strongholds can still be followed up to Bwlch Ehediad and down into Nantgwynant. Once the royal manor of Nant Conwy, Castell Dolwyddelan was the birthplace of Llywelyn Fawr and its tall rectangular keep tower probably dates from this time, about 1170. The now fragmentary west tower was probably built for Llywelyn Fawr himself at a later date. His grandson, Llywelyn ap Gruffydd, used the castle as his headquarters during the second war of independence until his assassination in 1282.

Dolwyddelan has two churches, a nineteenth-century building of no special interest and the old parish church of St Gwyddelan built in the early sixteenth century. The latter is small and neat, with slate floor and lime-washed walls; a robust little structure modestly appropriate to its mountainous surroundings. Inside there is a carved Gothic screen, a fine painted memorial to the Wynn family and a battered hand-bell of Celtic design reputedly dating from the tenth century. In the village there are also two early Nonconformist chapels (1825 and 1835) with attached minister's houses.

Below the village the road and railway run parallel to each other on opposite sides of the Afon Lledr. At Craig Lledr the single-track railway emerges from the woods, crosses both river and road over a castellated viaduct and disappears again into the Gwydir Forest. At Pont yr Afanc one can cross the bridge and rejoin the A5 on the east bank of the Conwy near Waterloo Bridge or, keeping to the west bank, follow the old road directly back to Betws-y-coed.

The A5 road, following Thomas Telford's road of 1805, continues through Betws-y-coed along the Llugwy valley to Capel Curig, passing on the way the Swallow Falls and the site of a Roman fort at Caer Llugwy. From Pont Cyfyng tracks lead to Moel Siabod (2,860 feet) which is worth climbing for the views of the surrounding mountains. The more interesting route to the summit follows the footpath through disused quarries to Llyn y Foel, nestling at the base of the mountain, and then up a rugged spur to the top; this way the view northwards to the great flanks of the Glyders and westwards to the towering Snowdon massif is made more exciting by the suddenness with which it unfolds. From Moel Siabod the way back can be made down the bold northern slopes of the mountain to Capel Curig passing the twin lakes of Llynnau Mymbr. The scenery is wild with rocky outcrops everywhere, small stunted trees in the valley and a magnificent view of the eastern approach to Snowdon seen across the placid waters of the lakes.

Capel Curig is a straggle of houses, inns and hotels and apart from its tiny medieval church its chief interest is in its splendid situation which makes it a superb centre for exploring the mountains. The largest inn, Plas-y-brenin, is now a centre of Central Council for Physical Recreation.

Telford's road follows the north bank of the Llugwy and then continues along the east side of Nant Ffrancon towards Bangor. An earlier road, constructed by Lord Penrhyn on the opposite side of the valley at the end of the eighteenth century, still survives as a track and is more suitable for walking. At Pont Rhyd-goch the infant Llugwy and Ffrancon rush down the boulder strewn slopes of Carnedd Llywelyn in parallel streams just a few yards apart until they reach the main valley where they suddenly diverge in opposite directions, the Llugwy to the south east and the Ffrancon to the north-west. The craggy peaks of Carnedd Llywelyn (3,485 feet) and Carnedd Dafydd (3,427 feet) rise up boldly to the north. The best route to the top is via a track to the lake of Ffynnon Llugwy and then steeply up to the ridge leading to Carnedd Llywelyn. From the summit return along the main ridge to Carnedd Dafydd and then down to the spur of Pen-yr-ole-wen (3,211 feet) dropping back to the valley at the side of Llyn Ogwen. From the highest ridge the mountain plateau dips steadily northwards towards the sea at Penmaen-mawr, providing the longest walks above the 3,000-feet-south of the Scottish Highlands. Here, in the north-facing gullies snow lies longer than in any other part of Wales. The triangular mass of Tryfan (3,010 feet), immediately south of the main road, rears up in magnificent splendour against the rugged background of its higher sisters. The upper half of Tryfan is solid rock with three perpendicular buttresses on the eastern side making it a favourite challenge for climbers. Beyond the peak stand two upright boulders, known as Adam and Eve, inviting the strong-nerved to jump from one to the other.

After rounding the shoulder of Tryfan the mile long Llyn Ogwen comes into view looking, as always, deceptively inviting and placid against the great bastion of Pen-yr-ole-wen. Beyond Llyn Ogwen the valley is suddenly transformed from an open V-shaped upland vale into a deep and trench-like defile. This is Nant Ffrancon, a perfect text-book example of a glaciated valley. Rhaeadr Ogwen, situated just beyond the lip of the lake, marks the point where the Afon Ogwen falls rapidly in a series of cascades from the upper to the lower valley and standing above the fall it is easy to imagine how a glacier once filled the valley. Ogwen Cottage, formerly an inn but now a mountain rescue centre, and a large Youth Hostel stand just above the falls. The place is usually busy with climbers and hikers for this is an ideal start for climbs and walks to both the Carneddau mountains and the Glyder range.

The Glyders form a seemingly inpenetrable barrier of rock to the south-west, enclosing within a roughly semi-circular escarpment three separate cwms with their own lakes each divided from the other by projecting ridges; seen from the rough plateau just behind Ogwen Cottage this is one of the grandest views in Wales – a magnificent panorama of rocks, buttresses, peaks and precipices. Llyn Idwal, the largest lake, occupies the central cwm; it is now a Nature Reserve and is renowned as an example of glaciation and for its rare Alpine flora. The most direct route to the Glyders is from the end of Cwm Idwal and up a narrow boulder-strewn shelf to the side of Twll Du, a dark vertical cleft popularly known as the Devil's Kitchen. A longer, easier and less exhausting route, though still a tough hike, is to approach the mountains from Llyn Bochlwyd sheltering in the shadow of Tryfan; from there scramble up to the col below the peak of Tryfan and follow the Bristly Ridge to Glyder Fach (3,262 feet). The main peak at Glyder Fawr (3,279 feet) is an easy walk along the top of the ridge, passing on the way a jagged outcrop of vertical rocks known as the Castle of the Winds. At any time this wasteland of scattered stones, rock piles and precariously positioned boulders make a strange scene, but in poor light or faint mists it is a view of utter desolation, unforgettably eerie and strange. A steep scree slope leads down to Llyn y Cwm, a moorland tarn lying in the saddle below Glyder Fawr, and the way back can be made via Y Garn (3,104 feet), with its superb views back to the Glyders and Snowdon, following its eastern ridge round Cwm Clyd and its two little lakes down to Llyn Idwal.

The Glyder range continues northwards in a long ridge, high above the floor of Nant Ffrancon. The northermost peak, Carnedd y Filiast (2,694 feet), has an inclined east face of rock which is still etched with wave-like ripples formed countless millions of years ago when the mountains were part of the sea bed. Further north the rock is vertically exposed by the enormous Penrhyn Quarries developed by Richard Pennant of Penrhyn in the late eighteenth century. Continuously worked until recently, the quarries at one time employed 3,500 men and ended up as the largest slate quarry in the world, forming a gigantic mile-long slash, nearly 1,200 feet deep, across the face of the mountain. Bethesda, named after a chapel built in 1820, developed as a quarrymen's village similar to Blaenau Ffestiniog but in a less dramatic setting. Architecturally, Bethesda's most impressive buildings are its chapels such as Bethesda itself, rebuilt in 1840 and Siloam, built in 1872. Cochwillan, two miles away to the north, is a very fine example of a fifteenth-century house which ended up being used as a barn; now reduced to a single rectangular hall, it still retains ornate hammer-beam roof trusses and a dividing screen.

A mile further on is Llandygai, a picturesque estate village, built by Lord Penrhyn at the gates of his vast pseudo-castle. The dwellings are semi-detached stone cottages in 'vernacular' Tudor style. The cruciform-planned church has a medieval core, but is mostly of sixteenth-century date. The nave was extended in 1853 and at the same time a new central tower was added to give the church its present lofty appearance.

Penrhyn Castle was designed by Thomas Hopper in the likeness of a Norman fortress and erected over a period of 13 years between 1827 and 1840. A colossal structure by any standards, it was constructed around the great hall of an earlier 'castle' (designed by Samuel Wyatt) which in turn incorporated the remains of a medieval mansion built by the Tudors of Penmynydd in the early fourteenth century. Penrhyn Castle has an irregular layout and displays to great effect a medley of rectangular, round and octagonal towers together with a monumental keep tower the design of which was based on the Norman castle at Hedingham in Essex.

The elaborately decorated interior rooms are grandly scaled, but it is the vast main hall with its enormous staircase which, in a somewhat nightmarish and oppressive way, impresses most. There is a Doll's Museum in the Castle and a good Railway Museum in the out-buildings which includes engines and equipment from the Penrhyn Quarry railway.

Port Penrhyn, built by the first Lord Penrhyn in 1790 for exporting slate from his quarries, lies at the entrance to Bangor. The handsome Port Office was designed by Benjamin Wyatt (elder brother of the more famous James Wyatt) who, as Lord Penrhyn's agent, was also responsible for a large number of other buildings in Bethesda, Bangor and the surrounding district.

Bangor, the largest town west of the Conwy, lies parallel with the Menai Strait in a short valley between two ridges. It was a centre of

Early Christianity and thus has one of the oldest bishoprics in Britain. St Deiniol had his church here in the sixth century and later Bangor became a haven of refuge for the Bangor Is-coed (Clwyd) monks who managed to escape the massacre which followed the fateful battle of Chester in the seventh century. Despite its fine setting between the sea and mountains and its lengthy history Bangor is a relatively undistinguished town and few of its older buildings have survived. By far the most splendid building is the University College magnificently sited on the northern ridge. Designed by R. T. Hare in Jacobean style and built in 1911 it is very much in the romantic spirit of the Gothic Revival and looks, with its soaring castellated central tower rising majestically above the roofs of the adjoining wings, more like a large monastic cathedral than a college.

The Cathedral, on the other hand, is disappointing; long and low with a squat tower, it is sited near the bottom of the valley and unnoticeable from a distance. The Cathedral is mostly thirteenth to sixteenth century in date, although parts belong to the early twelfth century; it was restored in 1868–80 by Sir Gilbert Scott and his son John Oldrid Scott, but the spire which they envisaged as part of the restoration scheme was, unfortunately, never carried out. The Town Hall, between the Cathedral and the University College, dates from the late fifteenth century when it was built as the Bishop's Palace. It was considerably altered and improved in the eighteenth and nineteenth centuries. Between the Cathedral and the Town Hall is an unusual garden devoted to flowers mentioned in the Bible.

The most attractive part of Bangor is up on the ridge behind the University College. Here, in College Road, is the oddly named Normal College (teacher-training), a sparse mid-nineteenth century building in Tudor dress, and the interesting Museum of Welsh Antiquities. Menai Road, running parallel with the coast, has fine views across the Menai Strait to the island of Anglesey, while at the point known as Garth there remains a late-Victorian pier from which ferry boats once plied regularly across the Strait to Menai Bridge and Beaumaris.

ELEVEN

Anglesey

Anglesey, although so physically different to the rest of Wales, yet retains within its folds the very essence of the Principality. A flattish island, pierced here and there by ancient rock outcrops which have been moulded on the eastern side into rounded hills and dip into the sea on the western side, Anglesey is one of Wales' richest repositories of prehistoric and historic sites, hoards and relics. It was also the island of the Druids and, in more recent times, of bards and poets. Isolated by the thin, waving line of the Menai Strait, the island has managed to preserve its Welsh culture and language to a greater degree than many other parts of the country although it is now, as a result of increased accessibility, losing its predominance as a Welsh-speaking area at a faster rate than other parts of Gwynedd. Though an island, Anglesey has always been an integral part of the Principality and was for long considered the 'granary of Wales', supplying the princes of Eryri and their people with grain and other foods in peace and war. When besieged the Welsh princes could hold out indefinitely as long as they controlled Anglesey, but once the island was invaded, as happened during Llywelyn ap Gruffydd's war of independence, the plight of the princes was precarious indeed.

A county in its own right until 1974 Anglesey is now once again, as it was during the Middle Ages, a district of Gwynedd. The cultural and economic links between the island and mainland Gwynedd have always been strong, but the physical links are tenuous; just two bridges – one constructed for road traffic and the other built for the railway – across the Menai Strait. The five ferries which once plied the Strait have ceased, and unless one swims or flies there is no alternative but to use one of the two bridges to reach the island. The Menai Bridge (or Pont y Borth in Welsh) carries the main road from Bangor high above the water to the little town also known as Menai Bridge on the Anglesey shore. The famous suspension bridge was designed in 1818 by Thomas Telford for the Holyhead Road Commissioners as part of the highway from London to Holyhead. At the time of its opening eight years later it was the longest iron bridge in the world, with a span of 579 feet between its two lofty stone towers. The task of bridging the Menai in those days was difficult enough, but the Admiralty ruled that there must also be a minimum clearance of 100 feet between the water and the roadway. Telford rose to the occasion in superb style and designed a bridge which looks, to our eyes, entirely appropriate to its picturesque setting. The bridge was partly reconstructed in 1940 to take modern traffic.

The town of Menai Bridge (Porthaethwy in Welsh) lies in the lee of the bridge and in fact owes its birth to the bridge's construction. Before the bridge was built there were only a few scattered groups of cottages making up the parish of Llandysilio and its only claim to fame was the fair, known as Ffair y Borth, held annually in October. The earliest evidence of the fair is a reference in 1691; since then it has been held each year. The town faces south across the Strait. Little crags of islands appear off shore while in the town itself rocky outcrops project here and there between the houses and hotels. Near the centre is the Museum of Childhood established in a modest double-fronted house. The fascinating miscellany of items collected there illustrate all aspects of childhood pleasures during the last century and a half, including dolls and dolls' houses, children's games, needlework, money boxes and music boxes.

A favourite walk in Menai Bridge is to the Belgian Promenade and Church Island. These can be reached along the back streets near the Menai shore and under the tall arches of the suspension bridge, passing on the way the circle of standing stones erected for the National Eisteddfod. The Belgian Promenade lies alongside the Menai Strait and is named after the 30 or so Belgian refugees who constructed the walk during the First World War as a tribute to the friendship of the local people. The walk skirts a delightful section of woodland (Coed Cyrnol) situated on a rocky headland. At the end of the Promenade a stone causeway provides a link with Church Island. Here is the tiny old parish church of St Tysilio, dating from the fifteenth century but built over the site of a far earlier – perhaps as early as the beginning of the seventh century – Celtic church. The church is hidden away near the shore, but the hill in the centre of the small island is crowded with the monuments, memorials and graves of a cemetery. The summit of the cemetery provides a splendid view up the Strait of the other famous bridge – the Britannia Tubular by Robert Stephenson – which was thrown across the waters in the nineteenth century to link Anglesey to the mainland (see page 144).

The main road from Menai Bridge to Beaumaris follows the coast closely, but because of the ruggedness of the terrain the road is narrow and winding. Large and small houses of all kinds are scattered on both sides of the road nearly all the way between the two towns. Most were built in the late nineteenth or early twentieth century and exhibit a most versatile imagination on the part of their builders. The view southwards across the Menai Strait to the peaks of Eryri is magnificent and one can easily understand how this stretch of road attracted the *nouveaux riches* away from their dark satanic mills.

Beaumaris is an attractive seaside town with the appearance of a well-mannered early nineteenth century spa. Partly this is because Beaumaris is still small and self-contained, with no suburban overspill to mar its edges, but also because of its neat and regular layout dating back to the fourteenth century. The main street, and indeed the town itself, turns its back on the sea and leads instead to the castle which has become a tourist asset even more popular than the sea. The castle was the last to be built in Wales by Edward I. It was something of an afterthought, not being started until the beginning of 1295, and then only as a counter to Madoc ap Llywelyn's capture of the 'impregnable' castle at Caernarfon in the previous year. It was never finally completed, but its present state differs little from when building operations ceased in the early fourteenth century. Though overshadowed by Caernarfon and Harlech in sheer grandeur and drama, it is perhaps the most attractive and architecturally satisfying of all of Edward's castles. Being sited on flat land near the sea, the royal architect was able to plan a perfectly symmetrical fortress unhindered by physical conditions. It has a square inner ward with two bold twin-towered gatehouses as well as corner and mid-wall towers. Surrounding this core is an outer wall with a dozen small round towers, all encircled in turn by a broad moat which is still filled with water. Near the entrance to the castle there is a small ship dock which was originally connected to the sea by a short canal. In design and layout Beaumaris Castle is a masterpiece of medieval planning, the epitome of the concentric ideal in which every part of the fortress and its immediate surroundings were covered by crossfire from the numerous towers.

Within a year of the castle's commencement Edward started building a 'new town' alongside, naming it, in Norman French, as Beau Marais ('fair marsh'). In order to establish the new town the King ordered that the existing community at Llanfaes, which had been developed by the Welsh princes as one of their main centres, be uprooted and moved to Niwbwrch on the west coast of Anglesey. Not all of the inhabitants wanted to go and a local doctor and 30 other former residents were fined for unreasonable delay.

The 'new town' for English settlers was planned to a grid layout alongside the castle, but it was not until after the Glyndŵr War of Independence in the early fifteenth century that the town walls were caused to be built. The large parish church, dedicated to Saints Mary and Nicholas, was one of the first buildings to be erected for the convenience of the new settlers. Sited near the centre of the town it is in the robustly masculine version of the Perpendicular style common to Gwynedd. The fine chancel was rebuilt in the sixteenth century and the odd-looking corner pinnacles were added in the nineteenth. Inside there are some handsome misericords brought from Llanfaes Friary and an interesting sarcophagus of Princess Joan, the wife of Llywelyn Fawr and daughter of the English King John. The graveyard at the rear of the church has been anaesthetized and laid out as a formal garden of rest.

The curiously shaped Court House opposite the castle dates from 1614 and is the oldest court still in use. The interior is paved with flagstones and divided into public and official areas by a massive iron railing while the roof is supported by a local version of hammer-beam trusses. Almost of the same date is the old Almshouses (Elusendai) just outside the town. By the 1930s it was falling into ruins, but it has since been restored into seven cottages and a chapel surrounding a courtyard. The most interesting nineteenth-century buildings in Beaumaris are the forbidding Gaol (1829) and Victoria Terrace (1835), the grandest and most Classical of the sea-front buildings, both designed by Joseph Hansom, better known as the inventor of the hansom-cab. The Gaol, after serving much of its life as a police station, has now been turned into a rather gruesome museum. It is well worth visiting if only to see the treadwheel (the only one remaining in Britain) and to try to imagine a criminal's last thoughts as he walked along the gangplank to the gibbet raised above the street in the outside wall.

Penmon lies almost at the end of Anglesey's windswept eastern peninsula. Here for 14 centuries has stood a church of one sort or another. Founded originally in the sixth century as a Celtic monastery it became one of the more important of the *clas* churches when it was rebuilt in the twelfth century. In the mid-thirteenth century it was taken over by the Augustinian Canons and became known as Penmon Priory. Architecturally it is of some interest as it has managed to retain a number of purely Celtic features such as its bare cruciform plan consisting of a short nave with two stubby transepts. Above the crossing is a squat central tower resting on corner piers protruding into the interior space. The simple, angular layout carries with it the hallmark of Celtic monasticism and similar church layouts of pre-Norman foundation can be found in all parts of Wales. Inside, Penmon Priory is dark and gloomy until one gets used to the light and then the cave-like interior has the effect of a piece of monumental sculpture carved out of a single block.

The chancel arch at Penmon, built a generation later than the rest of the church, shows Romanesque geometric influence in its bands of chevron and chequerwork patterns, but this is almost entirely absent in the arch over the entrance where a panel of naturalistic interlacing patterns and low-relief sculpture continue the best traditions of Celtic art. The monolithic Early Christian cross (late tenth or eleventh century) standing in the South Transept confirms the Celtic aura of the place. The base of another Early Christian cross has become the font and yet another cross stands just within the deer park a few hundred yards north-west of the Priory. In 1237 the monastery of Penmon was granted to the Prior of Ynys Seiriol (Puffin Island) by Llywelyn the Great. The prior apparently moved in to take up residence in his new property and subsequently set about adding to it. The disproportionately large chancel was rebuilt about this time (and rebuilt again in the nineteenth century), as also was the Prior's House (still lived in) and the large three-storey refectory and dormitory block on the south side of the Cloister Court. The domed dovecot nearby is much later (probably about 1600); inside there were nearly a thousand pigeon holes reached by a central pillar with corbelled steps.

Perhaps the most interesting building of all at Penmon is the tiny chapel of St Seiriol. St Seiriol, a descendant of Cunedda Wledig and the second cousin of King Maelgwyn Gwynedd, lived in the early sixth century. A square chamber, partly rebuilt in the eighteenth century, incorporates the ruins of the saint's cell with its well to baptize the converts; close by are the foundations of an oval hut where Seiriol lived 14 centuries ago. Fragments of St Seiriol's monastery stand on the rocky island of Ynys Seiriol off the point of Penmon and pre-dates the more famous sanctuary of St Columba at Iona off the Scottish coast. The monastery resembled Irish Celtic monasteries in its layout, which usually included a diminutive church in the centre of an oval enclosure with huts for the monks on the perimeter. The island is now deserted except for swarms of sea birds. The rabbits which once swarmed everywhere have been decimated by myxomatosis, allowing the plants to grow tall and unchecked, and even the puffins are on the decline.

From Penmon the northern part of the peninsula can be explored via narrow country lanes. Llaniestyn is a sparsely populated parish which has two pocket-sized churches set in open countryside but no village. Llaniestyn Church, near Llanddona, is simple and whitewashed and has a beautifully austere carving in stone of its patron saint. The church of Llanfihangel lies nearer the coast at the edge of Din Sylwy, an Early Iron Age fort occupied in Roman times. The fort, also known as Bwrdd Arthur (Arthur's Table), had thick parapet wall-walks. One can get a splendid and far-reaching view down towards Red Wharf Bay and along the east coast of Anglesey from the remains of the wall-walks.

Between Menai Bridge and Pentraeth the undulating landscape is broken by innumerable outcrops of rock and the trees all bend eastwards away from the wind which here meets higher ground for the first time after racing across the lowlands of Anglesey. Six roads meet at Pentraeth, a hilly village standing at the end of a sea estuary now filled-in by marshland. The name means 'head of the sands' and is a reminder that at one time this village was a port and that it was sea traffic rather than road traffic which provided its inhabitants with a living. A good stone chapel with rounded corners seems to recall Celtic architectural traditions. Neat new houses in white, stepped terraces and dark grey roofs add something to the character of the village, but other post-war housing a little further away are out of place and distracting.

Being an island, the interior of Anglesey tends to be off the beaten track for tourists. The natural tendency is to circulate around the coastal periphery where the most attractive scenery is generally to be found. The island's capital, Llangefni, however, lies right at the centre of Anglesey and in order to visit it a detour has to be made. Halfway between Penmynydd and Llangefni is Plas Penmynydd, a smallish farmhouse (not open to the public) important in Welsh and English history as the ancestral home of the Tudors. Although Owain Tudor, the lover of Henry V's widow Catherine de Valois, was not born here it seems to have been the home of his father Maredudd ap Tudur. The offspring of Owain and Catherine included Edmund, the father of Henry VII, and Jasper, Earl of Pembroke. By the time of Henry VII, however, the gulf between the remote country family in Anglesey and their royal kinsmen had become enormous and almost unrecognizable; so much so that a neighbour was able to describe the Penmynydd squire as 'a poor gentleman of mean living, who giveth himself only to good fellowship, pleasure and hunting, without respect of his profit, and of a plain wit'. Plas Penmynydd was rebuilt in 1576.

Llangefni appears to be hidden away from the main traffic routes, but it was not always so for though it has never been a large place it did at least stand directly on the old Holyhead road (until Telford built a new road to the south in 1815) and even the Afon Cefni was once navigable as far as the town. Prominent on the skyline south of the town is the tower of an old windmill. On market days Llangefni comes back to life, busy with farmers and livestock from all over the island. The stalls overflow into the streets surrounding the central square behind which looms the Victorian Gothic Town Hall. The elaborate white limestone clock tower in the square commemorates a Boer War victim, but the grandest memorial is Capel Moriah (the Calvinistic Methodist chapel) built to commemorate John Elias (1774–1841), a celebrated figure of the Methodist Revival in Wales.

The church, rebuilt in 1824 and altered in 1898, has iron traceried windows and stands outside the town centre at the edge of The Dingle, a deep wooded valley through which flows the Afon Cefni. A mile further up the river is Llyn Frogwi, a reservoir, surrounded by woods and divided into two parts by an embankment over which ran the old railway to Amlwch.

North of Pentraeth the coastal areas are sheltered from the south-westerly winds and have become the favourite seaside area of the island. Benllech, with its mile-long stretch of firm, smooth sands and nondescript bungalow development, is the centre of this holiday area. A modern Roman Catholic church in the town stands out as being the only building of any interest. In the vicinity of Benllech there are a number of Stone Age burial chambers. Those at Glyn and Pant-y-saer, together with the remains of an Iron Age hut group, are just to the south-west of the built-up area. In Benllech itself another burial chamber was discovered as recently as 1965; prior to being recognized as an ancient *cromlech* it had been used as a duck-house and then as a rubbish tip.

A mile west of Benllech is Brynteg where Goronwy Owen, poet and religious scholar, was born in 1723. Owen was one of the leaders of a renaissance in Welsh literature which demanded a return to the strict metres and difficult alliterative poetry known as *cynghanedd*, and as a result he scorned the popular songs and interludes of his contemporaries. Owen himself was scorned in turn by his elders and although he was the curate of his local parish church for a short time he was soon replaced by a person of 'superior' status and was never given a living in Wales. He moved from church to church in England, but was forever in dire poverty and always felt himself an exile. Eventually he left Britain to go and try his fortune in America. Misfortune dogged him even then for his wife and two of his children died on the ship crossing the Atlantic. Owen died in Virginia in 1769 at the early age of 46.

Moelfre, the next settlement along the coast, is a cosy little place in a charming position between a small bay and a rocky headland. Rocks shelve down to the water and a row of old stone cottages line the narrow road as it runs parallel with the side of the bay. The headland projects well out into the sea and provides a good lookout for the coast guard station there. From the cliff walk there are excellent views across the sea to Penmon Head, Ynys Seiriol and the Great Orme at Llandudno, with the high Carneddau range in the background. Being near the Irish Sea shipping lanes, as well as being on a rocky and dangerous part of the coast, Moelfre was an obvious place for a lifeboat station. It was near here that *The Royal Charter* was wrecked in 1859 on its way home from Australia. More than 450 people on the iron clipper died in the tragedy and they are commemorated by the memorial on the headland behind Moelfre. No single local cemetery could cope with the problem of burial at the time and so the bodies were buried in nine different graveyards in the district.

A mile inland there is an interesting group of monuments near Plas Lligwy farm. Nearest the road is a Stone Age burial chamber with a row of small upright stones supporting a giant 28-ton capstone over a natural fissure in the rock. When excavated the chamber revealed the remains of 30 bodies of prehistoric age. A footpath leads across the field to the craggy walls of the roofless Capel Lligwy, a twelfth-century church extended in the fourteenth century by the addition of a small crypt and chapel. The most unusual monument in the group is Din Lligwy, a fourth-century village or hut-group, in the next field. Here are well preserved walls of two circular and seven rectangular buildings, all surrounded by an outer perimeter wall and built on the edge of an escarpment. All the walls, which are roughly four to five feet thick and up to three feet high, are made up of two outer skins of large stone slabs, coursed wherever possible, with an infilling of earth and smaller stones. In some cases the stone gate-posts, up to six feet tall, and 'door steps' are still in position after 16 centuries.

Further west is Mynydd Bodafon, a geologically ancient outcrop of Pre-Cambrian age, which forms one of Anglesey's highest (584 feet) and most prominent hills. Traces of circular huts, known as Cytiau'r Gwyddelod, on the eastern slopes are evidence of man's presence here during the Bronze Age. The Marusiaid monument at the foot of Mynydd Bodafon commemorates the more recent activities of the Morris brothers who grew up at Pentre-eiriannell farm below the hill. Each of the brothers was connected in some way with the sea, but perhaps their chief interest is in the thousands of letters which they wrote to each other. These were fortunately kept and have provided a wealth of information about life in Wales, and particularly Anglesey, during the eighteenth century. John (1706–40), the youngest, joined the navy and died at sea. William (1705–63) spent all his life in Anglesey and became a Customs official at Holyhead. Richard (1703–79) left home at an early age to join the Navy Office in London where he founded the Honourable Society of Cymmrodorian to support and patronize Welsh scholarship and art. Lewis (1701–65), the eldest of the four, combined his work as a mining engineer and surveyor with his interests of collecting manuscripts and antiques, writing poetry and printing and publishing Welsh books. Lewis Morris was also a notable map-maker and it is for this that he is best remembered. The most important of his charts was a complete hydrographic survey of the Welsh coasts undertaken when he was employed as a customs officer at Holyhead. When it was published in

1784 as *Plans of Harbours, Bays, and Roads in St. George's and the Bristol Channels* a previously unrecorded reef was charted for the first time and thus, so it is said, put paid to a locally lucrative business in looting ships that had gone aground on it.

The most famous, though not the highest, prominence in Anglesey is Mynydd Parys which overlooks the small port of Amlwch at the north-eastern corner of the island. The fame of the mountain rests on its vast copper deposits which were discovered in 1768 and which, within a few years, made it the greatest single producer of copper ore in Europe. At the end of the eighteenth century more than 3000 tons of copper were mined annually, employing 1,200 men, women and children, and Anglesey copper dominated the European metal market. A century later the mines had closed due to falling quality and quantity allied to foreign competition. Now, though mining has long since ceased, the evidence of all that activity is still obvious in the extraordinary moon-landscape that remains. A great excavated chasm, more than a thousand feet deep, has been rent through the centre of the mountain. At the highest point of the hill is an abandoned windmill tower and in the distance the ruins of old mine buildings loom above the edge of the fantastic chasm like the craggy remains of some medieval castle. At the bottom of the mine lies a small lake, its water stained blood-red, while all around are rocks, screes, tips and slag heaps in a gorgeous range of colours – ochre, browns, coppery reds, mauve, blues and greys. The whole scene, though undoubtedly magnificent, is strangely eerie for there is no sound to be heard, apart from the wind, and no sign of life; grass does not grow here, insects and animals are conspicuous by their absence, shrubs and trees are non-existent and even the sky is empty of birds. Apart from the 'Keep out – Danger, Old Mine Shafts' signs and some of the rubbish of contemporary society the mines seem to have been abandoned for ever by all and sundry.

Amlwch lies in a scatter at the foot of Mynydd Parys and seems to cover a wide area for a town of less than 4,000 inhabitants. In its heyday, as the world's most important copper port, there were considerably more people and reputedly over a thousand ale houses! Without the copper industry Amlwch would have remained a village and despite its sudden growth and importance it still has a rural appearance. The harbour, long and narrow, is little more than a long gash hacked out of the cliffs, yet it was sufficient to shelter up to 30 200-ton ships during the copper era. The harbour walls are built of thin slabs placed upright in herring-bone fashion with here and there the natural rock showing through to give the place an atmosphere of antiquity.

Almost everything in Amlwch was brought about by the riches of the Parys copper mines. After being mined the copper ores were brought to Amlwch for initial smelting and then shipped to southern Wales for further smelting. A side effect of the copper bonanza was the introduction of a local mint. From 1787 onwards the Parys Mines Company cast more than 12,000,000 coins in penny or halfpenny denominations. Although handsomely designed, with a relief engraving of a druid's head on one side, they were really trade tokens, as was made plain by the inscription on the obverse side promising to pay the bearer 'on demand in London, Liverpool or Anglesey'. Shipbuilding was another industry encouraged by the copper boom, but perhaps the most interesting offspring of the flourishing trade was the tobacco industry. Tobacco was processed at a number of small works (there were still three tobacco factories in the town at the beginning of the century) and Amlwch Shag became very popular throughout northern Wales amongst pipe smokers. Apart from its pair of churches Amlwch has little of architectural interest. The parish church, built in 1800 in Classical style on the site of an ancient Celtic structure, was 'Gothicised' in 1867. The post-war Roman Catholic church has a parabolic concrete roof in modern Brazilian fashion. The great new aluminium and chemical works north of the town, though giving much needed employment to the area, has done little to improve the appearance of the splendid coastline.

Two miles east of Amlwch, near Point Lynas promontory, is Llaneilian Church, one of the three most interesting churches on the island. Its spacious and well-lit nave, complete with battlemented parapets, is of the late fifteenth century but the stumpy tower at the west end and its curious pyramidical spire date from the twelfth century. There is a robust rood-screen and good fittings inside. On the south side of the nave and attached to it by a passage is St Eilian's chapel – a *capel-y-bedd* or mausoleum of the saint – rebuilt in the fourteenth century on the side of the original sixth or seventh-century sanctuary.

The coastline and cliff scenery along Anglesey's north coast is superb, spoilt only by the enormous atomic power station at Wylfa built in 1969. The northernmost tip of the Anglesey mainland, halfway between Porth Wen and Cemaes Bay is occupied by an Iron Age promontory fort known as Dinas Gynfor. The fort is protected by two ramparts across the neck of the headland and entered along a natural gully. From the fort there is a splendid outlook along the coastline and to the north-west one can see Ynys Badrig (Patrick's Island), the most northerly Welsh island. Tradition recalls that St Patrick left from this part of the coast to go to Ireland, but as there are other reputed departure points in Wales and northern England one has to treat the story with caution. Nevertheless, Patrick may well have visited this part of the coast for there is a tiny church (Llanbadrig) on the cliffs a little further west dedicated to his memory. The interior of the church was transformed in 1884 by Lord Stanley of Alderley so that it no longer looks medieval.

The north-western corner of Anglesey is windswept and wild in appearance, reminiscent of St David's Head in Dyfed. Cemlyn Bay, shielded from the westerlies by the peninsula of Trwyn Cemlyn, has an inner lagoon separated from the sea by a raised storm beach which is a favourite gathering place for wildfowl in winter.

Llanfairynghornwy has a twelfth-century church (much restored by the Victorians) set in an oasis of trees. The village straggles towards the corner of the island where Carmel Head can be reached by footpath. From the cliffs there one can look out towards a group of small islands still known by their Norwegian name, The Skerries. The lighthouse on the island was the last privately built and owned lighthouse in Britain. It was eventually sold to Trinity House in 1841 for nearly half a million pounds.

Inland there are interesting medieval churches at Llanfechell and Llanbabo. Llanfechell church stands in the middle of the village, which is an unusually compact one for Anglesey. The tower of the church is sixteenth century and has a peculiar stone cone on top of it in place of a spire. Reputedly the cone was added to the tower in the eighteenth century at the insistance of the local squire to drown the sound of bells which he believed upset the fermentation of his home-brewed beer. North of the village are a number of prehistoric standing stones and a Bronze Age burial chamber. The little medieval church of Llanbabo stands in an isolated position three miles south of Llanfechell. Over its doorway are three crudely sculptured faces; inside there is a fine fourteenth-century grave-slab which is believed to be a memorial to St Pabo.

The once marshy valley of Cors y Bol south of Llanbabo was transformed in 1966 into a three-mile-long reservoir known as Llyn Alaw. This, the largest stretch of inland water on the island, has become a sanctuary for birds and wild swans, and ducks are often attracted to it. The Afon Alaw flows out of the reservoir at its western end and a mile beyond the dam passes the Bronze Age burial mound of Bedd Branwen (Branwen's Grave). This is the spot where, according to one of the stories in the *Mabinogion*, Princess Branwen was buried after dying of a broken heart when her marriage to an Irish king had resulted in war between Britain and Ireland.

Nearby, at Llanddeusant, there are two old mills. Melin Howell, on the banks of the Alaw, is a water-driven corn mill which has been lovingly restored and is still working. The last corn mill in Anglesey, it is a reminder of the time when the island was the chief grain area in

Wales and was known as *Môn mam Cymru* (Anglesey mother of Wales); now cattle and sheep have largely taken the place of corn. The windmill, on the other side of the village, was the last of Anglesey's many windmills to work. Only the arms of the sails are left and although it is now in poor condition it still retains its machinery.

Holy Island, three quarters of a mile off the west coast of Anglesey, is reached by the Stanley Embankment which Telford built in 1822 to cross the last natural obstacle on his London to Holyhead road. Once on Holy Island Telford's road and Stephenson's Irish Mail railway part company temporarily to pass on either side of a large aluminium smelting works before joining again in the centre of Holyhead at the end of the inner harbour.

Holyhead (Caergybi), the largest town in Anglesey, is also one of the main sea links between Great Britain and Ireland. The entrance to the inner harbour is shielded by Salt Island, a rocky islet which took its name from the salt which was extracted from the sea water there in the seventeenth century. The Doric triumphal arch (by Thomas Harrison) near the entrance to the island was erected in 1824 to commemorate George IV's unplanned stay in the town when he was held up for five days in 1821 while waiting for the weather to abate before sailing. The A5 road is therefore the only road in Britain which has a triumphal arch at the beginning (at Marble Arch, London) and the end (at Holyhead). The outer harbour beyond Salt Island is protected by a mile-and-a-half long breakwater built between 1845 and 1873 with rock quarried from nearby Holyhead Mountain. The breakwater is the longest in Britain and in the past has often given shelter to a hundred or more ships seeking refuge from stormy seas. The new pier at the end of Salt Island was constructed in the 1960s for use by the aluminium works.

Holyhead's history goes back to the third or fourth century when the Romans built a small 'shore fort' to protect this outpost of their decaying empire from barbarian raiders. The Welsh name by which Holyhead is known is a reference to this fort. The walls and corner towers of the fort are well preserved and enclose the parish church of St Cybi. The church, which was largely rebuilt in the fifteenth and sixteenth centuries (and much restored by Sir Gilbert Scott in the nineteenth century), has a cruciform layout with high ceilinged aisles separated from the nave by wide four-centred arches. The exterior walls and tower are battlemented and there are elaborate late Gothic carvings on the south porch and the parapet of the south transept. The little detached *capel-y-bedd* near the south gate was a medieval chapel built on the site of the original sixth- or seventh-century cell of St Cybi.

Much of Holy Island is wild and rugged, especially at the

spectacular north-western corner of the island where caves have been gouged out of the 400-feet-high cliffs by the sea. Just inland from these cliffs is Holyhead Mountain, at 720 feet the highest point in Anglesey. This is one of the best viewpoints in Wales, with a prospect extending south-east across most of Anglesey to the Snowdonian mountains and the whole length of the Llŷn peninsula and in good light westwards across the Irish Sea to the Wicklow Mountains in Ireland. The rocky summit of the mountain is partially enclosed by a strong rampart wall, still standing in places up to ten feet high, belonging to an Early Iron Age fort called Caer y Twr. The fort was probably used as an emergency refuge and there are therefore no remains of permanent habitation. A mile away downslope, however, there are impressive hut circle remains of an extensive settlement (marked as 'Cytiau Gweddelod' on maps, but as 'Holyhead Mountain Hut Circles' on the signpost) occupied in the second to fourth century A.D. Twenty huts, both circular and rectangular, now remain but in 1865 another 30 were recorded.

Beyond the hut circles the road drops down to the western tip of Holy Island and to South Stack Lighthouse. The lighthouse, built in 1808 and usually open to visitors, is set on a deeply eroded and rocky islet connected to the main island by a suspension bridge. There is spectacular cliff scenery all around which includes some text-book examples of rocks contorted and folded under enormous primeval pressures. This is also an excellent place to watch sea-birds, such as guillemots, razorbills, puffins, fulmars and the occasional chough, which breed among the cliffs.

The southern half of Holy Island has less dramatic cliff scenery, but the coastline is still lovely and there are a number of sandy coves. At the narrow waist of the island Trearddur Bay has become a rapidly growing holiday resort. Rhoscolyn, at the southern tip of the island, has two sheltered sandy bays and is less developed. Beyond the ancient well of Ffynnon Gwenfaen on Rhoscolyn Head there are remarkable cliff formations at Bwa Du ('Black Arch') and Bwa Gwyn ('White Arch').

A winding estuary-like channel separates the southern part of Holy Island from the Anglesey mainland. The old bridge at the village of Four Mile Bridge was the crossing point used by travellers at high tide before the Stanley Embankment, further north, was built. At low tide the channel is almost dry and travellers were able to cross further down the coast. The road leads to Valley and back to the A5. Valley Airfield is near the coast about three miles south of the village of that name, but actually in the parish of Llanfair-yn-Neubwll; presumably the name of the latter village was too difficult to pronounce for the hundreds of airmen that came to the airfield during the last years of the Second World War and so the English name Valley was used instead. The RAF airfield is now used for training pilots and as a rescue station for planes, and climbers in difficulties in Snowdonia.

There are a number of natural marshy lakes in the vicinity of Llanfair-yn-Neubwll. One of these, Llyn Cerrig Bach, was on the site of the airfield and when construction work began there in 1943 a vast hoard of Iron Age objects was scooped out of the lake. The deposit, which had been miraculously preserved in peat, included chariot fittings, horse trappings, swords and daggers decorated in the La Tène artistic tradition showing that during the last centuries of Celtic independence Anglesey had been an important focus of wealth. The Llyn Cerrig Bach hoard is now in the National Museum at Cardiff.

Rhosneigr is a popular holiday village on the coast between the sea and the attractive lake of Llyn Maelog. The lake is popular for yachting and fishing. North west of the village a fine stretch of sand sweeps round the bay towards Valley Airfield. On a headland south of Rhosneigr there is a famous burial chamber called Barcloddiad-y-Gawres ('the giantess's apronful'). Impressively sited above the sea it is a passage-grave which has been re-covered with a new mound. At the end of the long dry-stone passage inside the mound the upright stones of the burial chamber are decorated with pecked geometric patterns, making it one of the most remarkable and mysterious examples of Stone Age art in Great Britain.

Two miles further south is Aberffraw, once the royal seat of the Llywelyns. Its importance in the twelfth and thirteenth centuries led to the beginnings of an urban settlement, but the ending of native rule in 1283 destroyed any future that the embryo town may have had. It is now a village attractively sited on the west bank of the Afon Ffraw, facing a large warren of sand dunes across the ancient bridge. St Beuno's church in the village is a simple, tough twelfth-century building with a Romanesque chancel arch decorated with flat, but naturalistic, intertwined foliage and beak-heads.

In the rock-studded bay to the west of Aberffraw is a little island with a tiny church on it. Remote and isolated, St Cwyfan's church was rebuilt in the twelfth century and though in regular use until recent times seems hardly to have changed in 800 years. The circumference of the island is ringed by a stone wall built by the Early Christians to mark the limits of their circular *llan* or churchyard. There is another twelfth-century church at Llangadwaladr, two miles east of Aberffraw. The church is dedicated to King Cadwaladr and has a grave slab in the nave in memory of Cadwaladr's grandfather Cadfan, 'wisest and most illustrious of all kings' who died in the early seventh century.

Beyond Llangadwaladr the road veers inland to avoid the broad, sandy estuary of the Afon Cefni. It crosses the Cefni near the modern limit of the estuary at Malltraeth, a hamlet which once had its own shipyard. In the eighteenth century the estuary was 12 miles long (four times its present length), reaching nearly to Llangefni and almost cutting Anglesey in two halves. An embankment was thrown across the estuary at Malltraeth in 1818, the Afon Cefni canalized and the surrounding marshland drained. The low, flat alluvial plain that now exists in place of the former estuary looks like parts of the East Anglian fenlands except that it is all pasture land instead of arable fields. The area is bisected by long, lonely lanes which every now and then cross remnants of the original course of the Cefni.

Surprisingly, Malltraeth Marsh was the centre of Anglesey's coal industry until about 1870. Numerous small coal mines were worked for centuries on both sides of the marshland near Malltraeth itself and further inland around Pentre Berw. Two small lakes in the middle of the former marsh alongside the Afon Cefni are still known as Llynau Gwaith Glo (Coal Work Lakes); spoil heaps from the coal mines are still visible where the railway crosses the Cefni and at Pentre Berw there is also a chimney stack belonging to one of the pits. The local coal industry was eventually killed off by the geological difficulties of mining and by competition from other parts of Wales.

Niwbwrch, on the south side of the Cefni estuary, was established (as Newborough) by Edward I at the end of the thirteenth century to replace Llanfaes (at the eastern end of the island) from which the Welsh had been forcibly removed to make way for the new English borough of Beaumaris. Although Niwbwrch prospered as a market centre and was for a long time a centre of an important cord and net-making industry it never grew into a town.

The land south and west of Niwbwrch was once all sand dunes, with here and there an outcrop of rock. Since the Second World War a large part of this area has been transformed into a forest. A well-screened car park and picnic area has been hidden in the forest near the sea. From there one can walk out on to the immense curving sand beach and see a magnificent panorama of the Arfon mountains and the Llŷn peninsula across the sea to the south. Llanddwyn island is a long, rocky peninsula jutting out into the sea at the western extremity of the forest. It is part of the Newborough Warren National Nature Reserve and visitors are therefore expected to keep to the footpaths. Plants and flowers alongside the footpaths are neatly labelled in Welsh, Latin and English. On the summit of the island are the remaining three chancel walls of a medieval church. This was St Dwynen's Church built on the site of the fifth-century saint's chapel. A modern Celtic cross near the church commemorates the ancient Celtic monastery while the Latin cross was erected in memory of St Dwynen herself. At the far end of the 'island' there is a terrace of former pilot's cottages and a lighthouse. The Pre-Cambrian rocks and cliffs projecting from the sea are delightfully colourful and are of great geological interest, being amongst the oldest in Wales.

Newborough Warren extends beyond the forest down to the Menai Strait. This is a great area of silvery white sand dunes partly covered by marram grass which was first planted here in Elizabethan times to prevent the sand creeping further inland. At the time when Edward I removed the displaced villagers of Llanfaes to Niwbwrch most of the land west of the new borough was fertile. The new settlers, however, cleared the land too thoroughly, in order to make new fields, and left the ground exposed to westerly winds. The newly-won farmland was soon overwhelmed by mountains of sand and the ancient farms and fields have remained buried ever since. A mile-and-a-half long dune peninsula reaches out from Newborough Warren to Abermenai point less than half a mile from the opposite shore of the Arfon coast.

Dwyrain, to the east of Niwbwrch, is a scattered village in the parish of Llangeinwen. The interesting little church standing at the corner of a sharp bend in the road has early medieval grave slabs set into a buttress on the north side and a thirteenth-century decorated font. Long, narrow lanes lead down to the Menai Strait foreshore where there are splendid views of Caernarfon's town walls and castle across the water.

Llanidan, near Brynsiencyn, has two churches. The new church, at the side of the main road is Victorian. The old Church, half a mile up a side turning to the north, was abandoned when the new church was built and was partly demolished. Its fifteenth-century arcade, open to the sky and partly enveloped in vegetation and surrounded by trees, has become a romantic ruin heavy with the atmosphere of the past in its quiet beauty.

Brynsiencyn has a number of remains dating back to Roman times and earlier. Caer Leb, just north of the village, is a third-century rectangular settlement site defended by two lines of banks and ditches. Its low position in a marshy area allowed water to fill the ditches as an added protection. Castel Brynygwyn is a circular earthwork, dating from the first century A.D., which had probably been refashioned from a much earlier neolithic structure. Two standing stones nearby are the remains of an ancient stone circle. There are also remains of two burial chambers in the vicinity, the one at Bodowyr on the way to Llangaffo being the best. The Bodowyr cromlech has a large dome-shaped capstone delicately resting on three upright stones.

The most complete burial chamber in this area is Bryn Celli Ddu at Llanddaniel Fab. The great earthen mound covering the chamber has been restored and the chamber itself is reached by a long, dark, dry-stone passage. There is an obscurely carved standing stone within the chamber while the mound is surrounded by a ditch and concentric circles of stones.

Plas Newydd stands in its own park at the edge of the water in an enviable position overlooking a sweeping curve of the Menai Strait with the mountains of Eryri opposite. It was rebuilt between 1795 and 1806 in a curious mixture of Classical and Gothic design by James Wyatt and Joseph Potter and is now National Trust property open to the public. Within the mansion there is Rex Whistler's famous mural in the dining room complementing the marvellous view seen through the windows of mountains and Strait.

Almost the last thing to be seen in Anglesey (or the first thing, depending which way you are travelling) is the Anglesey Column at Llanfair-pwllgwyngyll. This was erected in 1816 to commemorate the first Marquess of Anglesey, who lived at Plas Newydd and led the cavalry at the battle of Waterloo, where he was second-in-command. For another great view of Snowdonia and the Menai Strait it is worth climbing the 115 steps to the top of the column. The statue of the Marquess at the top was not added until 1860.

Llanfair-pwllgwyngyll (St Mary's Church by the white hazelpool) is known locally simply as Llanfair P.G. It was lengthened by a local wit to Llanfair-pwllgwyngyllgogerychwyrndrobwll-llandysiliogogogoch to amuse and bewilder nineteenth-century tourists. Another claim to distinction by the village is that the first Women's Institute in Britain was founded here in 1915.

Both road and railway leave Anglesey at Llanfair-pwllgwyngyll by way of the Britannia Tubular Bridge across the Menai Strait. The bridge was designed by Robert Stephenson and Francis Thompson and built between 1845 and 1850 to carry the railway across the Strait in two separate metal tubes (one for each track) in four spans between five great stone pylons. The centre spans were built on land and then floated out on pontoons and slowly hauled up into position by hydraulic pumps. The great wrought-iron tubes were badly damaged by fire in 1970 and have now been replaced by cumbersome steel arches, carrying both the railway and a new road on separate decks, between the original stone towers. The well-fed stone lions (sculptured by John Thomas) guarding the bridge at either end are referred to in a Welsh nursery rhyme:

Pedwar llew tew heb ddim blew
Dau yr ochr yma a dau yr ochr draw.

(Four fat lions without any hair,
Two on this side and two over there).

TWELVE

Caernarfon, Snowdon and Llŷn

The best way to approach Caernarfon would be by sea, but as this is now impossible without a private boat the next best way is along the by-road which skirts the coastline west of the Afon Seiont on which the town stands. Either way one is confronted, across the river, with a magnificent view of the castle and town walls which makes Caernarfon unique. Failing these difficult and awkward entrances it is best to ignore the dismal suburbs as one approaches the town along the main roads from the east and only begin to look around as one enters the town's central market square; then one can hardly fail to sit up and take notice for before you is the most elaborately conceived castle in Wales and one of the most impressive in all Europe.

The castle was commenced in 1283 by Edward I after defeating the Welsh armies and took nearly half-a-century to build. It is difficult to believe, when seen from the outside, that this seemingly impregnable castle is now, some nine centuries later, nothing more than a hollow shell. But what a splendid shell it is! The formidable strength of Caernarfon Castle is nowhere more apparent than at its main entrance, the King's Gate, which was approached by a drawbridge and protected by no less than five gates and six portcullises with arrow-loops between the divisions and 'murder holes' in the vaulting above. The main towers of the castle are topped by tall octagonal turrets and the connecting walls are threaded with a multitude of internal shooting galleries in complicated arrangements at different levels. Altogether there are 11 immense towers (including two twin-towered gateways) and two smaller towers. The architectural treatment throughout is highly sophisticated for a military structure, with finely coursed masonry arranged in different coloured bands. No expense was spared by Edward I in building this spectacular citadel for it was intended to be seen not only as the status symbol of the conqueror, but also as the palace of the new Anglo-Norman 'Prince of Wales' and as the administrative headquarters of his principality.

The lavishness with which Edward I built his castles 'to embrace and grip the intractable heart of northern Wales' did little, however, to cow the native Welsh into submission and in September 1294 Madog ap Llywelyn lead a violent insurrection in Caernarfon. The town was overwhelmed and occupied in the rising, the walls thrown down and the castle burnt. For six months the great castle, built to overcome the Welsh, was in the hands of the Welsh and in the summer of 1295 Edward had to start again from the bare lower walls.

Alongside the castle Edward built a new town on the French *bastide* model, with a rectangular grid of streets encircled by stout town walls fortified with eight towers and two twin-towered gateways. Street layout, walls, towers and gateways have all survived and although built on a smaller scale than Conwy the medieval town of Caernarfon is much easier to appreciate because of its compactness and its subservient relation to the castle.Built into the north-west corner of the town walls is St Mary's Church, formerly known as the Garrison Chapel. It was erected in the fourteenth century and partly rebuilt in 1809 by Benjamin Wyatt. Although so perfect an example of a *bastide* town, Caernarfon is no longer as Pennant once wrote 'the badge of our subjection', for ironically Edward I's policy of enforcing an Anglo-Norman character on the town and district failed. The original Anglo-Norman settlers were soon assimilated within the surrounding Welsh community and within a few generations were as Welsh as the native-born Welsh; even the town gates became transformed in name from East Gate and West Gate to Porth Mawr and Porth-yr-Aur and are still known as such. Caernarfon is today one of the strongholds of Welsh culture and it is Welsh rather than English that is the language heard and spoken on the streets.

The name Porth-yr-Aur (Golden Gate) has an especial ring about it, recalling the more famous gateway at Constantinople and providing another link with the curious history of Caernarfon. To Edward I Caernarfon was a special case, symbolizing not only his pride but also the capture of one of the chief places of the Welsh princes – the Constantinople of Wales (Caer Cystennin, i.e. 'Fort of Constantine') as it was originally known. The castle in particular is full of architectural symbols and quotations, such as the angular towers which were designed to be almost identical (even to the alternating bands of stone) with the towers of the mighty town walls of the other Constantinople in Turkey. The three sculptured Roman eagles on the topmost turret of the Eagle Tower were designed to be both a tribute to the Roman fort of Segontium (which is clearly visible from the tower) and a reminder of Owain the Great, King of Gwynedd in the twelfth century and ancestor of the last Llywelyn.

Segontium itself, a mile south-east of the castle, was traditionally associated with Constantine and his mother Helen (wife of the emperor Magnus Maximus) and is referred to in the 'Dream of Macsen Wledig' in the *Mabinogion*. 'Macsen' is of course the Magnus Maximus who came to Britain and after travelling the country from sea to sea came to a mountain 'and from that mountain he saw a river flow through the land, making towards the sea. And at the river mouth he could see a great castle, the fairest that mortal had ever seen, and he came to the castle. Inside the castle he saw a fair hall . . . and he saw a maiden sitting before him in a chair of red gold'. The maiden Elen, or Helen, was the king's daughter and Macsen married her. For her maiden fee Elen named for her father the Island of Britain to be held under her as empress of Rome with her own chief stronghold in Arfon, and 'thereafter Elen thought to make high roads from one stronghold to another across the Island of Britain'. The latter tradition is perpetuated in the Roman road still called Sarn Helen (Elen's causeway) which runs from Segontium in the north to Carmarthen in the south.

Segontium, the original 'Caer yn Arfon', was founded by the Romans in the latter part of the first century as an auxiliary fort. It is bisected by the modern road, but the northern half of the fort was excavated by Sir Mortimer Wheeler in 1921–3 and has been left exposed to view. There is a good museum on the site which includes a Roman altar to Minerva found during the excavations. Nearby, remains have been found of a small temple dedicated to Mithras. Near the fort is Llanbeblig Church, the original church of Caernarfon, which dates back to the thirteenth century and is possibly a Celtic foundation. It was to this church that Edward I is reputed to have moved the tomb of Constantine for safe-keeping. The perpendicular-style Vaynol Chapel at the north-east corner of the church was added in the late sixteenth century.

Caernarfon has a number of memorable open spaces, unusual for any Welsh town. First there is a Castle Square (in fact a triangular space) ringed by a varied collection of buildings and overlooked at one end by the Queen's Gate of the castle. At the furthest corner of the square is a fine statue of Lloyd George (by W. Goscombe John), Member of Parliament for the borough for 55 years until his death in 1945. The open space between the castle and the river (now a car park) was once a vast slate quay, the scene of much activity in the early years of this century when Caernarfon was an important port for the export of slate. From the side of the Afon Seiont one looks across the river to a hill surmounted by a folly. This is Coed Helen (another reference to the mother of Constantine) which makes a suitable foil to the castle opposite. The promenade (known locally as the 'South of France') between the town walls and the mouth of the river leads to the old dock and overlooks the Menai Strait towards the Anglesey coastline.

The foothills between Caernarfon and Snowdonia are scattered with a clutter of sprawling, undistinguished villages; their appearance partly the result of geology and partly a consequence of the agriculture of the district, which together gave rise to a mixed economy of quarrymen crofters who slogged away at the slate when work was available and tended their small-holdings in between times. Kate Roberts, born in 1891, has vividly described this area in her novels, a number of which have been translated into English. The cottage where she was born at Rhosgadfan is open to the public.

The explorer John Evans was born at nearby Waunfawr (four miles south-east of Caernarfon) in 1770. In 1792 he went to North America in search of a tribe of Indians who were said to be of Welsh descent and got as far as St Louis before being imprisoned by the Spanish governor on suspicion of being an English agent. Later Evans worked for the Spanish Government and was able to explore and map the Missouri from St Louis to the foot of the Rocky Mountains where he came in contact with a tribe of Mandan Indians. Evans spent six months living with the Mandans, but never came across any evidence of their supposed Welsh descent and never heard a word of Welsh spoken by them.

The idea of Welsh Indians grew out of the legend of Madoc, supposedly a son of Owain Gwynedd, who, as we have seen, was reputed to have crossed the Atlantic in the twelfth century and was supposed to have discovered a new country rather like the Norwegian Leif Ericson had done in the ninth century. The legend was bolstered up in Elizabethan times to support the theory that the British had discovered America before Columbus and so dispute the Spanish claim to their newly found wealth. Despite John Evan's non-evidence the legend has persisted until recent times. Southey wrote a long poem called *Madoc*, a number of Welsh poets have found inspiration in the legend and as recently as 1950 a book was published in the United States 'proving' that America was discovered by Madoc ab Owain.

The man-made remains of the narrow band of straggling villages and townships that lie behind Caernarfon in a line from Pen-y-groes to Bethesda are mostly from the nineteenth and twentieth century. Llanrug, for instance, where the river unaccountably changes its name from Afon Seiont to Afon Rhythallt, has a gawky, early nineteenth-century Normanized castle at Bryn-bras. On the foothills around Llanrug there are remains of much older settlements such as Iron Age forts (Dinas Dinorwig on the east side of the Rhythallt is the most impressive) and Celtic hut-groups and field systems.

Beyond Llanrug the scenery suddenly becomes mountainous and one is at the threshold of Eryri and the Snowdonia National Park. The name Snowdonia (which now includes the mountains of Arfon and

Meirionnydd) was introduced by Thomas Pennant in the late eighteenth century. Eryri is a far older term, but is more restrictive, covering only the Snowdon, Glyder, Carnedd, Hebog and Siabod ranges. The Welsh name is appropriate, however, for it envelops the words for highland and eagle (*eryr*), both being developed from the same root *er*, and has come to mean 'eagle height' or 'eagles eyrie'. As a nesting bird the golden eagle has disappeared from Eryri, although from time to time occasional visitors in search of prey have been seen. Eryri still has its special bird, the chough, which elsewhere in Britain only survives amongst the sea-cliffs of western Ireland and the Hebrides. The chough, a crow-like bird with glossy purplish-black dress and bright orange-red legs and curved beak, nests in the high rock crevices of the mountains and can be often seen skidding along the turbulent up-currents of air near the precipitous cliffs.

Llanberis is the tourist centre for this part of the National Park and though unexciting in itself has a splendid situation near the neck of land between Llyn Padarn and Llyn Peris. Llyn Padarn is two miles in length, narrow and one of the most beautiful lakes in Snowdonia, especially when seen from the Fachwen (north) side. Llyn Peris is smaller and deeper and is flanked on the north side by the excavated terraces of the enormous Dinorwic Quarries which rise up in tiers from the lake's shore. The water level of Llyn Peris has recently been raised by constructing embankments at either end so that the lake can be used as the lower reservoir of a pumped storage hydro-electric scheme. The upper reservoir is Marchlyn Mawr, desolately situated 2,000 feet above sea level in a glaciated cwm below Mynydd Perfedd. The power station itself has been located out of sight in vast artificial caverns hewn out of the rock below the now disused Dinorwic Quarries.

The oak woodland alongside Llyn Padarn to the north of Dinorwic Quarries is a country park with way-marked footpaths to explore. From one of the paths, starting near the former quarry hospital, it is possible to explore one of the galleries of the derelict Vivian Quarry which has sliced the wooded hillside here with a giant gash. A narrow-gauge steam railway runs alongside Llyn Padarn from Gilfach Ddu Station to Pen-llyn. From the train there are superb views across the lake to Llanberis and Snowdon. Of the five engines working the line three (including the oldest built in 1889) were previously used at the Dinorwic Quarries. The old quarry workshops, near Gilfach Ddu, have become the North Wales Quarrying Museum. Built in 1879, in the manner of a colonial fort around an open quadrangle, the museum is an excellent place to find out about the slate industry which once dominated the lives of almost everyone in this valley.

Dolbadarn Castle stands on a rocky outcrop at the edge of Llyn Peris in a romantic setting almost at the foot of Snowdon and has changed little since Turner and others painted it at the end of the eighteenth century. The castle's most important feature is the large round tower attributed to Llywelyn Fawr. Of the rest of the castle only fragments of the curtain wall and two rectangular towers are now left. The history of this Welsh *castell* is obscure, but traditionally it is the place where Llywelyn ap Gruffydd imprisoned his brother, Owain Goch, for more than 20 years.

The mountains of Eryri, and Snowdon in particular, are deservedly popular for, though not the highest peaks in Britain (and diminutive when compared with the Alps), they look every inch like real mountains. Few of the peaks are higher than 3,000 feet yet the savagely raw topography of these mountains gives them a wild appearance that is out of all proportion to their height. The valley floors are bare and strewn with rocks and boulders and it is difficult to gauge the real height of the precipitous cliffs and knife-edged ridges. The intervening cwms were gouged out by glaciers 10,000 years ago, leaving behind grey-blue lakes, cold and lonely, beneath fearsome ice-etched crags. The mountains, contorted and compacted into a comparatively small area, are never far from the sea and the clear rain-washed air seems to emphasize their steepness and grandeur. Even so, despite the mountains' lack of height and the moderating effect of the nearby sea, the weather is often severe and snowstorms are not uncommon in April. Although nearly all the peaks can be reached fairly easily by a reasonably steady-headed and fit person, the mountains can be dangerous, particularly if the weather changes suddenly (as it often does), and all of them should be treated with respect and caution. Accidents in Snowdonia are, unfortunately, all too common.

Snowdon itself is the grandest of all the Welsh mountains and looks well from almost all directions. Its central peak, Yr Wyddfa (3,560 feet), is sharp and pointed as a mountain peak should be and falls away precipitously on the east side to Glaslyn nearly 1,600 feet below. From the summit five long, steepsided and rocky ridges branch out in different directions enfolding deep, glaciated cwms most of which contain lakes. The ascent of Snowdon can be made by following any of the ridges, but as they vary considerably in difficulty some are more popular than others. The most impressive, but most difficult, walk is along the famous horseshoe route (overlooking the twin lakes of Llyn Llydaw and Glaslyn) which, starting at the upper end of the Llanberis Pass, takes in the arête-like peaks of Crib-goch (3,023 feet) and Crib-y-ddysgl (3,493 feet) on the way up and cliff-edged Y Lliwedd (2,947 feet) on the way down. The easiest, longest and least attractive route is the footpath which follows the mountain railway from Llanberis. The walk will take a few hours and even from here there are many dramatic views, especially south to the vertical cliffs of Clogwyn du'r Arddu and eastwards into Llanberis Pass. It is quicker and easier still to go to the top by steam train but far less exciting. The narrow-gauge engines run on a rack-and-pinion track and have operated (in summer only) since 1896. The railway's only accident was on the day when it opened. There is a station and café just below the summit designed by Sir Clough Williams-Ellis; not, unfortunately, one of his better works. In summer the summit and the main footpaths can become crowded and it is therefore more pleasant to walk to the top in spring or autumn provided that the weather is fine. The views from the summit naturally vary with the weather; often it is too misty to see much, but occasionally one can get extensive views across the roof of Wales to the English border, across Cardigan Bay to St David's Head and across the Irish Sea to Eire and the Isle of Man. The time of day, and of the year, also make a difference. If one is fortunate to be there at the right time it is possible to see some breath-takingly colourful sunsets and sunrises, but in winter even the easy footpath up from Llanberis can turn into a terrifying nightmare.

Llanberis Pass is a long and deep defile between Snowdon and the Glyders. Starting from Llyn Peris the narrow, twisting road passes through Nant Peris (the old village of Llanberis with a medieval, oddly planned church) and then follows Nant Peris stream up through a wild terrain peppered with tumbled boulders bigger than houses and hemmed in by rocky outcrops. At the top of the pass (Pen-y-pass) there is a large Youth Hostel, café and car park. A fine three-mile walk starts at Pen-y-pass and goes alongside the lakes of Llyn Teyrn, Llyn Llydaw and Glaslyn, with its ruined copper mines, to the foot of Snowdon. A steep footpath, which requires some scrambling, zig-zags up to the saddle between Crib-y-ddysgl and Yr Wyddfa. A shorter route, to the saddle, known as the Pyg Track, also starts at Pen-y-pass but runs higher up between the lakes and the crest of Crib Goch.

A mile further on the road from Llanberis meets the main Capel Curig to Beddgelert road at Pen-y-Gwryd, a mountaineers' hotel standing on the site of a Roman camp. The road descends through the beautiful Nant Gwynant valley with its two lovely, placid looking lakes, Llyn Gwynant and Llyn Dinas, towards Beddgelert. At the upper end of the valley there is a marvellous panoramic view of the Snowdon massif; Yr Wyddfa and Crib-y-ddysgl lie dark and menacing in the background, Y Lliwedd prominent in the middle distance and the massive spur of Gallt-y-Wenallt tumbling down to the shore of the lake in the foreground. Bethania, lying between the two lakes, is the start of another footpath (the Watkin Path) up to the summit of Snowdon. The route follows the stream past some waterfalls and then enters a bowl-shaped cwm between the peaks of Y Lliwedd and Yr

Aran (2,451 feet) before climbing steeply up to the ridge at Bwlch-y-saethau. The footpath was opened by Gladstone when he was prime minister in 1892 and a plaque on Gladstone's Rock half way up the valley commemorates the fact.

The scanty remains of Castell Dinas Emrys stand on a wooded outcrop alongside the road in the shadow of Yr Aran. It was one of the strongholds of the princes of Gwynedd and built on the site of a Dark Age camp traditionally supposed to have been the court of Ambrosius, a fifth-century ruler.

Beddgelert is a pretty village of stone cottages splendidly situated at the junction of three valleys with mountains all around. The little church has some fine early thirteenth-century windows and arcading, but little else of interest although it is on the site of a sixth-century Celtic monastery. Near to the church is the supposed grave, or *bedd*, of Gelert after which the village was named. Who Gelert really was is unknown, but according to the local innkeeper in the eighteenth century it was the dog Gelert of the folk-tale who, when left to guard the house, saved his master's baby from a wolf and was then mistakenly killed by his master who on returning saw blood from the wolf and thought that Gelert had attacked the baby. To lend credence to the story the innkeeper added the grave. More probably Gelert was an Early Christian saint buried at the site of the monastery.

South of Beddgelert the Glaslyn valley narrows again between craggy cliffs at Aberglaslyn Pass. The route of the old Welsh Highland Railway can be followed alongside the river from Beddgelert to Aberglaslyn, where it disappears in a series of tunnels beneath the cliffs. Until the beginning of the nineteenth century, when the embankment at Porthmadog was constructed, the Glaslyn was tidal and the sea came in almost as far as the bridge at Aberglaslyn. The bridge has long been a favourite spot from which to view the picturesque gorge.

North of Beddgelert the countryside is more open, but still very mountainous. The large Beddgelert Forest spreads up little valleys on the west side of the road to the foot of Moel Lefn (2,094 feet) and Moel Hebog (2,566 feet). Hidden in the cliffs below Moel Hebog is Ogof Owain Glyndŵr, the cave where Owain is reputed to have hidden. To the east there are fine views of the back of Snowdon beyond Yr Aran's shapely peak.

From Rhyd Ddu a narrow, winding road runs between rough stonewalls through the unspoilt pass of Drws-y-coed. At Bwlchgylfin there is a wonderful view of the valley ahead, with the cliffs of Mynydd Mawr (2,290 feet) towering above long, wide scree slopes. From the north Mynydd Mawr looks like a recumbent monster and is often referred to as the 'Elephant Mountain'. Beyond Llyn Nantlle Uchaf (where Richard Wilson once painted a famous view of Snowdon) the road leaves the National Park and enters once again the world of derelict slate quarries and quarrymen's crofts. The quarries are smaller than those at Llanberis and Bethesda, being dug in pits along the floor of the valley between Nantlle and Talysarn instead of being excavated from the side of the mountains. They are still awesome features of the landscape and many, including the great Dorothea Quarry, have now filled with water. Pen-y-groes, the largest township of this singular area, stands at the entrance to the Llynfi Valley on the road to Caernarfon.

Llandwrog, a couple of miles to the north-west, is a pretty nineteenth-century model village with attractive stone cottages. It was built as the estate village for Glynllifon Park on the opposite side of the road. The centre of the village is marked by a handsome little church with a spire. Glynllifon itself is a large and rather dull mansion built in a monotonous Palladian style in 1836 for Lord Newborough; it is now an educational institution. In the extensive grounds are a number of interesting buildings such as Fort Williamsburg, which was erected in 1761 as a somewhat whimsical base for the Caernarvonshire Militia. It is a roughly rectangular enclosure with angle bastions and has a castellated tower and barracks. The uncompleted and now overgrown Newborough Mausoleum was begun in 1826 in the form of a truncated cone standing on a podium, but the chapel which was intended to crown the structure was never built.

Lord Newborough also built Fort Belan a few miles to the north as an obstacle to sea-borne invaders. It lies beyond Dinas Dinlle, with its long shingle beach, at the extreme tip of a low peninsula facing Anglesey and is reached by crossing a private airfield. Fort Belan comprises a fascinating group of buildings (now open to the public), comprising the miniature fort itself and a dockyard. The fort, set behind inverted ramparts and approached across a draw-bridge, was originally manned by the Loyal Newborough Volunteers, a garrison raised and maintained by Lord Newborough at his own expense. The dockyard was constructed in the nineteenth century as a replica of the old English Harbour at Antigua in the West Indies. The original workshops alongside the dock are now furnished as a well-laid-out museum and include a forge and a furnace for burning rust off chains.

The little village of Clynnog Fawr lies at the entrance to the long arm of Llŷn and stands on the pilgrim's road that once attracted Early Christian 'saints' to the island monastery at the end of the peninsula. The village is dominated by its grand, Perpendicular church which stands close to the road. This is the once wealthy collegiate church of St Beuno. The Welsh Saint, Beuno, was deeply revered and his importance and the love of the faithful for him is reflected in this building. Nobly proportioned on the outside and light and austere within, the church has a fine tower with diminishing storeys, large windows with precisely organized tracery and a good hammerbeam roof. St Beuno's Chapel lies at an angle to the main church and is linked to it by a rough stone passage. It is at least the third on the site and grey paving slabs in the floor mark the outline of the original chapel of the Saint. St Beuno's Well, consisting of a small rectangular pool in a walled enclosure, lies near the road just beyond the church.

Three miles further on the road curves inland up a valley between the craggy face of Moel Penllechog and the triple peaks of Yr Eifl to Llanaelhaearn where a secondary road leads to the hilly, northern side of Llŷn. After Llanaelhaearn the road skirts round the scree slopes of Yr Eifl on the right. Southwards one looks down on apparently flat lands, but westwards the view takes in a rugged outline of hills across the end of the peninsula – a bleak, windswept landscape of stone boundary walls, hardly ever a tree and only a few stunted bushes. Yr Eifl (unfortunately often anglicized into 'The Rivals') is less than 2,000 feet high, but as it rises straight from the sea's edge it looks wild and mountainous. The nearest peak is dramatically crowned by Tre'r Ceiri ('Town of the Giants'), a remarkable example of a Celtic town surrounded by a massive stone rampart up to 15 feet thick in places. Often shrouded in mists from the sea, it contains the remains of 150 roughly circular, stone dwellings arrayed across the ridge in bands. In clear weather the views are magnificent in all directions and it is well worth expending some energy on the half-hour walk to the top.

The northern side of Yr Eifl is scarred by granite quarries which in parts extend to sea level. The western side of the mountain frowns down on Nant Gwrtheyrn, a deep isolated little valley with a romantic appeal. It was to here that the arch villain Vortigern (possibly the last Romano-British governor of Britain) is reputed to have fled in the fifth century after his request for help from Hengist and Horsa had turned into an uncontrollable Saxon invasion. Porth-y-nant, near the mouth of the valley and only accessible by sea or on foot, was, during the early years of this century, a thriving quarrymens' village. After the Second World War it became deserted for many years and it is only now gaining a new lease of life as a residential centre for Welsh language students.

The Saint's Road to Bardsey continues on through Pistyll, where there is another church dedicated to St Beuno and, half a mile beyond the church on the south side of the road, a little medieval cross to guide pilgrims on their way. Nefyn, a mile further on, has a couple of good sandy beaches sheltered from westerly winds by the point of Penrhyn Nefyn and the long, rocky peninsula of Porth Dinllaen where there is a promontory fort. Today Nefyn is a pleasant fishing village and holiday resort; in the nineteenth century the owners of the Great Western Railway and William Maddocks seriously considered turning Porth Dinllaen into the main port on the London–Dublin route and a new town was planned on the site of the golf course high above the cliffs. In 1284 Edward I held a lavish festival at Nefyn to celebrate his triumphal conquest of Wales. The high point of these (to Welshmen, somewhat dubious) celebrations was a tournament.

Beyond Nefyn the arm of Llŷn widens out into a fist and in the middle of this bulge is Carn Fadrun, a rocky, treeless hill crowned by the rampart walls and ruined hut circles of an Iron Age settlement. The summit, 1,217 feet above the sea, has a small fort traditionally associated with the 'castle of the sons of Owain'. From the top there are splendid views across the peninsula to the sea in all directions. Carn Fadrun also looks down on two interesting medieval churches at Llandudwen (to the north) and Llaniestyn (to the south). Both are small and towerless; the former has transepts but no chancel and the latter is of the double-nave variety.

The northern coast of Llŷn between Tudweiliog and the end of the peninsula is wild and windswept, with dramatic cliff scenery and occasional unspoilt and secluded sandy beaches. At Porth Oer the 'whistling sands' are white and squeak underfoot. A mile beyond Tudweiliog a Stone Age burial chamber known as Coetan Arthur ('Arthur's Quoit') adds to the primeval appearance of the area and a mile or so further on at Llangwnnadl a standing stone reminds one that this is the Saint's Road to Bardsey. The Perpendicular-style church at Llangwnnadl is surprisingly large, being wider than its length, and it has a nave and two aisles.

Aberdaron nestles in a small valley on the edge of a sheltered bay near the tip of the Llŷn peninsula. It was here that the pilgrims stopped to rest while waiting for a suitable tide and wind before sailing across the rough waters to Bardsey. The simple but stark church at Aberdaron, originally founded in the sixth or seventh century, was rebuilt in the twelfth century, and a south aisle was added in the sixteenth century. It provided sanctuary for Gruffydd ap Rhys, prince of Deheubarth, in 1127 when he was forced to flee to Ireland. Above the cliffs at Braich-y-pwll, the most westerly point of Llŷn, there was another pilgrimage church, but hardly anything of it has survived.

Ynys Enlli, better known now as Bardsey Island (after Bardr, a Viking leader), lies two miles off the mainland coast and four miles from Aberdaron. From early times it has been renowned as a religious retreat and burial place for saints. There are, however, few visible remains of the once famous abbey (apart from the stump of a tower) and the island is now mostly visited by naturalists and artists. Some of the earliest Christian settlers on the island were monks who managed to escape the massacre at Bangor Is-coed in the early seventh century. The flourishing monastery is said to have been founded a century earlier by St Cadfan. It remained firmly Celtic and independent until the thirteenth century, when a new Abbey of St Mary's was built, and for long held high place in the annals of the Celtic Church. St Dubricius, the reputed founder of Llandaf Cathedral, died on Enlli in 612 and since then 20,000 other 'saints' are said to have been buried on the island. In the middle ages three pilgrimages to Ynys Enlli were equal to one to Rome. In the early nineteenth century the island provided a home for almost a hundred people, but now only about a dozen fisher-farmers and lighthouse keepers live there. Boats from Aberdaron visit Bardsey, weather and tides permitting, and anchor out of sight of the mainland beyond the 500-foot-high Mynydd Enlli, near a narrow isthmus joining the main part of the island to its rocky 'tail'.

The southern coast of Llŷn is more subdued in character than the northern, but it can still show some bulky, cliff-ringed headlands such as Trwyn Cilan and Trwyn-yr-wylfa to the south of the holiday village of Abersoch. Between most of the headlands there are fine stretches of sandy beaches. Porth Neigwl has a four-mile-long beach, reached by footpath from the car park near Llanengan, and is popular for surfing although in rough weather it can be dangerous for bathing. A good view of Porth Neigwl, or Hell's Mouth as it is otherwise known, can be had from the road which climbs up to skirt the slopes of Mynydd Rhiw. Plas-yn-rhiw, just above the road, is a pleasant seventeenth-century and Regency House, the property of the National Trust and often open to visitors. From the idyllic gardens, which drop down in terraces below the house, one can look out across the sea to Cadair Idris in Meirionnydd. Nearby are the remains of two Stone Age burial chambers and, on Mynydd Rhiw itself, traces of a Stone Age axe factory.

Llanengan, at the eastern end of Porth Neigwl, has one of the best churches in Llŷn. It was mostly rebuilt in the sixteenth century and includes a fine roof-screen and loft and open truss roof. Llangian, a mile north, is the prettiest village in the peninsula, while Capel Newydd at Nanhoron, on the road between Botwnnog and Llanbedrog, is the oldest Nonconformist chapel in Gwynedd. Built in 1769 by the Congregationalists and carefully restored in 1956, the chapel still has an earthen floor and raised box pews. Llanbedrog is an attractive holiday village sheltering behind the headland of Mynydd Tir-y-cwmwd. Its church is built on the slope of the wooded hillside above the sea and still retains a medieval rood-screen.

The chief market and administrative centre of Llŷn is Pwllheli, an old-established borough which was given new life by the arrival of the railway in the nineteenth century. Pwllheli is also an important holiday resort, although the dour, dark stone buildings of the older part of the town do not give this impression. A large harbour divides old Pwllheli from its West End and South Beach, where there is a promenade and the beginnings of a new town started in the late nineteenth-century with grandiose terraces but never completed. East of the harbour there is another four-mile-long beach backed, this time by sand dunes.

Inland from the beach is the enormous Butlin's holiday camp. The camp was originally built in haste in 1940 to serve as a training camp for the Admiralty. Immediately after the Second World War the location and permanent use of the camp as a holiday centre was hotly disputed by local amenity centres. Ten years earlier in 1936 a RAF 'bombing school' at Penrhos, on the other side of Pwllheli, was burnt by three Welsh Nationalists in an historic protest against the swamping of a wholly Welsh-speaking area by the introduction of a large English-speaking settlement. When the matter was taken to court at Caernarfon the jury failed to agree and the case was then transferred to the Old Bailey in London where the men were convicted and sent to prison. David Lloyd George, the Liberal leader and prime minister during the First World War, was aroused to anger when he heard of the transfer and confessed that it was 'an outrage which makes my blood boil'.

Lloyd George (1863–1945), although born in Manchester, was of Welsh parentage and was brought up at Llanystumdwy (six miles east of Pwllheli) from the age of two. He was elected as member of parliament for the Caernarvon Boroughs in 1890 and became one of the greatest orators of the century. His passion and fire made people either love him or hate him. A sensitively designed memorial grave by Sir Clough Williams-Ellis is sited high above the Dwyfor river where Lloyd George used to walk. The Lloyd George Museum is in Llanystumdwy itself.

Cricieth, a mile and a half further on, was an important though small, Edwardian borough before it was developed as a resort in the last century. The town slopes pleasantly down from The Green towards the coast where the princes of Gwynedd built one of their larger castles on a rocky spur overlooking the sea. Although captured and partly rebuilt by Edward I the major features of the castle, including the massive twin-towered gateway, belong to the earlier Welsh period. In the early fifteenth century the castle was captured by Owain Glyndŵr. After that it fell into disuse and was allowed to crumble into ruins.

Four miles north of Cricieth a minor road from Dolbenmaen leads to the lovely Cwm Pennant of which the poet Eifion Wyn asked, with some justification, 'O God, why didst thou make Cwm Pennant so beautiful and the life of a Shepherd so short?'. After passing the simple, box-like church at Llanfihangel-y-Pennant the valley becomes suddenly restricted by a rocky spur and then widens out again below the massive shoulders of Moel Hebog and Craig Cwm Silyn. The valley is a cul-de-sac and the only way out at the northern end is on foot via the track over Bwlch-y-ddwy-elor to Rhyd Ddu.

The main road back to Porthmadog and the coast passes through Penmorfa and then drops down quickly to flat fields on the floor of the valley. Penmorfa means 'head of the marsh' for until William Maddocks built his famous embankments between 1797 and 1811 this was part of Traeth Mawr, a tidal and marshy estuary which reached almost as far as Aberglaslyn a few miles to the north-east. Maddocks started by constructing a small embankment to enclose land on which to build his model town of Tremadoc in a dramatic position below the rugged cliffs of Allt Wen. The town (built between 1800 and 1811) was intended to serve, among other things, as a coaching stop on the proposed London-Porth Dinllaen-Dublin route. Holyhead, however, became the main port for Ireland and Tremadoc never saw any of the hoped-for traffic although one of its streets was, and still is, known rather optimistically as Dublin Street. Tremadoc remains a delightful little town with a well-proportioned market place in the form of a Renaissance *piazza*. Three sides of the market place are enclosed by a continuous terrace of two-storey houses while the north side has an attractive town hall-cum-market-cum-theatre with an open arcade on the lower floor. Immediately outside the town Maddocks built one of the earliest Gothic revival churches in Wales on one side of the main road and opposite it an elegant neo-classical chapel.

The high point of Maddocks' endeavours came when he constructed the mile-long embankment (known as the Cob) across the mouth of Traeth Mawr. The Cob was started in 1808 and completed in 1811 although a year later it was temporarily breached by tremendous winter gales. As a result of this embankment many square miles of marshland became farmland, a new road (the A497) was brought in from the south-east and Porthmadog was developed into a sizeable town. A dock at Porthmadog provided an export outlet for the local slate industry and in 1836 a railway was opened between the town and Blaenau Ffestiniog. Porthmadog, originally intended as the port for Tremadoc, became itself the new town that Maddocks had envisaged, although as most of it was developed after his death he had little hand in its layout. Although the slate trade has gone Porthmadog remains a prosperous-looking little town with wide streets and a friendly atmosphere; the dock has become a yachting basin with attractive, close-packed holiday houses on nearby Ballast Island, and the

Festiniog Railway is now one of the most popular narrow-gauge steam railways in Wales.

Moel-y-gest rises in a massive lump behind Porthmadog on the west side and is an ideal place for shortish hillwalks. Beyond Moel-y-gest, at Morfa Bychan there are miles of sandy beaches between Ynys Cyngar and Graig Ddu ('Black Rock'). Near the little lake between Porthmadog and Morfa Bychan is Garreg Wen, the setting for the lovely air 'Dafydd y Garreg Wen' ('David of the White Rock'). David Owen (1712–41), the composer of this and other songs, including 'Codiad yr Ehedydd' ('The rising of the lark'), lived in the parish and is buried in the lonely little church of Ynyscynhaearn on the edge of the Ystumllyn marshes a couple of miles east of Cricieth.

THIRTEEN

Meirionnydd

From Porthmadog there are two direct ways into Meirionnydd – the Festiniog Railway and the A487 road. Both use the Cob, the great embankment that Maddocks built in 1811 to cross the Traeth Mawr Estuary. The Meirionnydd landfall is at Boston Lodge (where there is a road toll) on the hilly Penrhyn peninsula which separates Traeth Mawr from Traeth Bach.

The Festiniog Railway, the oldest surviving steam-hauled, passenger-carrying, narrow-gauge railway, was constructed in 1836 to carry slate from the Blaenau Ffestiniog quarries to the harbour at Porthmadog. The railway was built on a continuous gradient, allowing the early trains loaded with slate to be worked by gravity; horses were also carried on the down journey and used to haul the empty train back up to the quarries. Steam locomotives were introduced in 1863 and passenger services started in 1865. The railway continued in operation until 1946 and was then re-opened for passenger services in 1955 (at first only between Porthmadog and Boston Lodge) as a result of considerable voluntary effort. The original railway had its own locomotive works at Boston Lodge (named after William Maddocks' parliamentary constituency in Lincolnshire) and some of the original engines are still in use. The railway, 14 miles long, runs through delightful scenery from Porthmadog to Blaenau Ffestiniog. Most of the way it follows the side of the Vale of Ffestiniog, climbing all the time as it runs through forests, snakes sharply around Llyn Mair and does a spiral at Dduallt before going into a tunnel to come out alongside Tanygrisiau Reservoir.

On the Penrhyn peninsula the chief place of interest is Portmeirion, the romantic holiday village designed and built by Sir Clough Williams-Ellis from 1926 onwards. There is a toll at the entrance near Minffordd, imposed partly to help pay for the upkeep of the place and partly to reduce the number of visitors to sizeable proportions. Portmeirion is an architectural folly – and therefore not to everyone's taste – but what a marvellous folly it is. The first impression one gets is of a Mediterranean-type coastal village, yet there are no tight-knit streets and alleys – only collections of eclectically designed buildings apparently sited at random, but in reality carefully related to each other so that wherever one looks the groupings seem perfect. The architecture is gay and uninhibited and, though not particularly Welsh in flavour, there is a kind of Celtic richness in the profuse intricacy of the forms and styles and in the interplay of these with each other and the landscaping. Portmeirion started with the conversion of an early Victorian house into a hotel with its own promenade and lighthouse. Since then the village has developed and grown and now includes amongst its re-erected buildings a richly decorated ballroom from Emral Hall in Clwyd (now part of the 'Town Hall'), a Gothic porte-cochère from Nerquis Hall and a splendid eighteenth-century colonnade from Arnos Court, Bristol. Surrounding the village on the landward side of the peninsula are extensive wooded grounds which include many exotic trees and shrubs.

Penrhyndeudraeth is in two parts. The lower village near the main road, was laid out on reclaimed land in the mid-nineteenth century by David Williams. The older and upper part comprises the hillside terraces on either side of the Beddgelert road. From the upper village one can make a short detour northwards across part of the reclaimed land of Traeth Mawr to Garreg with its pretty houses. Plas Brondanw, which was the home of Sir Clough Williams-Ellis, is on the other side of the ridge. It has some imaginatively laid out gardens with fine views of Snowdon and, nearby, a statue of Neptune overlooking the land reclaimed from the sea. A minor road through Cwm Croesor leads to the foot of Cnicht (2,265 feet), a sharp-faced mountain which looks inviting in profile. The walk up is a bit of a grind, but worth the effort for from the summit there are marvellous panoramic views of Eryri to the north and the coasts of Llŷn and Meirionnydd to the south west.

From the little slate quarrying village of Croesor there is a minor road, with many steep hills, back to the Vale of Ffestiniog at Tan-y-bwlch passing on the way, Llyn Mair in its sylvan setting. Much of the oak woodland (now a National Nature Reserve) around the lake formed part of the estate of William Oakley (the owner of the Oakley Quarry at Blaenau Ffestiniog) who lived at Plas Tan-y-bwlch, a largish house now used as a residential study centre for the Snowdonia National Park.

Maentwrog nestles prettily below wooded hills on the opposite side of the Afon Dwyryd. It is an estate village of houses built in a brownish-grey slate-stone and has a charming little church (remodelled 1896 by John Douglas) with a spire. The village gets its name from Maen Twrog ('St Twrog's Stone'), a sandstone pillar standing outside the west end of the church. The poet and scholar

Edmwnd Prys (1541–1623) lived at Maentwrog for the greater part of his life and died there. He is reputed to have spoken eight languages and became a canon of St Asaph in 1612. He is chiefly remembered today for his Metrical Psalms. There is a good waterfall, Rhaeadr Du, on the Afon Prysor a mile south of the Maentwrog where the river flows through a deep ravine (Ceunant Llennyrch) from Llyn Trawsfynydd down to the main valley. An early hydro-electric power station stands near the side of the Harlech road at the lower end of the ravine.

Llyn Trawsfynydd also serves the nuclear power station up on the moorlands at the north-eastern corner of the enlarged lake. It has been built on a gargantuan scale and is an unfortunate visual intrusion, both disconcerting and awesome in its raucous and spine-chilling disregard for its surroundings. A mile east of the nuclear power station is Tomen-y-mur where there are numerous earthwork remains of a Roman fort, including an amphitheatre and practice camps. The motte within the Roman fort was erected in the eleventh century. In Trawsfynydd village itself there is a bronze statue to the memory of the poet-shepherd Ellis Humphrey Evans, better known by his bardic name 'Hedd Wyn'. He was born on a local farm and was largely self-educated. In 1917 one of his poems won the Chair prize at the National Eisteddfod, but when it was announced that he had been recently killed in action in France the Chair was draped in black.

The foothills between the mountains and the coast road are rich in prehistoric monuments, this area being (like Anglesey and the Llŷn peninsula) open to the cultural influence of immigrants using the western seaways. There is a fine selection of sites along the high road to the east of Harlech which include 13 standing stones (known as Meini Hirion) between Llanbedr and Moel Goedog marking a Bronze Age trackway. On Moel Goedog itself there are remains of stone circles and hut groups and an Iron Age hillfort. South of Llanbedr there are a number of Stone Age burial chambers in various states of preservation at Dyffryn Ardudwy, Cors-y-gedol and on Mynydd Egryn (marked on maps as 'Carneddau Hengwm'). Pottery found in the Dyffryn Ardudwy cromlech during excavations in 1962 dates the burial chamber to about 3000 B.C. There are remains of Iron Age hillforts at Pen Dinas on Mynydd Egryn and at Craig-y-dinas in the Ysgeithin valley east of Dyffryn Ardudwy.

The coast road to Harlech follows the southern side of the Afon Dwyryd as far as Talsarnau before taking a sharp turn across the Morfa Harlech flatlands. Talsarnau is a comparatively recent village set on the edge of land reclaimed from the sea in 1810 behind a two-mile long earth embankment. The parish church at Llanfihangel-y-traethau ('St Michael's Church of the estuaries'), a mile to the west, was, before the construction of the embankment, isolated on a largish, rocky island surrounded by tidal saltings and creeks. The church was rebuilt in 1871. A six-foot-high inscribed stone in the churchyard commemorates Wleder, who built the original church during the time of 'King Owain' (Owain Gwynedd) and is thus a contemporary record of an important figure in early Welsh history. Morfa Harlech is now largely covered with sand dunes, but until the eighteenth century it was mostly marshlands and tidal saltings. The northern part of the Morfa (meaning 'sea edge land') is a National Nature Reserve while the southern part has the famous Royal St David's golf course on it.

Harlech is a small and attractive town dominated by an Edwardian castle. Harlech Castle, started in 1283, is a superb example of the concentric type and is splendidly situated high above the old coastline on a steep cliff. The castle has a strikingly regular plan consisting of a quadrangle with massive round towers at the four corners linked by high curtain walls and a majestic gatehouse in the centre of the eastern side, all enclosed by lower walls. A dry moat is cut into the rock on the town side. Nevertheless, despite the castle's great strength it was successfully besieged and captured in 1404 by Owain Glyndŵr and became, for a few short years, one of the chief administrative centres of independent Wales. It was recaptured in 1408 and Owain's wife Margaret Hanmer and his daughter were taken prisoners. The march *Gwyr Harlech* ('Men of Harlech') is associated with the stand made later by Dafydd ab Ifan during the Wars of the Roses. The castle was held by Dafydd for the Lancastrians for eight years and was the last to fall, in 1467, to the Yorkists. Nearly two centuries later, in 1647, Harlech was the last castle to hold out for the king during the Civil Wars.

Harlech is a town of narrow streets and twisting lanes perched on the hillside at the rear of the castle. The most interesting building after the castle is Coleg Harlech which was built as a private house in 1910 and converted into a residential college in 1927. Constructed in the dark, local stone its design, by George Walton, is in the spirit of the Arts and Crafts movement. The extrovertly modern theatre block and 11-storey tower was added in 1973. The tiny medieval parish church at Llandanwg, on the seashore two miles to the south, was abandoned to the slowly encroaching sands after a new church was built in Harlech in 1841.

Llanfair, on the main road south of Harlech, was once a slate quarrying village with its own port at Pen-sarn near the mouth of the Afon Artro. The Old Llanfair Quarry Slate caverns are now open to the public and are entered through a twin archway known as 'The Crypt'. The main cavern, known as 'The Cathedral', leads on to a number of old chambers linked by access tunnels. Llanbedr, a mile further on, is a substantial village attractively grouped around a bridge over the Artro. The little church, north of the bridge, contains a Bronze Age stone with an incised spiral and has two ancient standing stones in the churchyard. West of Llanbedr is Mochras (Shell Island), a long peninsula which was an island until shifting sands moved the mouth of the Artro on to a more northerly course. The peninsula, accessible from Llanbedr at low tide for an admission fee, has a good bathing beach and has long been popular with shell collectors for the great variety of sea shells found there.

Inland from Llanbedr there are two beautiful valleys leading to the heart of Ardudwy – the local and historic name for this part of Meirionnydd – and the mountains. One minor road follows the Artro along the more northerly of the two valleys through patches of woodland and wild stretches of rocky moorland to the attractive lake of Llyn Cwm Bychan lying in a craggy hollow formed by the surrounding hills. South-east of the lake one can climb up the infant valley along a line of carefully engineered steps, known as the Roman Steps, to Bwlch Tyddiad. In former centuries the pass provided an important trading route through the mountains from Harlech to Bala and to ease the passage of pack-horse traffic the steps were constructed, probably during the Middle Ages, along the roughest and steepest section of the journey.

About a mile east of Llanbedr another minor road follows the other valley alongside the Afon Cwmnantcol to the foot of the Rhinog mountains. Just after leaving the Artro the road passes the little eighteenth-century Capel Salem which was made famous by Sydney Vosper's nostalgic painting 'Salem'. The painting shows the interior of the Baptist chapel and depicts an old lady in traditional Welsh costume holding a prayer-book in the foreground; the face of the devil can be seen amongst the folds of the woman's cloak. Vosper's life-study was widely illustrated and reproductions of Salem now hang in thousands of homes throughout Wales. At the end of the valley is Maes-y-garnedd, which was the birthplace of Colonel John Jones, brother-in-law of Cromwell and a signatory of Charles I's death warrant.

The upper reaches of Cwm Nantcol merge into Bwlch Drws Ardudwy, a deep defile between the mountains of Rhinog Fawr and Rhinog Fach. It is one of the most impressive and desolate passes in Wales and in times past was, as its name implies, the 'door of Ardudwy' for those approaching from the east. Today it is only accessible on foot.

Rhinog Fawr (2,362 feet) is a great craggy dome which, though steep sided, can be reached either from Llyn Cwm Bychan, via the Roman Steps, or from Cwm Nantcol. From the summit there is a magnificent view, in clear weather, of the mountains of Snowdonia to the north. Rhinog Fach (2,333 feet), Y Llethr (2,475 feet) and Diffwys (2,462 feet), lying further south are the other main peaks in the long rugged chain of mountains which run majestically through the length of Ardudwy from the shores of Llyn Trawsfynydd to the Mawddach estuary near Barmouth. Of all the numerous tarns nestling in the bare folds of these rocky mountains Llyn Hywel has the most awesome setting in a deep hollow between Rhinog Fach and Y Llethr; from its wild shores the broken rock face of Rhinog Fach rears up above mounds of boulders and scree while Y Llethr rises straight out of the chilly waters at an angle of fifty degrees in a series of gigantic rock slabs. Diffwys, at the southern end of the chain, looks across the peerless Mawddach estuary towards the northern precipices of Cadair Idris. The mountains of Ardudwy offer some of the most marvellous hill-walking country in Wales, but though exhilarating it is usually tough going; there are acres of heather and rock, but very little grass and hill-walking here is not recommended for strollers nor, especially in the vicinity of Llyn Hywel, for the nervous.

At the southern corner of Ardudwy the mountains come almost to within spitting distance of the coast. After passing Egryn Abbey (really a late medieval hall-house) the road and railway cling to an ever decreasing gap between the hillside and the sea. At Llanaber there is a well-preserved example of an important thirteenth-century church sited on a ledge overlooking the sea. This is the parish church of Barmouth, a mile and a half further south, and although smallish it has clerestoreyed aisles and is exceptional for the austerity of its detailing. Barmouth (Abermaw, but 'Bermo' in colloquial Welsh) is dominated by the towering cliffs against which it nestles. Although still a small town it has grown considerably since the days when it was merely a little fishing village. Near the old quay is 'Tŷ Gwyn yn Y Bermo' ('White House in Barmouth') a fifteenth-century house said to have been built by Griffith Vaughan of Cors-y-Gedol for the use of Henry Richmond, later King Henry VII. The older part of Barmouth climbs up the hillside along narrow winding lanes and straggling steps. St John's church built in 1898, has a large tower and stands in an imposing position on the edge of the hillside. From near the church footpaths lead to Dinas Oleu, the first piece of land ever acquired by the National Trust (given by Mrs G. T. Talbot in 1895), and to the minor peak of Garn.

The Mawddach estuary begins at Barmouth and can be seen to advantage from the half-mile long footbridge (toll) which runs alongside the railway bridge across the mouth. The estuary winds gracefully inland almost as far as Dolgellau, in a scene of sublime splendour edged with wooded hills on both sides. Beyond the foothills the Ardudwy mountains stand out to the north and the crags of Cadair Idris to the south. A higher level view of the Mawddach estuary can be had by climbing up to the delightful Panorama Walk just east of Barmouth.

The main road to Dolgellau follows the north bank of the Mawddach in a serpentine fashion. It passes on the way, Caerdeon, where the Revs. W. E. Jelf and J. L. Petit built St Philip's church in 1862 on the model of a rustic Alpine village church. Bontddu, two miles further on, is a handsome little village of rough, grey stone houses. A minor road through a wooded ravine north of Bontddu leads to the Hirgwm valley, which was once the main centre of gold-mining in Wales. The Clogau gold mines flourished in the mid-nineteenth century and have been worked on and off since. They are the traditional source of gold for royal wedding rings.

At Pen-y-bryn a minor road leads down to the river and crosses a wooden toll bridge to Penmaenpool on the far side. Another minor road follows a steep, wooded valley towards Llyn Cwm-mynach ('Lake of the Monk's Valley') in a hollow below the rocks of Diffwys. The monks referred to in the lake's name were from the Cistercian abbey at Cymer just across the old bridge at Llanelltud. The abbey was founded in 1199 by Gruffyd ap Cynan as an offshoot of Cwmhir in Powys. It was the smallest of the Cistercian abbeys in Wales and its substantial remains look befittingly austere in its peaceful site alongside the river.

East of the abbey a steep track leads up to the famous Precipice Walk encircling Foel Cynwch (1,068 feet). The three-mile-long walk looks down, on the western side, straight into the deep, wooded middle reaches of the Mawddach valley and backwards towards Cadair Idris; the eastern stretch of the Walk follows the side of the graceful Llyn Cynwch. The New Precipice Walk starts at Llanelltud and skirts Foel Ispri on the northern side of the valley.

Four miles up the valley from Llanelltud is the little village of Ganllwyd lying in an open clearing at the centre of Coed-y-Brenin, a vast 25-square mile area of forest (mostly Forestry Commission conifers but with, here and there, patches of older, deciduous woodland). Many miles of forest trails have been opened for walking but the chief interest here are the waterfalls. Rhaeadr Ddu is the main fall in a series of cataracts on the Afon Gamlan lying a quarter of a mile from the main road near Dolmelynllyn. The other waterfalls, Pistyll Cain and Rhaeadr Mawddach, lie two miles further upstream to the east of the main road and can be reached along the forest tracks from Pont-ar-Eden. A quarter of a mile upstream of the Rhaeadr Mawddach there are adit levels and some buildings remaining from the gold mines which were worked here from about 1840 to the 1930s.

Dolgellau is on the Afon Wnion, a tributary of the Mawddach, in a fine position below the northern flanks of Cadair Idris. As a town it is not everyone's 'cup of tea', but it has a strong, rugged character and is unique in Wales for the consistency with which the dark, coarse-grained granite has been used for nearly all its buildings. Dolgellau's somewhat higgeldy-piggeldy layout turns out to be, on closer investigation, based on a number of open squares of differing sizes. They are linked by narrow lanes and crooked streets which climb up and down providing marvellous compositions of traditional single-storey terraces (with slate dormers) hard up against later three-storey terraces. If there is such a thing as a Welsh character in architecture then Dolgellau is thoroughly Welsh (as it still is also in speech) and has a sense of appropriateness to the surrounding scenery which is undeniably right.

Despite Dolgellau's generally early nineteenth-century appearance it is, in fact, far older and is one of the few Welsh towns not established by Norman and Edwardian conquerors or inflated by nineteenth-century industrialists. The busy, bustling heart of Dolgellau is Eldon Square. It lies grandly at the centre of the town and would look well as a pedestrian *piazza*. Close behind the square, off a narrow lane, is Eglwys Fair, the parish church built in 1716 in local stone. Outside, it has a massively rugged character and a handsome tower. Inside, it is dark and gloomy with gaudily coloured Victorian glass in the windows and an unusual carved ceiling to the nave supported on wooden columns. The old Shirehall (designed by John and Edward Haycock, 1825) by the bridge is a Classical building with Doric pilasters and wide, attractive overhanging eaves. The Roman Catholic church (partly designed by its parish priest) is an elaborate Norman design built over a long period and consecrated in 1967. The bronze Crucifixion on the outside was designed and made in Italy. The 'Parliament House', which was reputedly used by Owain Glyndŵr for some of his parliaments in the early-fifteenth century, was removed to Newtown in 1885.

Almost as well known as the Precipice Walk north of Dolgellau is the Torrent Walk east of the town. To reach it take the Machynlleth road for a mile and then turn down the lane to the lower end of Afon Clywedog. The walk can be followed upstream for nearly a mile along a well-built footpath through picturesque scenery which includes a number of waterfalls as the stream tumbles down on its headlong course. The walk emerges from the upper end of the woodland valley near Brithdir where there is an unusual church. St Mark's Church was designed by Henry Wilson 'as if it had sprung out of the soil instead of being planted on it', and was built in 1897 using local materials. Outside it is dark and bold with a great sweeping roof ending in a massive stone hood at one end; inside, despite its small, narrow windows, it is light and airy. The nave is painted white and the barrel-vaulted chancel red and blue; the doors are inlaid with mother of pearl and the lovely altar has a beaten copper font and pulpit.

Cadair Idris (2,927 feet), the 'chair' of the giant Idris, dominates the skyline south of Dolgellau and is one of the most popular mountains in Wales although it just fails to reach 3,000 feet. Its nearness to the sea and its immensely rugged escarpments give it the feel of a much higher mountain. The summit, Pen-y-gadair, lies on a narrow ridge overlooking two rocky cwms. The northern cwm, cradling the waters of Llyn-y-gadair, is the traditional 'chair' from which the giant, who was supposedly astronomer, philosopher and poet, is said to have studied the stars. The southern cwm is the more dramatic of the two, however, and almost encircles Llyn Cau lying nearly 1,500 feet below the summit. There are a number of routes to the top of the mountain, the best known being the Fox's Path which starts near Llyn Gwernan on the minor road two miles south of Dolgellau. A longer route, starting near the lovely twin lakes of Llynnau Cregennen, follows the main ridge over the shoulder of Tyrau Mawr (2,200 feet). All along the ridge there are magnificent views across the Mawddach estuary northwards to the mountains of Ardudwy.

From Dolgellau the main road to Tywyn and Aberdyfi runs parallel to the southern side of the Mawddach estuary between hills covered in forests as far as Arthog. There, after passing a large disused quarry, the land on the north side of the road opens out into a short marshy strip of lowland facing Barmouth on the far side of the estuary. The relatively young resort of Fairbourne is built against a bar of sand dunes projecting across the mouth of the Mawddach. A two-mile-long miniature (15-inch gauge) steam railway follows the sand bar out to the Barmouth ferry.

Beyond Fairbourne the coastal shelf virtually disappears and both road and railway are squeezed in between the sea and foothills, which rise up almost sheer from the waters. After Llangelynin, where there is a primitive-looking, single-chamber medieval church resting on a narrow rock shelf, the road turns sharply inland to Llanegryn whose little church has one of the finest rood-screens north of the Black Mountains. The sixteenth-century screen is reputed to have come from Cymer Abbey and is intricately and delicately carved in pierced panels with elaborate abstract and curving designs. Peniarth, a large mansion nearby, was the home of W. W. E. Wynne, who amassed a superb collection of early Welsh manuscripts in the nineteenth century. Many of the most famous manuscripts assembled there had come from Hengwrt (near Llanelltud), where they had been brought together in the seventeenth century by Robert Vaughan; in 1909 they were transferred to the National Library at Aberystwyth to form the basis of the great collections there.

East of Llanegryn the broad valley of the Dysynni stretches back lazily towards the heart of the Cadair Idris range. Half way along the valley is Craig-yr-Aderyn ('Bird Rock'), a tremendous rock buttress rising up vertically over 700 feet above the dead flat floor of the valley. It forms an unexpected inland nesting place for cormorants.

Two miles further up the valley are the ruins of Castell-y-Bere perched on an isolated rock outcrop. The south face of the outcrop is precipitous and the footpath curls three-quarters of the way around the ridge before reaching the castle entrance. The remains of the castle appear to consist of a haphazard jumble of walls clinging to the bare rock at different levels; excavations have shown, however, that this was one of the most richly ornamented as well as being one of the largest of the native Welsh castles. It was built by Llywelyn Fawr in the early thirteenth century as his headquarters and must have been, in its heyday, a very impressive structure. The plan of Bere is highly irregular, for the layout was designed to fit the contours of the ground itself in Celtic fashion, and the central courtyard seems to have been slung in a saddle between two higher points each defended by formidable towers soaring above the cliffs. From the castle there are fine views down Dyffryn Dysynni, past Craig-yr-Aderyn, towards the sea and also inland up towards the end of the valley and the summit of Cadair Idris four miles away.

Llanfihangel-y-Pennant, half a mile further on, is a tiny village with just a few houses clustered around the church's circular churchyard. There are ruins of a couple of other houses nearby and perhaps it was from one of these that 16-year-old Mary Jones walked barefoot in 1800 25 miles over the mountains to Bala to get a Bible. Mary was the daughter of a poor weaver and had saved for years to acquire a Bible which, she had been told, could be obtained from the great revivalist preacher Thomas Charles. When she arrived at Bala, Thomas Charles said at first that he had sold out of his stock of Bibles, but he was so impressed with Mary's effort that he gave her his own copy. Charles realized then that there was a world-wide hunger for Bibles and the incident eventually led to the formation of the British and Foreign Bible Society.

Half-way between Castell y Bere and Craig-yr-Aderyn the Afon Dysynni breaks through a mountain ridge to cross from one valley to another. The two valleys lie parallel to each other and are perfectly straight, both being the result of geological faults in prehistoric times. The Dysynni actually starts in the Tal-y-llyn valley (a famous example of a fault-valley) on the southern slopes of Cadair Idris and after crossing through shallow Tal-y-llyn lake carries on down towards Abergynolwyn before turning sharply north to gouge its way through to the next valley. Abergynolwyn was an important slate-quarrying village, but is now better known as the terminus of the Talyllyn Railway. The seven-mile-long narrow-gauge railway, built in 1866 to take slate down to the quay at Tywyn, has been run by a preservation society since 1951. The restored railway runs regular services in the summer and still has two of the original steam locomotives in use.

Both road and railway run through the narrow Fathew valley before emerging from the mountains to enter the flat alluvial plain near Tywyn. The resort has a rather drab mixture of developments, with little in the way of a climax when one gets to the town centre some way inland from the sea. Tywyn's parish church, though on a site dating back to the sixth century and an important collegiate church in the medieval period, is disappointing. Of more architectural interest is the modern Roman Catholic church (1969), the roof of which is funnelled up to form a tower over the centre of the octagonal nave. Tywyn was developed into a prosperous seaside resort in the 1870s by John Corbett, but his ambitious ideas for the town were never quite realized. As a result the grand esplanade along the sea front was not completed and the land behind this had to wait three-quarters of a century before being developed. There is a Narrow Gauge Railway Museum alongside the Talyllyn Railway station.

Aberdyfi, four miles to the south is squeezed in between a range of steep hills and the Dyfi estuary at the southernmost corner of Meirionnydd. The little slate port was developed into a fashionable resort by the Victorians and Edwardians. There was, fortunately, little room for later expansion and thus Aberdyfi still retains the character of a fishing port, particularly at high tide. One is unlikely, however, to hear the famous 'Bells of Aberdovey' tolling from the sea the fate of the legendary Cantre'r Gwaelod under the waters of Cardigan Bay. According to folklore Cantre'r Gwaelod, or the 'Lowland Hundred', was a low-lying tract of land belonging to Prince Gwyddno which was 'drowned' when a young and rather dim-witted maiden let loose all the water from the well after she had been over-feasting. A later version of the story attributes the disaster more plausibly to a drunkard named Seithennin who left open the sluice-gates of the protective embankment. The song 'Bells of Aberdovey' was composed in 1785 by Charles Dibdin. The bells of the parish church, however, are still more recent and only date from the time when the church was built in 1837.

From Aberdyfi the road and railway interlace their ways along the shore of the Dyfi estuary towards Machynlleth. At Cwrt, near Pennal, the old mail-coach road leads back to Tywyn through the pleasant valley of Cwm Dyffryn, passing close to Llyn Barfog. The track of a still older drovers' road goes straight across the mountain ridge to the Fathew valley near Bryn-crug.

Pennal is a small village of low, slate-built cottages and a handsome classical-style church. Owain Glyndŵr summoned one of his Parliaments to Pennal in 1404 and long before that the Romans built a small fort there.

After passing close to Machynlleth (see Chapter Four) one can follow the road along a winding route up the Dulas valley to Corris which, until recently, was the chief centre of the slate industry in the southern half of Meirionnydd. At Llwyngwern Quarry there is now a very interesting Centre for Alternative Technology which aims to show that people can live happily on limited material resources without producing unnecessary waste and pollution. The Centre has an exhibition hall and some fascinating equipment in the grounds displaying ways of producing energy from wind and water-power and solar energy and growing food cheaply by organic means only.

Abandoned slate quarries tend to give Corris a decayed air, but there are fine walks on the hills and along the hidden valleys. At Aberllefenni a minor road leads into the large Dovey Forest and through it back down to the Dyfi valley at Aberangell. Beyond Corris Uchaf the main road goes on to the head of the Tall-y-llyn valley and enters the lower end of Bwlch Llyn Bach, a magnificent fault-valley pass between awesome cliffs. The craggy line on the northern side of the pass belong to a spur of Cadair Idris and the mountain can be climbed, from a point near Minffordd, through an arid, rocky cwm encircling the deep, silent waters of Llyn Cau.

At Cross Foxes one can go back down to Dolgellau (three miles to the west) or eastwards through another bleak pass, Bwlch Oerddrws, on a long downhill glide to Dinas Mawddwy in its idyllic setting on the Afon Dyfi. It was not always so pleasant for in the sixteenth century the area was renowned as the centre for a band of red-haired bandits known as Gwylliad Cochion. They were a kind of Welsh Mafia, terrorising the countryside, stealing sheep and cattle and killing anyone, including the King's judge who got in their way. They were eventually rounded up in 1555 and more than 80 of the bandits condemned to death. At Dinas Mawddwy there is a woollen mill open to the public.

North of the village a three-mile journey up to the craggy head of the lovely Cywarch valley takes one to the foot of Aran Fawddwy (2,970 feet), the highest peak south of Snowdon. The western side of the mountain is gentle and unexciting, but the eastern side has a shattered rock face rising up from the edge of Craiglyn Dyfi, birth-place of the Afon Dyfi.

The Dyfi can be followed almost to its source along another minor road through Llanymawddy, with its delightfully simple church, to Blaen Pennant where there is a good waterfall in the gorge below Ogof Ddu. From there the narrow road climbs steeply up the hillside to Bwlch y Groes ('Pass of the Cross'). At the top (1,790 feet) the road divides, one branch going east to Lake Vyrnwy and the other continuing north along the Twrch valley to Llanuwchllyn and Llyn Tegid.

Llanuwchllyn ('Church at the head of the lake') has no particular interest architecturally. It was, however, the birthplace of two men important in Welsh affairs at the end of the last century and the beginning of the present century. Michael D. Jones (1822–98) succeeded his father as Principal of Bala Independent College and was a staunch nationalist. He was one of the main protagonists of the plan to found a 'New Wales' in Patagonia, South America. The plan became a reality when 153 men, women and children embarked at Liverpool in 1865 and sailed across the Atlantic to Patagonia, where they were able to establish a mini-colony amongst the Indians of the Chubut Valley. The community managed to survive in spite of a number of disasters and though life was often exceedingly harsh they raised townships throughout the valley, built chapels and succeeded in holding their own annual *eisteddfodau.* At first Welsh was the only language of the colony, but after Patagonia became incorporated into Argentina Spanish became more and more commonly used and the old language began to die out. Nevertheless, even today, more than a century after the first landing, the descendants of the original settlers still maintain strong ties with Wales.

The other notable son of Llanuwchllyn was Sir Owen Morgan Edwards (1858–1920) who, humiliated in childhood by an English schoolmaster, became an ardent advocate for the teaching of Welsh. A brilliant history scholar at Oxford, he later became Chief Inspector of the new Welsh Education Department when it was set up in 1907 and did much to champion the cause of Welsh learning, encouraging and writing many books for children. His son, Sir Ifan ab Owen Edwards (1895–1970), was the founder of *Urdd Gobaith Cymru* (The Welsh League of Youth), an estimable organization which manages to blend together culture, artistic activity, outdoor pursuits and Christian piety. Glanllyn, a handsome nineteenth-century mansion overlooking the western end of Llyn Tegid, is now used by the *Urdd* as the main centre for its summer camps.

Llyn Tegid is the longest natural lake in Wales and stretches for nearly four miles along the valley bottom between Llanuwchllyn and Bala. The River Dee (known here as Afon Dyfrdwy) flows through the lake following, in part, the great series of geological fault lines which cut across Wales diagonally north-east to south-west from Corwen to Tywyn. The lake has a lovely setting with the Berwyn mountains to the south and Arenig Fawr rising up more gently to the north and is an ideal place for sailing and fishing. Llyn Tegid supports numerous varieties of fish but its pride is the *gwyniad*, a whitefish member of the salmon family found only in this lake.

Roads run along both sides of the lake while on the southern side there is also a narrow-gauge railway connecting Llanuwchllyn to Bala. Bala is a neat looking town with a broad, tree-lined High Street running through the centre. Although an important market centre for many centuries it has, surprisingly, no military relic other than a low Norman mound (Tomen y Bala) which survives in the middle of housing. Home-spun Bala stockings were once famous – George III, for instance, always wore them – but the flannel industry has now disappeared from the town. The best building is the nineteenth-century Town Hall which has round arches on the ground floor and a clock tower rising from the roof. The largest building is the former Calvinistic Methodist College (founded in 1837) on the Ffestiniog road.

From Bala's thoroughly Welsh background have come poets, politicians and preachers as well as an unusual nurse. The nurse, Elizabeth Davies (1789–1860), was from the start a spirited young girl. Before she was 15 she ran away to Liverpool and, after a number of years in service, began a career travelling all around the world working on ships going to the West Indies, Australia, India and South America. Late in life she trained to be a nurse and at the age of 65 followed Florence Nightingale out to Turkey, and then of her own accord went on to Russia where she became one of the first women to go to the Crimea to work in the hospital at Balaclava. The poet was Evan Lloyd (1734–76), the son of an impoverished squire. He was educated at Oxford and became a convivial parson with a liking for *penillion* singing, and he wrote four long poems, one of which, 'The Curate', is a satirical portrait of a bishop. Thomas Edward Ellis (1859–99) became Liberal M.P. for the district and rose to become Chief Whip; his statue is in High Street surrounded by traffic. Ellis was the son of a tenant farmer and was much concerned with land reform, but he is chiefly remembered for his strenuous efforts to achieve Welsh home rule, the disestablishment of the church in Wales, and better education. Thomas Charles (1755–1814) was not born in Bala, but came to the town after joining the Methodists in 1784. He became one of the leaders of Welsh Methodism and took an important part in founding the British and Foreign Bible Society. He is chiefly remembered, however, for his work in establishing the Sunday School system in Wales and for his writing and publication of childrens' religious books. A statue of Thomas Charles stands outside the Welsh Presbyterian Chapel in Tegid Street.

From Bala there is a pleasant road northwards through the Treweryn valley to Ffestiniog. It passes close to Llyn Celyn, a reservoir which caused more of a furore than almost any other land-thirsty project in recent Welsh history. It is neat and tidy, simply landscaped and shelters below the lonely peak of Arenig Fawr (2,800 feet) which now, without Cwm Treweryn at its feet, looks tamed and less unattainable than in former years. At the side of Llyn Celyn there is a dignified, rustically modern Memorial Chapel built in 1971 to commemorate a village that was 'drowned' by the new reservoir and which in the late 1960s became a rallying point for all those concerned about the destruction of Welsh-speaking communities in the face of 'progress'. The stone and slate chapel is a poignant memorial, for in this part of a lovely and once thriving valley the people – and with them their culture, language and religion – have now gone forever.

INDEX

Abbeycwmhir 34, 38, 166
Abercamlais 21
Aberconwy 97, 114, 119
Abercynrig 16
Aberdaron 155, 156
Aberdyfi 168, 170
Aberedw 28–29, 31
Aberffraw 141
Abergele 55, 95, 96
Aberglaslyn Pass 152
Abergwesyn 32
Abergynolwyn 170
Aberllynfi 25
Abermule 41, 44
Abersoch 156
Aberysgir 18
Aled, Tudor 96
Amlwch 136–137
Aran Fawddwy 103, 171
Arenig Fawr 173, 174
Arthog 168

Bala 49, 164, 169, 172, 173–174
Bangor 93, 126–127
Bangor Is-coed 55, 72, 73, 127, 156
Bannau Brycheiniog 22
Bardsey (Ynys Enlli) 103, 121, 154, 155–156
Barmouth 165, 166, 168
Basingwerk Abbey 81
Beaufort, Margaret 74, 77, 80, 81
Beaumaris 127, 129, 130–131, 142
Bedd Branwen 138
Beddelgelert 151, 152
Benllech 134
Berriew 44
Bersham 58, 75–76
Berwyn Mountains 8, 45, 49, 54, 61, 63, 65, 69
Bethesda 126, 148, 153
Betws Pen-pont 21
Betws-y-coed 70, 102, 119, 123, 124
Beulah 32
Black Mountains 7, 8, 10, 11, 12, 13, 14, 24, 25, 26, 27, 57
Blaenau Ffestiniog 121–123, 126, 158, 160, 161
Blaenllyfni 14
Blaen-y-Glyn (waterfall) 15
Bodelwyddan 93
Bodnant Gardens 115
Bodrhyddan Hall 94
Bontddu 166
Brecon 8, 9, 12, 13, 14, 15, 16–18, 24
Brecon Beacons 7, 8, 10, 11, 12, 15, 16, 18, 19
National Park 7, 11, 13, 22
Brithdir 167
Bronllys 24
Brut y Tywysogion 106
Brycheiniog 8, 9
Brymbo 58, 75
Bryn Glas 9
Brynich 16
Brynsiencyn 143
Bryn-tail Lead Mine 38
Buckley 78
Builth Wells 9, 29, 30, 31, 107
Bwlch 13, 14
Bwlch Drws Ardudwy 164

Cadair Idris 8, 19, 103, 165, 166, 167, 168, 169
Caer Aranrhod 104
Caergwrle 54, 77, 78
Caerhun 76, 116
Caernarfon 76, 105, 107, 109, 116, 130, 143, 145–147, 148

Caersws 8, 40, 41, 76
Caerwys 54, 83, 84, 96
Camddwr Bleiddiad 32
Cantref 19
Cantre'r Gwaelod 104, 170
Capel Curig 124
Carnedd Dafydd 124
Carnedd Llywelyn 124
Carno 40
Carrog 69
Castell Cefnllys 34
Castell Collen 8, 34
Castell Cwmcamlais 20
Castell Dinas Bran 58, 65, 66, 67
Castell Dinas Emrys 152
Castell-y-Bere 169
Cathedin 15
Catrin o'r Berain 92
Cefn Mawr 64
'Ceiriog' (John Ceiriog Hughes) 41, 53
Cerrig-y-drudion 70
Charles, Thomas 169, 173–174
Chartists, The 37
Chirk 58, 63–64, 75
Cilcain 84
Cilmeri 31
Clocaenog 87
Clough, Sir Richard 58, 89, 91, 92
Clun-gwyn Waterfalls 20
Cwm-wysg 22
Clynnog Fawr 153–154
Clyro 8, 26, 27
Cnicht 121, 161
Coke, Thomas 17
Colwyn Bay 96, 97, 111
Conwy 56, 111, 113–115, 116
Corris 171
Corwen 69–70, 71, 173
Craig Cerig-gleisiad 19
Craig Pwll-du 28
Craig y Cilau 13
Craig-y-Nos 22–23
Craig-yr-Aderyn 169
Cregina 29
Creigiau Eglwyseg 65, 67, 68
Cricieth 157, 159
Crickhowell 12, 13
Croesor 161
Crug Hywel 13
Cunedda Wledig 105, 132
Cwm Pennant 157, 158
Cymer Abbey 166, 168
Cynwyd 71

Dan-yr-Ogof (cave) 22
David, Prince 31, 79, 107
Davies, David 40, 43
Davies, Elizabeth 173
Davies, Robert and John 58, 75, 85
Dee, River 8, 53, 54, 56, 64, 66, 72, 73, 76, 79
Deganwy 112–113
Denbigh 57, 58, 88–90, 93
Derwen 87
Dinas Dinlle 153
Dinas Mawddwy 171
Din Lligwy 135
Dinorwic Quarries 149
Diserth 94
Dolbadarn Castle 149
Dolbenmaen 157
Dolforwyn 41, 44
Dolgarrog 116
Dolgellau 42, 57, 103, 165, 166–167, 168, 171
Dolwyddelan 123
Druids 104, 128
Dwyrain 143
Dyffryn Ardudwy 162
Dylife 38, 39

Edmwnd, Dafydd ab 53, 73
Edward I 78, 93, 94, 106, 107, 113, 114, 116, 130, 142, 143, 145, 146, 147, 155
Edwards, Sir Owen Morgan 73
Eisteddfod, International 66–67
  National 70, 129, 162
Elan Valley 10, 35
  Village 32, 35
Elenydd 32
Ellis, Thomas Edward 173
Erddig 58, 73, 75
Eryri 102, 109, 130, 144, 148–149, 150, 161
Evans, John 148
Evans, Ellis Humphrey ('Hedd Wyn') 162
Everest, Sir George 12
Ewloe Castle 79

Fairbourne 168
Ffestiniog 121
  Railway 159, 160
Ffordd Gam Elin 61, 71
Fforest Fawr 7, 11, 18, 19, 20, 21
Ffrwd Fawr (waterfall) 38

Flint 55, 58, 80
Forden 8, 47
Fort Belan 153
Four Mile Bridge 140
Fychan, Ednyfed 97
Fyrnwy, Afon 8

Gee, Thomas 53, 91
Geufron 38
Gibson, John 114
Giraldus Cambrensis 15, 18
Glasbury 27
Glascwm 29, 30
Glaslyn (lake) 150, 151
Glyder Fawr 125
Glyn Collwn 15
Glynceiriog 63
Glyndŵr, Owain 9, 12, 39, 42, 45, 53, 56–57, 60, 69, 73, 93, 107, 109, 113, 152, 157, 163, 167, 171
Glyndyfrdwy 56, 57, 69
Glynllifon 153
Glyntawe 22
Goch, Iolo 68
Graig Lwyd 104, 115
Great Orme's Head 101, 111, 112
Gregynog Hall 43–44
Gresford 58, 75, 77
Griffiths, Ann 48
Griffiths, Moses 82, 109
Gruffydd ap Cynan 83
Gruffydd ap Llywelyn 55, 106
Gruffydd ap Rhys 15
Gwern-vale 12
Gwernyfed, Old 25
Gwrych Castle 95
Gwydir Castle 117–118
Gwydir Forest 120, 123
Gwynedd, Owain 98
Gwytherin 96

Hanmer 72–73
Harlech 57, 69, 130, 162, 163, 164
Harris, Howell 9, 24, 25
Hawarden 78, 79, 107
Hay-on-Wye 7, 25–26
'Hedd Wyn' (Ellis Humphrey Evans) 162
Henllan 91, 93
Henry III 44, 45, 106, 113
Henry VII (Henry Tudor) 9, 45, 57, 82, 88, 108, 133, 165
Herbert, George 45
Holt 76
Holy Island 103, 139, 140
Holyhead 139, 158
Holywell 55, 58, 80, 81–82
Hughes, John Ceiriog ('Ceiriog') 41, 53
Hundred House 30
Huntingdon, Countess of 25
Hyddgen 9

Jones, Inigo 94, 118
Jones, Jack ('Jac Glanygors') 70
Jones, John ('Talhaiarn') 96
Jones, Mary 169
Jones, Michael D. 172
Jones, Theophilus 17, 31
Jones, Thomas 30

Kilvert, Rev. Francis 26–27

Lake Vyrnwy 48–49
Leeswood Hall 75, 85
Leighton Park 45
Llan Ffestiniog 121
Llanaber 165
Llanaelhaearn 154
Llananno 34
Llanarmon Dyffryn Ceiriog 62, 63
Llanbabo 138
Llanbadarn Fawr 34
Llanbadarn-y-Garreg 29
Llanbedr 162, 163, 164
Llanbedrog 156
Llanbedr-y-cennin 116
Llanberis 149, 151, 153
Pass 151
Llanbrynmair 39
Llandanwg 163
Llanddaniel Fab 143
Llanddeusant 138–139
Llan-ddew 18
Llanddwyn 142
Llandefalle 25
Llandeilo Graban 28
Llandinam 40
Llandrillo 54, 71
Llandrillo-yn-Rhos 97–98
Llandrindon Wells 8, 33–34
Llandudno 94, 102, 104, 111–113, 134
Llandwrog 153
Llandygai 126
Llanefydd 91, 93

Llanegryn 168, 169
Llaneilian 137
Llaneilian-yn-Rhos 97
Llanelieu 25
Llanelltud 166, 168
Llanelwedd 27, 30
Llanengan 156
Llanfaes (Beaumaris) 130, 131, 142, 143
Llanfaes (Brecon) 18
Llanfair 163
Llanfair Caereinion 47
Llanfair Dyffryn Clwyd 88
Llanfair-pwllgwyngyll 144
Llanfair Talhaearn 96
Llanfair-yn-Neubwll 140, 141
Llanfairynghornwy 138
Llanfechell 138
Llanferres 85, 86
Llanfihangel-y-Pennant (Llyn) 158
Llanfihangel-y-Pennant (Meirionnydd) 169
Llanfihangel-y-traethau 162
Llanfilo 25
Llanfrynach 16
Llanfyllin 48, 49
Llangadwaladr 141
Llangaffo 143
Llangammarch Wells 31
Llangar 71
Llangasty Tal-y-llyn 15
Llangattock 12
Llangedwyn 61
Llangefni 133–134, 142
Llangeinwen 143
Llangelynin 168
Llangernyw 96
Llangian 156
Llangoed Castle 28
Llangollen 53, 63, 65–67, 68
Llan-gors Lake 14
Llangurig 32, 35, 36
Llangynog 49
Llanidan 143
Llanidloes 34, 36, 37–38, 40
Llaniestyn 132
Llanilltud 19
Llanllwchaiarn 42
Llanrhaeadr-ym-Mochnant 54, 61, 62, 71
Llanrhaeadr-yn-Cinmerch 88
Llanrhychwyn 117
Llanrug 148
Llanrwst 115, 117, 118–119
Llansanffraed 14, 15
Llansanffraed Cwmteuddwr 34
Llansannan 96
Llansilan 60
Llanstephan 27, 28
Llantysilio 68
Llanuwchllyn 172, 173
Llanwnnog 41
Llanwrtyd Wells 31, 32
Llanwyddan 48, 49
Llanynys 89
Llanystumdwy 157
Llowes 27
Lloyd George, David 147, 157
Llwyd, Humphrey 53, 90–91
Llyn Alaw 138
Llyn Celyn 174
Llyn Cerrig Bach 141
Llyn Clywedog 38, 40
Llyn Conwy 121
Llyn Cowlyd 116, 117
Llyn Crafnant 117
Llyn Cwm Bychan 164
Llyn Dinas 151
Llyn Dulyn 116, 117
Llyn Eigiau 116, 117
Llyn Geirionydd 117
Llyn Gwynant 151
Llyn Hywel 165
Llyn Idwal 125
Llyn Llydaw 150, 151
Llyn Maelog 141
Llyn Mair 160, 161
Llyn Ogwen 124, 125
Llyn Padarn 149
Llyn Peris 149, 151
Llyn Stwlan 122
Llyn Tegid 172, 173
Llynnau Mymbr 124
Llys Helig 104
Llyswen 24, 27
Llywel 21
Llywelyn I (the Great) (Llywelyn ab Iorwerth) 28, 30, 34, 45, 80, 106, 117, 119, 123, 131, 169
Llywelyn II (the Last) (Llywelyn ap Gruffydd) 9, 20, 29, 30, 31, 34, 41, 44, 46, 56, 93, 94, 106–107, 113, 123, 146, 150
Long Mountain 9

Mabinogion 105, 138, 147
Machynlleth 9, 38, 39, 56, 85, 170, 171
Maddocks, William 117, 155, 158, 160
Madoc 98, 148
Maenan Abbey 114, 116, 117, 118
Maentwrog 161–162
Maes-yr-onen Chapel 27
Malltraeth 142
Marchwiel 73
Marford 77
Mathrafal 47
Meifod 48
Menai Bridge 127, 128–129, 133
Menai Strait 31, 103, 104, 105, 127, 128, 130, 143, 144, 147
Migneint 102, 111, 121
Mochras 164
Moel Famau 86
Moel Hebog 103, 152, 158
Moel Hiraddug 47
Moel Siabod 103, 121, 123, 124
Moel Sych 61
Moelfre 134–135
Moelwyn Mawr 122
Mold 39, 54, 58, 75, 84–85, 86
Monmouthshire & Brecon Canal 12, 15
Montgomery 8, 9, 41, 44–45
Morgan, (Bishop) William 60, 61–62, 93, 120
Morris Brothers 135
Morus, Edward 70
Morus, Huw 53, 60, 63
Mostyn 82, 83
Mynydd Du, Y 7, 11, 12, 18, 22
Mynydd Epynt 7, 18, 33
Mynydd Llangatwg 12, 13
Mynydd Mawr 152
Mynydd Parys 108, 136
Mynydd Rhiw 104

Nanhoron 156
Nannerch 84
Nant Ffrancon 124, 125
Nant Gwrtheyrn 154
Nant Gwynant 151
Nantlle 153
Nant, Twm o'r 53
Nefyn 154–155
Nerquis Hall 58, 85
Newbridge-on-Wye 32, 33
Newmarche, Bernard de 9, 17
Newtown 9, 41–43, 167
Niwbwrch (Newborough) 130, 142, 143
Northop 80

Offa's Dyke 8, 45, 55, 63, 77
Ogof Agen Allwedd (cave) 13
Ogof Eglwys Faen (cave) 13
Ogof Ffynnon Ddu (cave) 22
Overton 72
Owain Tudor 108, 133
Owen, Daniel 53, 84
Owen, Goronwy 134
Owen, Robert 42–43

Painscastle 28
Pantasaph 82
Parliament 39, 42, 167
Parys, Mynydd 108, 136
Patrisio 13
Patti, Adelina 22–23
Penn Cerrig-calch 13
Pencelli 16
Pencerrig 30
Penegoes 39
Pengenffordd 13
Penmachno 120
Penmaen-mawr 102, 104, 115
Penmyndd 93, 108, 133
Penmon 131–132, 134
Pennal 57, 170–171
Pennant, Thomas 82, 109, 146, 149
Pennant Melangell 49
Penrhyn Castle 126
Penrhyndeudraeth 161
Penry, John 31
Pentraeth 133, 134
Pentre Foelas 71
Pen-y-Crug 18
Pen-y-fan 19
Pen-y-groes 148, 153
Pistyll Cain (waterfall) 166
Pistyll Rhaeadr (waterfall) 62
Plas Mawr 114
Plas Newydd 144
Plas Têg 58, 78
Pont Cysyllte 64, 65
Pontneddfechan 20
Porth Neigwl 156
Porth-aml Fawr 24
Porthmadog 117, 152, 158, 159, 160
Porth-yr-Ogof (cave) 20

Portmeirion 160–161
Powis Castle 46
Prestatyn 94–95
Price, Sir John 17
Price, Thomas 12
Prys, Edmwnd 162
Prys, Thomas 71
Puffin Island (Ynys Seiriol) 103, 112, 132
Pumlumon 7, 9
Pwllheli 157

Radnor Forest 7
Raikes, Robert 15
Rhaeadr Cynfal (waterfall) 121
Rhaeadr Ddu (waterfall) 166
Rhaeadr Mawddach (waterfall) 166
Rhaeadr Ogwen (waterfall) 124
Rhaeadr-y-cwm (waterfall) 121
Rhayader 34, 35, 36
Rhinog Fawr 164
Rhodri Mawr 105
Rhoscolyn 140
Rhosllanerchrugog 75
Rhosneigr 141
Rhos-on-Sea 97
Rhuddlan 93–94, 95
Rhulen 29, 30
Rhwng Gwy a Hafren 7
Rhyl 54, 87, 95
Roberts, Samuel 39
Rolfe, Frederick (Baron Corvo) 81
Roman Steps 164
Rossett 76
Ro-wen 116
Ruabon 53, 58
Ruthin 54, 57, 58, 75, 85, 86, 87, 88–89

Saints' Road 154, 155
St Asaph 54, 55, 93
St Patrick 137
St Winifred's Well 81
Salesbury, William 53, 96
Sarn Helen 19, 147
Scwd Ddwli (waterfall) 21
Scwd Gwladys (waterfall) 21
Scwd-yr-Eira (waterfall) 20
Segontium 105, 146–147
Sennybridge 21
Severn, River 6, 7, 10, 35, 36, 40, 41, 44, 45, 46, 57
Siddons, Sarah 17
Skerries, The 138
Snowdon 103, 109, 124, 125, 149, 150–151 (see also under Yr Wyddfa)
Snowdonia National Park 11
Stanley, Henry Morton 90
Staylittle 38
Swallow Falls 119
Sycharth 56, 57, 60–61

Talerddig 40
Talgarth 13, 24, 25
Talhaiarn 53
Taliesin 117
Talsarnau 162
Tal-y-bont 15, 16
Tal-y-llyn 169, 170, 171
Three Cocks 25
Torpantau 15
Towyn 95
Traeth Mawr 117, 160, 161
Trawsfynydd 122, 162
Treberfedd 15
Trecastell 21
Trefeca 24, 25
Trefriw 117
Tregynon 43
Tremadoc 158
Tre'r Ceiri 104, 154
Tretŵr 13, 14, 24
Treweryn 174
Tryfan 124, 125
Tudweiliog 155
Twm o'r Nant 91–92
Tywyn 168, 170, 173

Urdd Gobaith Cymru (Welsh League of Youth) 172
Usk, River 7, 12, 13, 15, 16, 21, 22, 24

Valle Crucis Abbey 66, 68
Valley 140, 141
Vaughan, Henry 14
Vortigern 154

Wat's Dyke 73, 77
Waunfawr 148
Welshpool 7, 9, 44, 45, 46–47
Whitford 82
Williams-Ellis, Sir Clough 28, 151, 160, 161
Williams, Jane 24
Wilson, Richard 30, 39, 85, 86, 153

Wrexham 53, 58, 59, 72, 73, 74–75, 76, 77, 93
Wye, River 7, 13, 24, 25, 27, 30, 33, 35, 36
Wyn, Eifion 157
Wynn family 114, 117–118, 119

Yale, Elihu 74
Ynys Badrig (Patrick's Island) 137
Ynys Enlli (Bardsey) 121, 154, 155–156
Ynys Seiriol (Puffin Island) 103, 112, 132, 134
Ynyscynhaearn 159
Yr Aran 152
Yr Eifl 154
Yr Wyddfa 121, 150–151 (see also under Snowdon)
Ysbyty Ifan 120–121
Ysgeifiog 84
Ystrad Marchell 47
Ystradfellte 20, 21